The Family in Modern Germany

The Family in Modern Germany

Edited by Lisa Pine

BLOOMSBURY ACADEMIC
LONDON • NEW YORK • OXFORD • NEW DELHI • SYDNEY

BLOOMSBURY ACADEMIC
Bloomsbury Publishing Plc
50 Bedford Square, London, WC1B 3DP, UK
1385 Broadway, New York, NY 10018, USA
29 Earlsfort Terrace, Dublin 2, Ireland

BLOOMSBURY, BLOOMSBURY ACADEMIC and the Diana logo are trademarks
of Bloomsbury Publishing Plc

First published in Great Britain 2020
This paperback edition published in 2021

Copyright © Lisa Pine, 2020

Lisa Pine has asserted her right under the Copyright, Designs and Patents Act, 1988,
to be identified as Editor of this work.

Cover image: (from left to right) Ernst Budde, unknown, Gerhard Budde, Dr. Karl Budde
and Elsbeth Budde (parents to Ernst and Gerhard) on a walk, 1900
(© Gunilla Budde (granddaughter to Gerhard)/Family Archive)

All rights reserved. No part of this publication may be reproduced or transmitted in any
form or by any means, electronic or mechanical, including photocopying, recording,
or any information storage or retrieval system, without prior permission in
writing from the publishers.

Bloomsbury Publishing Plc does not have any control over, or responsibility for,
any third-party websites referred to or in this book. All internet addresses given in
this book were correct at the time of going to press. The author and publisher regret
any inconvenience caused if addresses have changed or sites have ceased to exist,
but can accept no responsibility for any such changes.

A catalogue record for this book is available from the British Library.

A catalog record for this book is available from the Library of Congress.

ISBN: HB: 978-1-3500-4770-9
PB: 978-1-3502-5313-1
ePDF: 978-1-3500-4771-6
eBook: 978-1-3500-4772-3

Typeset by RefineCatch Limited, Bungay, Suffolk

To find out more about our authors and books visit www.bloomsbury.com
and sign up for our newsletters.

In memory of Rose and Michael Pine

Contents

List of figures and tables	viii
Notes on contributors	ix
Acknowledgements	xi
Glossary of abbreviations and terms	xii
Introduction *Lisa Pine*	1
1 The family in Imperial Germany *Gunilla Budde*	27
2 Rejuvenating the family: The struggle between tradition and modernity in Weimar Germany *Michelle Mouton*	59
3 'The germ cell of the nation': The family in the Third Reich *Lisa Pine*	91
4 Post-war paternalism and modern mothers: Changing families in 1950s West Germany *Alexandria N. Ruble*	117
5 Continuities and ruptures: Women's agency and the West German family, 1960s–1980s *Sarah E. Summers*	141
6 Vanguard of the working mother: The East German family between change and continuity *Donna Harsch*	171
7 German family policy since reunification *Sigrid Leitner*	201
Conclusion *Lisa Pine*	229
Select bibliography	235
Index	239

Figures and tables

Figures

5.1 Number of births per year based on age of mother	146
7.1 The expansion of childcare for children under three	205
7.2 Attitudes towards the ideal weekly working times of parents with a child aged two years	212

Tables

5.1 Women's employment, 1950–89	144
5.2 Employment rate of mothers in West Germany, 1950–85	145
5.3 Birth rate developments in West Germany, 1950–90	145
5.4 Marriage and divorce rates in West Germany, 1950–88	148
7.1 Benefits from long-term care insurance in euros per month	216

Notes on contributors

Gunilla Budde is Professor of German and European History at the University of Oldenburg, Germany. She obtained her doctorate in 1993 and her habilitation in 2002 at the Free University of Berlin. Her main research interests are the history of the European bourgeoisie, the history of the GDR, emotional history of the First World War, family history, the history of consumption, music and history, and gender history. Her major publications are *Auf dem Weg ins Bürgerleben. Kindheit und Erziehung im deutschen und englischen Bürgertum* (1994), *Frauen der Intelligenz. Akademikerinnen in der DDR 1945 bis 1975* (2003) and *Blütezeit des Bürgertums. Bürgerlichkeit im 19. Jahrhundert* (2009). She is co-editor of the book series *Kritische Studien zur Geschichtswissenschaft*.

Donna Harsch is Professor of History at Carnegie Mellon University, USA. She is the author of *Revenge of the Domestic: Women, the Family, and Communism in the German Democratic Republic, 1945–1970* (2007) and *German Social Democracy and the Rise of Nazism, 1928–1933* (1993). With Karen Hagemann and Friederike Brühöfener, she is co-editor of *Gendering Post-1945 German History: Entanglements* (Berghahn Books, forthcoming). She is working on a book-length comparative study of infant mortality in the German Democratic Republic and the Federal Republic of Germany from 1945 to 1990.

Sigrid Leitner is Professor of Social Policy at the University of Applied Sciences in Cologne, Germany. She studied political science at the University of Vienna and the Institute for Advanced Studies in Vienna. She was a research fellow at the Austrian Academy of Sciences and an Assistant Professor at the University of Göttingen. Her research focuses on familialism in conservative welfare states, policies of childcare and elderly care, pension systems and the gendered effects of social policy. She teaches social policy and social work.

Michelle Mouton is Professor of History at University of Wisconsin Oshkosh, USA, where she teaches a variety of courses in European and German history. She is the author of *From Nurturing the Nation to Purifying the Volk: Weimar and Nazi Family Policy 1918–1945* (2007). While Weimar continues to be an interest, her current research focuses on German children during the Second World War and the early Cold War.

Lisa Pine is Associate Professor of History at London South Bank University, UK. She obtained her doctorate from the University of London in 1996. She is a Fellow of the Royal Historical Society. Her main research interests are the social history of Nazi Germany and the Holocaust. Her major publications are *Debating Genocide* (2018), *Life and Times in Nazi Germany* (2016), *Education in Nazi Germany* (2010), *Hitler's 'National Community': Society and Culture in Nazi Germany* (2007, 2017) and *Nazi Family Policy, 1933–1945* (1997).

Alexandria N. Ruble is Assistant Professor of History at Spring Hill College in Mobile, Alabama, USA. Her research interests include modern German and European history and women's and gender history. Her current book project explores how marriage and family law reforms in East and West Germany between the mid-1940s and late 1960s became a battleground of the broader Cold War struggle between the two post-war German states. Her work has been supported by the Social Science Research Council, the Fulbright US Student Program, the Central European History Society, the German Academic Exchange Service and the American Council on Germany.

Sarah E. Summers received her PhD in Modern European and Women's and Gender history from the University of North Carolina at Chapel Hill, USA. She is currently teaching Global and European history at Wilfrid Laurier University in Ontario, Canada. She is also completing a manuscript tentatively titled 'Reconciling Family and Work: Women's Emancipation and the West German Gendered Division of Labor, 1960s–1990s', which analyses the relationship between the West German women's movement, broadly defined, and family policy development. She recently published an article in *German Politics and Society* on green feminism and has a chapter in the edited volume *Gendering Post-1945 German History: Entanglements* (Berghahn Books, forthcoming).

Acknowledgements

I would like to thank my contributors for all their hard work in producing their excellent chapters and adhering to deadlines. I am extremely grateful to my daughter Gaby Fields and her friends, Miles Clifford and Kit Grange, for letting me stay with them in Southampton in July 2018 at a crucial point in the preparation of the manuscript, allowing me to retreat from my usual activities in university and home life, to focus on it without any distractions. I am also thankful to the LSS Research Fund at London South Bank University for research support in the form of a writing retreat in July 2019, enabling me to complete the final manuscript and submit it to the publisher in good time. I would especially like to express my gratitude to my editor, Rhodri Mogford, for all his continued help and good advice throughout the publishing process. I am grateful to the proposal reviewers for their insightful suggestions that helped me to refine my early ideas and to the manuscript reviewers for their useful advice and comments, as well as a number of colleagues who read and offered me advice on parts of the final manuscript. Together with the publisher, I would like to thank Gunilla Budde for permission to reproduce the cover image. Finally, I would like to take the opportunity, in this book on the subject of the family, to dedicate it to the memory of my parents, Rose and Michael Pine.

Lisa Pine
London, 2019

Glossary of abbreviations and terms

BDF	Federation of German Women's Organisations
BDM	League of German Girls
Betreuungsgeld	cash transfer for children
BGB	German Civil Code
Bildung	education
CDU	Christian Democratic Union
CSU	Christian Social Union
das ganze Haus	the whole house
DDP	German Democratic Party
DM	*Deutschmark* (unit of currency)
DNVP	German National People's Party
DVP	German People's Party
Ehegattensplitting	tax benefit for married couples with only one earner or a low-earning second earner
Elterngeld	Parental Benefit
Elterngeld Plus	Parental Benefit Plus
Erziehungsgeld	parental benefit or upbringing money
Erziehungsurlaub	parental leave
Familie	family
Familienzeit	family time
FDP	Free Democratic Party
Frauenpolitik	women's policy
FRG	Federal Republic of Germany
GDR	German Democratic Republic
Gleichberechtigungsgesetz	Equal Rights Act
Grundgesetz	Basic Law
Hausfrau	housewife
Hausmutter	mistress of the household
Hausvater	patriarch

Herdprämie	bonus for stay-at-home-mothers
Hilfswerk 'Mutter und Kind'	Mother and Child Relief Agency
Kaiserreich	Imperial Germany
Kinderladenbewegung	Store Front Daycare Movement
kinderreich	'rich in children'
KPD	German Communist Party
Lebensborn	Well of Life (Nazi maternity programme)
Mutterschaftsurlaub	maternity leave
Mutterschutzgesetz	mother protection law
Muttipolitik	mother's policy
NSDAP	National Socialist German Workers' Party (Nazi Party)
NSV	National Socialist People's Welfare
Partnerehe	partnership marriage
Pflegegeld	cash benefit for homecare
Pflegezeit	care leave period
RM	*Reichsmark* (unit of currency)
SED	Socialist Unity Party
SPD	Social Democratic Party
SS	*Schutzstaffeln* (Protection Squads; Nazi elite formation)
Volk	nation
Volksgemeinschaft	'national community'
Wehrmacht	armed forces
Wirtschaftswunder	economic miracle

Introduction

Lisa Pine

This book examines the history of the family in modern Germany from 1871 to the post-reunification era. It contributes a primary point of reference in the field and fills a significant gap in the historiography because there is no recent book published in English on this subject. There are, of course, a number of German scholarly works published in this field, although these mainly date back to the 1970s and 1980s.[1] The only book in English that is at all similar was published in the early 1980s and is very dated now.[2] There have been a number of monographs that deal with the history of the family in Germany in a particular era, as well as general histories of the family or the European family.[3] However, the trend in historical writing in recent decades has not been on the history of the family. Historiographical developments have been more focussed on women's history and gender studies, and also on sexuality, but not so much on the family. Recent historical writing has covered many subjects that are tangential to the history of the family – not only the ones just mentioned, but also the history of emotions, memory and food. The time is ripe to return to a history of the family that incorporates recent historiographical trends.[4]

This book comprehensively and chronologically treats the history of the family in modern Germany, tracing how the family has developed over time from the *Kaiserreich* (Imperial Germany) until the contemporary era. It analyses large forces of historical change and their social effects – for example, industrialisation, economic depression and the impact of war upon the family. Furthermore, it explores how different political systems and laws engendered changes in the German family. What were the norms of family life? How did they differ across the time period? The book examines the impact on the German family of the late nineteenth century transition from a predominantly agrarian to an industrialised society. It looks at the development of liberal and progressive family policies in the Weimar Republic and then the return to a more traditional view of the family during the Third Reich (1933–45). It considers the great social upheaval brought about by both the First World War and the Second World War, and the effect of these protracted conflicts upon the family. It examines the different approaches to the family taken by the West German state and the East German state in the Cold War era. Finally, it analyses the changes to the family brought about by the process of German reunification and its aftermath. In each chapter, we explore the connections between political developments and economic changes with the history of the family.

The family is a fluid institution, not a static one. This book evaluates how the family has changed over time, examining popular assumptions about the family as well as the impact of modernity upon the German family. In particular, it demonstrates the effect on the family of political and social change in modern German history. The book considers different family structures and types, such as extended, conventional nuclear and patriarchal. It explores the constitution of the household – family members, a married couple, dependent children, grandparents, non-family members in the household such as labourers or household staff. It discusses instances in which the household was matrifocal – that is, organised by the mother – such as, when men were at war. It examines the impact of this matrifocality and the double burden placed upon women in such circumstances. The book analyses changes in the gender and constellation of the family breadwinner – just the father; just the mother; neither (in periods of unemployment) or both (as in the neo-conventional family or new nuclear family, headed by a married or a cohabiting couple, both working). The book also examines the relationship between the family and (legal) sexuality. It traces the changes to the law in regard to same-sex relationships over time: from the illegality of homosexuality; to its legality; to cohabitation of same-sex couples but ineligibility to marry under German law; to the most recent development of legalised same-sex marriages in October 2017. It is possible to obtain a snapshot of the family in time at any historical moment, but this book seeks to investigate and explore longer-term trends and changes.

In addition, it is important to consider gender roles in the family, and also the impact of class and position in society on a family. Women at times have had a double burden of work and household. At many times, they have had a triple burden, where in addition, they do the emotional work in the family – that is, ensuring family members' well-being and happiness and holding relationships together. In this book, we analyse trends in domestic division of labour – from segregated conjugal roles in which men and women have had different functions and interests, to integrated conjugal roles in which men and women have had similar roles, interests and use of leisure time. We make reference to the place of the family in the primary socialisation of children, as well as expectations about the functions of the family and how these changed throughout the different political systems that have made up the modern German era.

Theoretical perspectives on the family and on the role of family members have developed over time and have had an impact on discourses about the family and its functions in modern and contemporary times. Sociologist Talcott Parsons described the distinction between the 'expressive' role of domestic chores, taking care of the household and children, traditionally carried out by the wife/mother, and the 'instrumental' role of the breadwinner, outside the household, traditionally done by the husband/father.[5] Michael Young and Peter Willmott put forward the 'march of progress' concept, which encapsulated a movement towards equality in the division of labour in the household, and a blurring of expressive and instrumental roles.[6] Feminist critiques of the family, especially during the 1970s and 1980s, objected to the so-called 'natural' division of labour and maintained that patriarchal society benefited from its perpetuation. Instead, some feminists called for a radical overhaul of family roles and relationships, across a variety of theoretical perspectives, including 'the personal is political'. They advocated a quest for a fundamental change in power relationships in the family and a negotiation of roles in the household.[7] These discourses have had an impact upon attitudes and policies towards the family in modern and contemporary society.

Each chapter analyses trends in family type, size and structure, as well as examining the relationship between the family and the state and the impact of family policies and laws. As the book moves through the modern period of German history, the reader will be able to identify continuities and changes in the history of the family in Germany. By the end of the book, the reader will be able to evaluate the impact of modernity on the German family and to draw conclusions about how the family changed over the course of history from the late nineteenth century to the start of the twenty-first century.

Context

Before we begin, it is useful to sketch in broad strokes a brief overview of family forms in Germany in the period prior to the era covered in the first chapter, in order to provide the historical context for the discussion of the complex processes of continuity and change in the German family after 1871 examined in this book. In the early modern period, the predominant German family form was that of the *Haushaltsfamilie* or *das ganze Haus* ('the whole house').[8] This 'domestic community' was composed not only of blood relations, but also of individuals who worked for the household, such as servants, farmhands, apprentices and journeymen. In preindustrial society, the household functioned as a unit of production and thus required a clearly defined and strict hierarchical social structure. The household was run jointly by the *Hausvater* ('patriarch') and the *Hausmutter* ('mistress of the household'), although each had different areas of authority. The *Hausvater* exercised legal guardianship rights over all members of the household.[9] In most cases, the *Hausvater* headed the family and was responsible for the general organisation of the household, wielding authority over his wife, children and employees. The *Hausmutter* was in charge of the internal economy of the household, which was her exclusive domain.[10]

The Industrial Revolution brought in its wake a dramatic change to the traditional German family model, as a separation of workplace and residence occurred.[11] The decline of the household's role in production was accompanied by the demise of the 'domestic community' that had defined at the household. Members of the household who had worked in productive activities, but were not bound by kinship, increasingly resided elsewhere.[12] The social unit of the household gradually became the *Familie* ('family'), composed of parents and their offspring. This transition instigated the new era of the bourgeois family, which became a private domain of social interaction and reproduction. Domestic servants were not included in this intimate sphere, although they still often lived in the family house. In the family, privacy and sentimentality prevailed and the relationship between parents and children was strengthened. The 'household of the family' became the dominant form. However, changes in the family form from the pre-industrial period to the era after the Industrial Revolution must be assessed with care. There was still no general historical trend from the large family to the small family or from a multi-generational family type to an isolated nuclear family form.[13] Contrary to popular belief, changes in the family were not the result of a reduction in the size of the family per se, but of the transformations in the constitution of the household, engendered by the changes in its functions. As the family lost its function as a unit of production, its perceived size declined as servants and other non-related persons were now outside it.[14]

The separation of dwelling and workplace also engendered a redefinition of the division of labour within the family unit, as productivity was removed from the household. The former close collaboration between the *Hausmutter* and *Hausvater* in administering the household – in which the former was an active partner – gave way to a completely different situation, in which male and female spheres became separate, both in location and activity.[15] From the 1820s onwards, the term *Hausmutter* was increasingly replaced by the word *Hausfrau* ('housewife') with the transition from the traditional household to the bourgeois family.[16] Her role changed from that of domestic producer to that of domestic consumer.

Middle-class wives and mothers believed that the new, bourgeois family form was superior to the rural family, on the one hand, and the aristocratic family, on the other. They looked down upon rural wives as vulgar, unfeminine and unsophisticated, and disdained aristocratic women as selfish, egotistical, immoral and dishonourable. The new bourgeoisie of the late eighteenth and early nineteenth centuries disassociated itself from both, as well as from the old middle class of guilded craftsmen, innkeepers, retailers and merchants, in whose households – as was the case of farming families too – women were still fully integrated into the production process. The new bourgeoisie created its own family ethos and sought to differentiate itself from other classes. The main factor that distinguished a middle-class lifestyle was the absence of work among women, as the bourgeois household could live on the income of the male provider, and employ domestic servants to do the housework. In contrast to the leisure of the middle-class woman, the working-class woman had to work an average of twelve to fourteen hours a day, as well as look after a large number of children and take care of her household.[17] Working-class women were employed in the textile industry as semi-skilled labour, but also in the food, paper and tobacco industries and in domestic service.[18] The working-class family was very much dependent upon the mother's as well as the father's income, and children aged ten and over were also obliged to work.

The rural household remained a unit of production. In agricultural families, where subsistence depended upon what was produced on the farm, the division of labour was based on gender. The farmer and household head took care of the fields, with the assistance of his sons and farmhands. His wife had many important functions of her own. She took care of the household in terms of bedmaking, linen and clothing, washing, sewing and cleaning. She supervised work in the dairy barns, the kitchen and cellar, as well as the rearing of livestock. She was in charge of training her daughters and supervising the work of female servants.[19] In such families, with distinct labour functions, the work of the *Hausmutter* and *Hausvater* was of equal value and importance in maintaining the estate. But men and women did not have equal status within the family hierarchy. In the majority of cases, the traditional patriarchal family structure remained firmly entrenched, with the *Hausmutter* being subordinate to the *Hausvater*.[20]

The same family structure with the man as indisputable head of the household and guardian of his wife and children also applied to families of the upper class. But the family of the nobility had a different lifestyle altogether. In aristocratic families, children were isolated from their parents, reared and educated instead by household servants, governesses and private tutors. As in other strata of society, daughters were brought up with the aim of marriage, but relations between marital partners were often rather distant. Many aristocratic couples lived quite separate lives – with separate bedrooms, frequent absences from home on the part of the husband, leisure trips, for example to spas, on the part of the wife, so that they were held together only by joint social duties. Women, free from the burden of work and of raising their children, were able to indulge in leisure pursuits and other activities, including, if they so wished, extra-marital affairs.

The nineteenth century saw the further development of the bourgeois family, with a distinctive style of furnishing and design (*Biedermeier*), for which the housewife and mother took responsibility.[21] Her role was to create a cohesive and stable home environment and to rear and protect her children. Middle-class women were the providers of family cohesion. The socialisation of children took place within the family. The mother brought up her children with values of industriousness, ambition, self-control and thrift. Women had three roles – as wives, mothers and housekeepers. Their priorities lay in that order too – to their husbands first, then their children, and finally their household. A woman's work in the household made possible and safeguarded her husband's success outside it. In this period, the bourgeois family had servants to do menial tasks and housework, such as scrubbing, heavy cleaning, washing and ironing, and nannies to look after the children and take them out for walks. Hence, the middle-class housewife's duties were more concerned with supervising such staff and keeping up the appearance of her household in line with its social status. The bourgeois family was portrayed as a haven of order and tranquillity. The image of idyllic family life prevailed as the norm, with the housewife's qualities of grace and effortlessness perceived as charming, feminine virtues. The household was a centre of warmth and love.

The mid-nineteenth century witnessed the emergence of a wider urban middle class, whose core was made up of civil servants, judges, lawyers, doctors, professors and teachers. This new urban bourgeoisie distinguished itself from the other inhabitants of the large towns in terms of its professional practices, dress, housing and cultural norms. Men of the professional middle class met in clubs and coffee houses and became more and more oriented to the world outside the home. In contrast, their wives remained very much inside the household. Their role was to supervise their servants, to keep up the appearance of wealth and luxury, to decorate their homes lavishly and to host tea parties and dinner parties, in order to demonstrate the success of their husbands' business or profession. Hence, while men became increasingly involved in the public sphere, women remained within the private sphere. Women's work within the domain of the home complemented that of men outside it.[22] The notions of natural gender polarity and of separate but complementary spheres of action for women and men were the key aspects of change in gender relations that began during the last decades of the eighteenth century and characterised the nineteenth century.[23] This was an important feature of this era of German social history.

Marriage was the only acceptable status for the daughters of the middle class. A married woman shared the social position and standing of her husband. But the marital relationship was unequal. The German Civil Code of 1900 placed a series of legal restrictions upon married women.[24] A married man could annul any contract made by his wife and disallow her to earn her own living. In addition, the German Civil Code granted all responsibility for marital affairs to the husband, not the wife. The husband also controlled his wife's dowry, property and inheritance. As parents, it was the father, not the mother, who took the major decisions about their children's education and future. Children also had to seek their father's consent before marrying. The marital relationship was very different for a man than for a woman. For a man, marriage was only part of his life, which was supplemented by his profession and social contacts outside the home. For a woman, the domestic sphere was her only one. Her relationship with her husband and the bearing and rearing of her children made up her entire world. Very few opportunities existed for married women to earn their own living. In keeping with tradition, only those women who were unmarried could seek employment.

Outline

In Chapter 1, Gunilla Budde examines the development of German families in the late nineteenth century. She shows how previously, a variety of types of family life had existed side by side, and more were added during the social upheavals of the nineteenth century. Earlier family structures began to dissolve or were slowly overlaid by new forms and patterns. During the mid-nineteenth century, the number of rural lower-class families had increased quickly as part of the general rapid growth of the German population. A significant group of the lower class previously had lived away from their own families for long periods of time. Journeymen and apprentices had lived as tenants or night lodgers at their masters' family households. In this earlier period, *das ganze Haus* ('the whole household'), as we have already noted, had comprised of relatives and non-relatives who had lived and worked together, and had shared the rare moments of leisure time.

Budde analyses the development of the bourgeois ideal of the family in the nineteenth century. Love as the sole motive of marriage and ultimately as the unifying bond of all family members was the core idea of the family of the newly emerging middle class during the nineteenth century. Family members held a shared ideal of family life and values. The middle class regarded itself as the foundation and bearer of 'bourgeois society' designed as a meritocracy and without any birth-class privileges. Its vision of a social order was determined by reason, individuality, humanity and its own 'civil culture'. The core elements of this 'civil culture' included a positive attitude towards self-determination and regular work, duty in professional and private life, the tendency to a sophisticated lifestyle, the emphasis on *Bildung* (education) and training, and the conception and realisation of a specific family ideal. In opposition to the world of economy and politics, the family entailed a private sphere, a separate and complementary world, a place of leisure for women and children, a serene space in the busy world of the bourgeois meritocracy.

Budde's chapter also explores the place of education and the position of children within the family. A good education prepared middle-class citizens for successful participation in civic life. It supplied the necessary rules and forms, for example, in table manners and social rituals, including forms of greeting and conversation patterns, in behaviour and dress codes. Behind the doors of family houses, these social forms were exercised during family celebrations, dinner parties and outside the house, on the usual Sunday walk to church or visits to museums, galleries or public parks. At the same time, the existence of a special sphere for children became the signifier of what the French historian, Philippe Ariès, described as the 'discovery of childhood'.[25] This idea of the child's own rights and development was reflected in a booming toy industry, the publication of new children's books and the emergence of a children's clothing industry. A mythologising of the role of the mother occurred in parallel with this new appreciation of children.

This chapter also examines developments in working-class families during the late nineteenth century. Budde demonstrates that urban working-class families experienced the largest growth in Imperial Germany. Despite a variety of different circumstances, there were also certain analogies that allow us to regard the working-class family as one type of family form in Imperial Germany. Work determined the communal life of all family members. The kind of work and its location defined the structure, lifestyle and habitus of family members in working-class families.

The First World War acted as a catalyst for social and economic change. Its modernising impact was felt throughout society as it brought about a significant upheaval in family life and created substantial transformations in traditional attitudes and values. The First World War engendered a disruption of family life. The calling up of some 9 million men – half of who were married – by the end of 1915 meant that families suddenly lost their breadwinners.[26] Conscription meant a decrease in family income, as the wartime supplements to soldiers' families were inadequate to meet their basic requirements. In addition, conscription created a social vacuum, as countless families now lacked the patriarchal authority upon which the functioning of family life had previously depended.[27] In many cases, women had to go out to work in order to make up for the shortfall in family income. Furthermore, in the factories, as women replaced men who had been conscripted, the distinctions between separate spheres of work for men and women were no longer clear. The number of women working outside the home had in any case been growing in the decades prior to the outbreak of war, and the war accelerated this trend, as well as breaking down traditional notions about the types of jobs for which women were suitable.[28]

The immediate aftermath of the war brought a host of economic and social problems, including inflation and unemployment. Inflation eroded the material foundations of middle-class family life. It meant that many families lost their savings and no longer had the financial resources to uphold the lifestyle to which they had been accustomed. At the more personal level too, the war engendered difficulties, including bereavement for fathers and sons who had died in battle and also the burden of many men who returned home crippled or psychologically disturbed. In addition, there was a significant trend of 'homecoming divorces'. As society readjusted to peacetime conditions, women were expected to leave their jobs to make room for demobilised men and to facilitate men's re-entry into family life. The impact of the war and the revolution of November 1918 created important changes in German society. The old imperial order collapsed, making way for a new experiment in liberal democracy. One of the most significant provisions of the new constitution of the Weimar Republic was that women achieved equal suffrage.[29]

In Chapter 2, Michelle Mouton analyses the struggle between tradition and modernity in the Weimar Republic. The Weimar Republic was a time of ambivalence of attitudes – the breaking of old taboos and the simultaneous conservative backlash – as society modernised. Germany's first parliamentary government, founded amid the chaos of a lost war, set out to rejuvenate German society and the German family. Concern for the family was widespread during the Weimar era. Family policy was evaluated not only for its specific and immediate impact, but also for its broader economic, demographic, social and moral implications. Politicians agreed that the family needed support, but they disagreed about the source of the trouble and the solution to the problem. Mouton examines the divergence of opinions in Weimar society – while traditionalists argued that the restoration of the family lay in a return to patriarchal authority and domestic roles for women, those advocating modernity saw equal wages, state support of families and greater rights for women as the solution. For German families – and, indeed, for society as a whole – the outcome of these political discourses played a fundamental role throughout the Weimar era. Politicians believed that national restoration depended upon the support of the government and the encouragement of stable family life. Mouton shows how not only Germany's politicians, but also physicians, judges, social workers, feminists, eugenicists and church leaders, weighed in on issues affecting the family. As legislators began their debates over providing assistance to families, it became clear that there were fundamental disagreements about how best to develop policy.

Mouton demonstrates that ultimately Weimar legislators did provide support for families. They ratified the Reich Youth Welfare Law, increased financial assistance for illegitimate children and large families, introduced marriage certificates and celebrated Mother's Day. At the local level, judges, social workers, youth department workers and physicians shifted policy and practices on a case-by-case basis in response to families' evolving needs and their own understanding of the right of the state to intervene in families. But with the advent of the Great Depression in 1929, the fragile state welfare system was overwhelmed and the economic security of German families was destroyed. In the face of this upheaval, conservative and right-wing politicians blamed women for overstepping their domestic roles, and an anti-feminist backlash nourished traditionalist critiques of modernity. New legislative alliances led to support for laws against 'double-earners', 'modern' marriage, birth control, liberalised abortion and divorce reform. The economic crisis also provided the opportunity for the National Socialists to become vocal in criticising the failure of parliamentary democracy to save the German family from peril. Adolf Hitler promised to revive the family and to reassert traditional gender roles in order to bring about national renewal.

In Chapter 3, I examine the family in the Third Reich. My chapter analyses the attempts of the National Socialist regime to redress both the 'crisis of the family' and the decline in the nation's birth rate. The Nazis proclaimed the family as 'the germ cell of the nation', the foundation on which the survival and the success of the German *Volk* (nation) depended. The Nazi leadership capitalised on the conservative backlash against changes in family life during the Weimar years and claimed that it would restore traditional models of the family. Point 21 of the NSDAP's Programme specified that 'The State must ensure that the nation's health standards are raised by protecting mothers and infants'.[30] A woman's 'most glorious duty', according to Joseph Goebbels, Nazi Minister of Popular Enlightenment and Propaganda, was 'to present her people and her country with a child'. My chapter analyses the policies towards the family implemented by the Nazi regime, as well as their impact. It examines a whole series of measures and incentives designed to achieve the goal of increasing the birth rate. These included: the Marriage Loan Scheme which was set up in June 1933 to promote marriages between healthy 'Aryan' partners; the symbolic tribute to mothers with large families in the form of the Cross of Honour of the German Mother, awarded to prolific mothers, in bronze, silver and gold, for four, six and eight children, respectively; the introduction of a new divorce law in 1938, which allowed for a divorce if a couple had lived apart for three years or more, and if the marriage had effectively broken down; the banning of contraceptives and the closure of family planning centres; and the tightening up of abortion laws. Furthermore, the chapter analyses Nazi policies of welfare for mothers and children.

My chapter also explores the more blatantly sinister side of Nazi family and population policy. Legal measures were introduced to prevent marriages between Jews and 'Aryans' (Nuremberg Laws, September 1935) and to prevent marriages between healthy 'Aryans' and those deemed 'unfit' for marriage due to physical or mental illness (Marriage Health Law, October 1935). Compulsory sterilisation was the principal method used by the Nazi regime to prevent people it considered 'undesirable' from having children. On 1 January 1934, the Law for the Prevention of Hereditarily Diseased Offspring came into effect, putting into practice Nazi eugenic ideas. This chapter also examines the *Lebensborn* ('Well of Life') organisation, established in December 1935 'to further the number of children in SS families, protect and administer to all mothers of good blood, and care for needy mothers and children of good blood'.

My chapter shows how the Nazis' aims of an increased birth rate, racial homogeneity and a regimented social life invaded the private domain of the family quite profoundly. Hence, the home was not a safe haven insulated from National Socialism. In the end, the Nazis stressed the importance of the family, but in reality, only cared about it as a vehicle for their own aims. Marriage and childbirth became racial duties, instead of personal decisions, as the Nazi regime systematically reduced the functions of the family to the single task of reproduction. The Nazi government encouraged families it regarded as 'valuable', but aimed to eradicate those it considered 'undesirable' or 'inferior'. Finally, the chapter considers the impact of the outbreak and duration of the Second World War on the German family and the legacy of the Nazi dictatorship in this area of life for the post-1945 period.

Indeed, the Second World War had far-reaching implications and consequences for family life, creating almost impossible circumstances for intimate and stable family life to be conducted. Men at the front suffered physical mutilation and psychological scarring, unsure if they would survive the war to resume family life. Many women who were used to their husbands making the decisions and dealing with family finances had to manage on their own. The conscription of farmers and male farm labourers created additional hardships for rural women, who had to cope with both their sources of livelihood and their families single-handed. In the cities and industrial areas, women bore the strains of factory work and the maintenance of their families on their own, struggling to survive under circumstances of rationing, bombings and fear. Their daily life was dangerous, demanding them to be 'both mindless and brave'.[31] There was much solidarity among women, who found themselves in similarly desperate situations. Female relatives helped each other with work, shopping and looking after children. In the absence of relatives, women turned to female colleagues, friends and neighbours for help and support. Networks of support among women were widespread and provided much-needed mutual relief. Air raids disrupted normal life and many families were made homeless and dispossessed. Many women and children were evacuated from the cities to rural areas, and families separated in the process. At the end of the war, flight from the advancing Red Army and the post-war expulsion of Germans from formerly Nazi-occupied lands led to further social dislocation, separation of family members and loss of homes.

As a consequence of the war, water and gas supplies to many homes had been destroyed, and food and clothing were in short supply. These problems were worse in urban areas than in the countryside, but the aim everywhere was simply 'to get through'.[32] Women cut clothes out of old military uniforms, formed knitting needles out of bicycle spokes and made yarn out of potato sacks. Food rations were meagre and shortages were severe, especially in the winter of 1946–7. One Berlin woman recalled the situation: 'During the war we were bombed, but had assurances of getting food supplies; when the war ended, there were no more bombing raids, but there was also nothing to eat.'[33] Hence, the immediate post-war period brought about feelings of joy and relief, but also disappointment.

By the end of the war, the German economy was shattered, and some two-fifths of the population had been displaced and dispossessed. There was a tremendous housing shortage, as the effects of the war destroyed about one quarter of all homes. In the cities, more than 50 per cent of housing had been devastated. In 1946, there were some 6 million dwellings too few for the needs of the German population.[34] People whose homes had survived the war had to make rooms available to refugees or homeless families. The impact of the war upon family life had been disastrous. The heavy death toll, as well as the large number of German men who were prisoners of war, meant that millions of German women had to be self-reliant. Lack of food and sleep brought emaciation and chronic exhaustion to many women who had to work as rubble clearers or in semi-skilled and unskilled jobs, and who often gave up their food for their children. The search for food included desperate foraging expeditions to the countryside or buying food on the black market for those women who could afford the elevated prices. Women had to be resourceful and good at improvisation, as they were forced to prepare meals with few ingredients and sometimes without energy supplies. A study of 498 Berlin families in 1946–7 concluded: 'The burden of day-to-day work carried out by most women has become not only more complex and difficult, but is also increasing disproportionate to the scant opportunity they have to recover their strength through eating and sleeping.'[35]

The homecoming of husbands and fathers had been long awaited by families that had been separated for between three and nine years. Women hoped that with the return of their husbands, their lives would be made easier. However, when men returned home, many women could scarcely recognise their husbands. The women faced perhaps their hardest task, to provide the understanding, emotional balance, rebuilding of confidence and encouragement needed by so many totally beaten and desperate men.[36] The process of recovery and rehabilitation was a lengthy one, and its strain frequently resulted in the physical and psychological exhaustion of women. Many men were unable or unwilling to adjust to their new situation, which exacerbated the already difficult circumstances of their families. For example, they often refused to change their attitudes and expectations, and despite their powerlessness, acted like domestic tyrants. This often resulted in conflicts and arguments between spouses. Rising divorce rates, reaching a post-war high of 87,013 in 1948, demonstrated that it was not easy for married couples to reformulate their relationships after years spent apart, as too much had changed.[37] To be sure, years of separation took their toll on family life. Both men and women were confronted with changes in the physical appearance of their partners. Feelings of reserve and alienation made it hard for many married couples to communicate with each other. In addition, it was difficult for them to recount painful experiences to each other. Other problems also contributed to the destabilisation of families, such as sexual distance between spouses and difficulties in the relationships between children and their recently returned fathers.[38]

In Chapter 4, Alexandria Ruble explores the effects of the Second World War and its immediate aftermath on familial structures, laws and family policies, and everyday life in the 1950s in the Federal Republic of Germany (FRG). She draws from statistics, reports, parliamentary protocols, and personal letters to illustrate the shifting norms of West German families and policies towards the family in the 1950s. Immediately after the end of the war, the Western Allies had had to cope with the 'surplus' of 7 million women – many of whom had worked outside the home and raised families on their own during the war. Families headed by single mothers, remarriage, illegitimate births and other new familial arrangements became commonplace in the late 1940s. These trends were not new to Germany, which had seen some similar patterns after the First World War. The demobilisation of the *Wehrmacht* (armed forces) and the return of prisoners of war further affected familial arrangements and labour market structures. Moreover, the influence of the Western Allies, who brought their own ideas of 'gender equality' and family life to Germany, was significant. In 1946, the Allied Control Council created policies on marriage and the family to deal with the perceived crisis of the family. When the Allies overturned old Nazi policies, they were pressed to fill a legal vacuum and harked back to the regulations in the 1900 Civil Code on marriage and the family for inspiration for their own policies. The resulting statutes reinforced the idea of a male-breadwinner/female-homemaker model. Furthermore, the burgeoning Cold War struggle between East and West pushed German legal experts on both sides of the Iron Curtain to formulate proposals in opposition to the other Germany.

After the formal establishment of the FRG in 1949, West German politicians embarked on overhauling two major laws – the *Mutterschutzgesetz* and the family law sections of the Civil Code – and implementing several new family policies. The ruling Christian Democrats, who controlled the federal government and held the majority in the Bundestag, spearheaded these discussions. The conservative Adenauer administration set up Germany's first ever Ministry of the Family in 1953, as a demonstration of the commitment of the federal government to family values. Discussions of these laws and policies revealed a deepening rift between the ruling Christian Democrats, who hoped to retain a male-breadwinner/female-homemaker model, and their main parliamentary opposition, the Social Democrats, who saw the post-war era as an opportunity to emancipate women and acknowledged the changed nature of German families after two world wars. Their debates placed issues such as out-of-wedlock births, divorce, alimony and paternal authority at the fore. This chapter demonstrates that in West Germany in the 1950s, the Christian conservative-led government responded to the perceived post-war crisis of the family with a series of paternalistic laws, which were designed to reinforce the male-breadwinner/female-homemaker family model. It also reveals, however, that the concept of the family was highly contested in the 1950s. Furthermore, families in West Germany in the 1950s adapted and embraced governmental plans with varying degrees of acceptance.

In Chapter 5, Sarah Summers builds upon the previous chapter by examining the West German family and family policies from the 1960s to the 1980s. She demonstrates how the male-breadwinner family and nuclear family ideal remained strong in cultural norms and state policy due to Cold War discourses on the family and concerns over the socialisation of young children, even as rising divorce rates, declining birth rates, the increased employment of mothers and critiques from the women's movement contested its hegemony. The first part of the chapter focuses on a top-down analysis of the continuities and changes of West German family policy and marriage law from the 1960s to the 1980s. Beginning in the 1960s, the increased desire and demand for employment from women and mothers, and the needs of the West German labour market, resulted in family and education policies that supported the part-time employment of women. This 'modernisation' of the West German division of labour was viewed as a compromise between the perceived cultural necessity of the role of the mother in the socialisation of children and the practical desires and choices of West German mothers. The election of the reform-minded left-wing Social Democratic Party (SPD) and liberal Free Democratic Party (FDP) coalition to the parliamentary majority in 1968 resulted in the liberalisation of divorce law and the Civil Code in 1977 to promote flexibility in the construction of gender roles in the family. However, attempts by the SPD/FDP to reform family policy to better reconcile family and employment for working mothers highlight the continuing significance of the conservative Christian Democratic Union (CDU) and Cold War discourses of the family in informing family policy development. The 1970s ended with the passing of a paid maternal leave policy. Summers's chapter moves on to examine developments in the 1980s, when the CDU was again elected into the parliamentary majority. While the CDU continued to promote the male-breadwinner family model and the stay-at-home care of children under three, it nevertheless passed new legislation in 1985, which granted paid parental leave for both parents, while also providing a subsidy to parents (mostly mothers), for parents who were not employed before the birth of the child. Overall, between the 1960s and 1980s, family policy and marriage legislation gradually recognised working mothers and the equal role of both parents in the raising of children, even while in practice promoting the care of children by mothers.

The second part of the chapter analyses the continuities and changes in the structure of the West German family, and the related norms and functions of the family. An examination of the public discourse of the family in major newspapers and magazines reveals contestation over the structure of the family and the role of parents in the household, not least due to the impact of Second Wave feminism in the late 1960s. Furthermore, after the liberalisation of divorce laws in 1977, single parenthood became more prominent and accepted in public discourse. Statistical analysis confirms that contestation over family norms reflected gradual changes in the structure of the family. The two-parent nuclear family remained the norm in West Germany, although a rise in single parent homes became evident. Employment rates of mothers rose steadily, but baby breaks, the prevalence of part-time employment for mothers and the dramatic decrease in the birth rate apparent by the end of the 1970s, reflected the impact of state policy upon family decisions. The Federal Republic also introduced some modifications to Paragraph 218, the abortion law, in 1976.

In Chapter 6, we turn to parallel developments in the history of the family in East Germany in the post-war period. Donna Harsch shows that in 1966, more women in the German Democratic Republic (GDR) worked for wages than anywhere else in the industrialised world, comprising 49.1 per cent of the entire workforce. Even more path breaking was the very large percentage of employed mothers in East Germany. In 1967, 55 per cent of women with three or more children had a job. Like the USSR, the GDR stood at the vanguard of a major social trend in advanced economies: the ever-increasing employment of married women and mothers. Whether in the proud eyes of East German Communists or the hostile view of West German anti-Communists, the 'working mother' represented the East German woman and defined the East German family. Harsch's chapter approaches the history of the family from the perspective of maternal employment, on the one hand, and the history of Communist economic and social policy through the lens of the family, on the other. Maternal employment produced cascading social effects on the family, but these changes were not always those predicted or wanted by the ruling Communist Party, and sometimes forced revisions in state policy. Maternal employment also did not change the family – or at least it did not transform the fundamental gender dynamics of the two-parent family. The chapter traces the intertwined complexities of continuity and change in private life and public policy over time. It begins with an examination of the condition of the family in the rubble of post-war Germany and traces its development through to its situation at the demise of socialism in 1989–90. It considers marriage rates, birth rates, divorce rates and the domestic division of labour. It explores popular attitudes about wives and husbands, mothers and fathers, and their private and public roles. It reconstructs everyday gender and generational relations in the family and reflects on the role of the family in child development and its relationship to East German society and social mores.

In addition, Harsch discusses the combination of socialist ideology, economics and culture that shaped state policy towards the family. She argues that East German Communists never actively entertained a revolutionary transformation of domestic relations, but did expect women's employment to make the family into an egalitarian institution. The chapter demonstrates that initial plans for a smooth increase in women's employment and a concomitant transition to women's social and domestic equality seriously underestimated the forces of resistance to these plans. They were distorted and bent by various obstacles, including male workers' opposition, husbands' resistance, wives' reluctance, the lack of service infrastructure to support maternal waged labour and the competing commitment of the state to a high fertility rate. The chapter examines how and why the state responded in both discourse and practice to these oppositional winds. Rhetoric about the importance of family life, Harsch shows, became louder, not quieter, over time. The state never questioned its commitment to the wage labour of women, but the tools and incentives it used to reach and maintain that goal evolved over time.

In 1990, the separate paths of the two German states reconverged with German reunification. In the last chapter, Sigrid Leitner examines contemporary German family policy. She demonstrates how post-reunification Germany has seen a fundamental change in family policy, which has left the post-war male-breadwinner model of West Germany behind and has aimed at a new understanding of shared parenthood and the continuous labour market participation of both parents. This development arose first with the expansion of public childcare for children aged three to six years in the mid-1990s, and subsequently also for children under three years of age. Since 2013, every child over one year old has had a legal right to a childcare place. As a result, the acceptance of childcare, previously widespread in East Germany, has increased in West Germany too. Improved childcare has enabled parents – particularly mothers – to return to work quickly after the birth of a child and to work longer hours. In 2007, the introduction of an earnings-related parental leave benefit created further incentives for an early re-entry into the labour market after the first birthday of the child. Moreover, the parental leave reform reserved two months of paid leave exclusively for fathers and thus promoted gender equality in parenting – or at least enhanced the participation of fathers in childcare.

This development reflects not only changed attitudes within the younger generations, but also different traditions between East and West Germany regarding the roles and responsibilities of mothers and fathers. The traditional male-breadwinner/female-homemaker model has been increasingly replaced by a one-and-a-half-earner model or by a two-full-time-earner model. However, the picture has remained mixed, with policies in place that continue to support a traditional division of labour within the family, such as the *Ehegattensplitting* (a tax benefit for married couples with only one earner or a low-earning second earner). The new family policy has been linked to European Union employment strategy, aiming at the mobilisation of human resources in order to increase economic growth. As a result, German labour market policy has become very rigid in terms of enforcing labour market participation. Thus, the political aim of increasing parental employment has been framed primarily by an economic rationale. Long-standing feminist demands for gender equality in the labour market and within the family have been only secondary drivers of the policy changes. Nevertheless, gender equality arguments have been prominent in political discourse about the family.

In addition to a description of policy change and a consideration of its main drivers, Leitner's chapter also analyses empirical data on the development of parental employment, the expansion of childcare and the introduction of parental leave by fathers in order to give a fuller picture of contemporary family life in Germany. Moreover, the shortfalls of the new family policy are discussed. On the one hand, parental leave regulations have continued to reproduce social inequalities and the rigid demand for labour market participation has been most coercive for parents with low incomes. Thus, the choices parents have about their labour market participation and the sharing of childcare have been highly dependent upon their socio-economic status. On the other hand, the current feminist debate on care has criticised the new adult worker model as described in family policy for neglecting care responsibilities, especially in regard to old age care. Sociologists Jean Duncombe and Dennis Marsden, in 1993, described women's 'triple shift' – consisting of firstly, the family and household, secondly, paid work, and thirdly, 'emotion work' with regard to family members. Leitner's chapter arguably shows a 'quadruple' shift – that is, the care for elderly and frail parents, as increasing life expectancy, medical advances, better nutrition and public health measures have contributed to longer lifespans. Leitner's chapter finishes by outlining the implications of these latest developments for the situation of families in contemporary German society. Finally, we shall draw together some summative comments in the conclusion to the book.

Notes

1 I. Weber-Kellermann, *Die deutsche Familie: Versuch einer Sozialgeschichte* (Frankfurt am Main, 1974) and R. Sieder, *Sozialgeschichte der Familie* (Frankfurt am Main, 1987).
2 R. Evans and W. Lee (eds), *The German Family: Essays on the Social History of the Family in nineteenth- and twentieth-century Germany* (London, 1981).
3 These include R. Moeller, *Protecting Motherhood: Women and the Family in the Politics of Postwar West Germany* (Berkeley, 1993); L. Pine, *Nazi Family Policy, 1933–1945* (Oxford, 1997); M. Mouton, *From Nurturing the Nation to Purifying the Volk: Weimar and Nazi Family Policy, 1918 to 1945*

(Cambridge, 2007); D. Harsch, *Revenge of the Domestic: Women, the Family, and Communism in the German Democratic Republic* (Princeton, 2007); M. Mitterauer and R. Sieder, *The European Family: Patriarchy to Partnership from the Middle Ages to the Present* (Oxford, 1982); A. Prost and G. Vincent (eds), *A History of Private Life. V: The Riddle of Identity in Modern Times* (London, 1991); L. Davidoff, M. Doolittle, J. Fink and K. Holden, *The Family Story: Blood, Contract and Intimacy 1830–1960* (London, 1999); D. Kertzer and M. Barbagli (eds), *Family Life in the Twentieth Century* (New Haven and London, 2003); P. Ginsborg, *Family Politics: Domestic Life, Devastation and Survival 1900 to 1950* (New Haven and London, 2014); Q. Skinner (ed.), *Families and States in Western Europe* (Cambridge, 2011). A number of interesting contributions relating to Germany may be found in the journal, *The History of the Family*. These include: R. Gehrmann, 'German Towns at the eve of industrialization: household formation and the part of the elderly', *The History of the Family* Vol. 19, No. 1 (2014), pp. 13–28; R. Gehrmann, 'Infant mortality in town and countryside: northern Germany, ca. 1750–1850', *The History of the Family* Vol. 7, No. 4 (2002), pp. 545–56; S. Stöckel, 'Infant mortality and concepts of hygiene. Strategies and consequences in the Kaiserreich and the Weimar Republic: the example of Berlin', *The History of the Family* Vol. 7, No. 2 (2002), pp. 601–16. For a useful comparative European overview of family and social policy, see C. Saraceno, 'Social and Family Policy', in Kertzer and Barbagli (eds), *Family Life in the Twentieth Century*, pp. 238–69. For wider overviews of world histories of the family, see M. J. Maynes and A. Waltner, *The Family: A World History* (Oxford, 2012) and G. Therborn, *Between Sex and Power: Family in the World, 1900–2000* (London and New York, 2004). For comparative work, see also L. Davidoff and C. Hall, *Family Fortunes: Men and Women of the English Middle Class 1780–1850* (London and New York, 2019); K. Rowold, *The Educated Woman: Minds, Bodies, and Women's Higher Education in Britain, Germany, and Spain, 1865–1914* (New York and London, 2010) and K. Rowold (ed.), *Gender and Science: Late Nineteenth-Century Debates on the Female Mind and Body* (London and New York, 1996).

4   For example, see T. Evans, 'Secrets and Lies: The Radical Potential of Family History', *History Workshop Journal* Vol. 71 (Spring 2011), pp. 49–73; T. Evans, 'How do Family Historians work with Memory?', *History Workshop Journal* Vol. 87 (Spring 2019).

5   T. Parsons and R. Bales (eds), *Family, Socialisation and Interaction Process* (New York, 1955).

6 M. Young and P. Willmott, *The Symmetrical Family* (London, 1973).
7 For example, see C. Delphy and D. Leonard, *Familiar Exploitation: A New Analysis of Marriage in Contemporary Western Societies* (Cambridge, 1992).
8 This term, however, has been rejected by a number of historians, including Michael Mitterauer and Reinhard Sieder. They suggest instead the term *Hausgemeinschaft* ('domestic community'). See Mitterauer and Sieder, *The European Family*, p. 9.
9 I. Weber-Kellermann, 'The German Family between Private Life and Politics', in A. Prost and G. Vincent (eds), *A History of Private Life. V: The Riddle of Identity in Modern Times* (London, 1991) p. 504.
10 On the role of the *Hausmutter*, see M. Gray, 'Prescriptions for Productive Female Domesticity in a Transitional Era: Germany's *Hausmütterliteratur*, 1780–1840', *History of European Ideas* Vol. 8 (1987), pp. 413–26.
11 Weber-Kellermann, 'The German Family between Private Life and Politics', p. 504. On the changes to the household in this period, see H. Medick, 'The proto-industrial family economy: the structural function of household and family during the transition from peasant society to industrial capitalism', *Social History* Vol. 1 (1976), pp. 291–315 and E. Shorter, *The Making of the Modern Family* (New York, 1975).
12 Mitterauer and Sieder, *The European Family*, pp. 6–7.
13 Ibid., p. 43.
14 See H. Rosenbaum, *Formen der Familie: Untersuchungen zum Zusammenhang von Familienverhältnissen, Sozialstruktur und sozialem Wandel in der deutschen Gesellschaft des 19. Jahrhunderts* (Frankfurt am Main, 1996).
15 U. Frevert, *Women in German History: From Bourgeois Emancipation to Sexual Liberation* (Oxford, 1997), p. 15.
16 Gray, 'Prescriptions for Productive Female Domesticity', p. 413.
17 On the experiences of working class women, see L. Abrams, 'Martyrs or Matriarchs? Working-class women's experience of marriage in Germany before the First World War', *Women's History Review* Vol. 1 (1992), pp. 357–76.
18 Frevert, *Women in German History*, pp. 85–93.
19 Gray, 'Prescriptions for Productive Female Domesticity', p. 422.
20 Frevert, *Women in German History*, p. 23.
21 Ibid., pp. 66–7.
22 On this, see K. Hausen, 'Family and Role Division: The Polarisation of Sexual Stereotypes in the Nineteenth Century – An Aspect of the

Dissociation of Work and Family Life', in Evans and Lee (eds), *The German Family*, pp. 63–4.
23 L. Abrams and E. Harvey (eds), *Gender Relations in German History: Power, Agency and Experience from the Sixteenth to the Twentieth Century* (London, 1996), pp. 19–20.
24 Ibid., p. 322.
25 P. Ariès, *Centuries of Childhood* (London, 1996).
26 Frevert, *Women in German History*, p. 154.
27 Sieder, *Sozialgeschichte der Familie*, p. 212.
28 On women's work in the First World War, see U. Daniel, *The War from Within: German Working-Class Women in the First World War* (Oxford, 1997), pp. 37–126.
29 On the background to the achievement of women's suffrage, see R. Evans, 'German Social Democracy and Women's Suffrage, 1891–1918', *Journal of Contemporary History* Vol. 15 (1980), pp. 533–57.
30 Cited in L. Pine, *Hitler's 'National Community': Society and Culture in Nazi Germany* (London, 2017), p. 19.
31 A. Tröger, 'German Women's Memories of World War II', in M. Higonnet et al (eds), *Behind the Lines: Gender and the Two World Wars* (New Haven, 1987), p. 297.
32 Sieder, *Sozialgeschichte der Familie*, p. 240.
33 Cited in S. Meyer and E. Schulze, *Wie wir das alles geschafft haben: Alleinstehende Frauen berichten über ihr Leben nach 1945* (Munich, 1984), p. 92.
34 C. Kleßmann, *Die doppelte Staatsgründung: Deutsche Geschichte 1945–1955* (Göttingen, 1982), p. 39.
35 H. Thurnwald, *Gegenwartsprobleme Berliner Familien. Eine soziologische Untersuchung* (Berlin, 1948), p. 86.
36 U. von Kardorff, *Berliner Aufzeichnungen. Aus den Jahren 1942–1945* (Munich, 1962), p. 293.
37 Moeller, *Protecting Motherhood*, pp. 29–30.
38 Sieder, *Sozialgeschichte der Familie*, pp. 237–8.

1

The family in Imperial Germany

Gunilla Budde

Introduction: The family becomes a topic of discussion

The word 'family' entered the German vocabulary 'with a vengeance', Jacob and Wilhelm Grimm noted in the early nineteenth century. 'Compound words' became multisyllabic and their 'inexhaustible array' showed 'how deeply the word has taken root among us'.[1] Their linguistic research beginning in 1838 yielded ninety compounds in all, ranging from *Familien-Abenteuer* (family adventure) and *Familien-Glück* (family happiness) to *Familien-Zwist* (family feud). Just as quickly as the new word spread, the family became omnipresent as a topic of contemporary discourse. This was all the truer in Imperial Germany, when social analyses flourished and crisis scenarios came to dominate them. People realised that something was happening to the family as an institution; the family became part of the historical process and thus dynamic and subject to evolution. In other words, it acquired its history as a natural entity, a history that has been written over and over since the mid-nineteenth century. This historicity that the discourses now accorded the family was also reflected in other forms. Eighteenth-century German plays had revolved around the family. Tragedies such as *Kabale und Liebe*, *Emilia Galotti* and *Miss Sara Simpson* presented the family as a fragile, imperilled and damaged institution. But in the less dramatic political literature, a romantically glorified image of the family dominated. This was also the case in Carl Rotteck's and Carl Welcker's well known *Staats-Lexikon*, where the article on the family calls it 'the foundation of all noble human and civil life, all human and civil happiness'.[2]

To what extent did family realities in Imperial Germany live up to this ideal? What were the prevalent ideal notions of the family, where were they best realised, and where did ideal and reality diverge most widely? What changes became evident in Imperial Germany in contrast to the first half of the century? What changes became apparent after the turn of the century?

The bourgeois family: Ideal and reality

If the family became a topic of conversational culture, it was above all members of the German upper middle classes who led the discussion. More influentially than anywhere else in Europe, comparative studies have shown, men and women of the German upper middle classes, although numerically a minority of around 5 per cent, put their stamp on their society.[3] At the beginning of the century, the educated bourgeoisie, and not least members of the higher civil service, led the way. Their main focus was the nobility, a social caste from which they wished to distance themselves in lifestyle and life plans. With self-confidence, the bourgeoisie as a new class set its own values against aristocratic ones. It conceptualised its own bourgeois culture in which, always with an eye to the aristocracy as a contrasting backdrop, achievement was opposed to birth, moderation to extravagance, and tolerance to narrow-mindedness.

The heart of this bourgeois culture was a specific ideal of the family. In this ideal, the family was supposed to be founded on affinity and held together by love. It was conceived of largely as a two-generation nuclear family composed of father, mother and children, and clearly sealed off from the world of profession and work. Its chief task was to raise children according to their peculiarities and needs and to cultivate a clear gender-specific division of labour, with the adequate income of the husband and father and the work of maids providing the necessary financial means and leisure.

Such ideas were expressed in a variety of normative writings, and their realisation was, by and large, what the bourgeoisie aimed to achieve. And not only the bourgeoisie; other social strata considered the bourgeois family ideal worth striving for, even if they frequently lacked the material means to do so consistently. On the one hand, the family suffered a decisive loss of traditional functions through the separation of work and family life. It evolved from a sphere of production to one of pure reproduction and recreation. The world of work moved more or less away from the domestic four walls, but in any case out of the immediate sight of women and children. On the other hand, the family attained a higher conceptual value, since it was projected as a harmonious refuge from the demanding outside world.

The division of tasks within the family, which assigned middle-class men the professional world outside the family and women the family sphere, was declared to correspond to 'innate' gender character and was thus dubbed 'natural'. Contemporary lexicon articles did their part to provide this model with a normative foundation. They described women as passive, conservative, emotional, irrational, adaptable, fickle, industrious and modest, and men as active, independent, brave, rational, energetic, future-oriented and farsighted. Such a polar gender order not only solidified inequalities, but also rooted them in a system of domination and subordination. Decisions were made by the husband and father, and all family members were subject to his absolute authority.[4]

But how did the idea of female subordination fit with that of equal opportunities and the freedom of all to develop their potential – without regard to birth, and hence also to sex? In any case, even the masterminds of the utopian programme of civil society were troubled by this inconsistency of argumentation, and diligently sought justifications. In so doing, they used some rather serpentine arguments. According to Johann Gottfried Herder (1744–1803) in his journal *Adrastea*, for instance, since women perpetually lived in the 'paradise' of 'domestic society' and were thus mistresses of the space of the 'purely human' – unlike middle-class men, who were out bustling in the professional world – they had no need for compensation in the guise of the public sphere. Accordingly, middle-class women had already found their 'destiny' as 'educators of humanity', while middle-class men had to seek their own forms and institutions outside the family in the process of finding themselves and their proper personality.

Man and woman were supposed to come together in marriage. In the bourgeois view, marriage as a life-long bond was not an institution dedicated to securing political and economic authority, such as it continued to be instrumentalised into the nineteenth century by the European nobility, with its orientation towards class privilege and outward conventions. Instead, it was an emotional relationship between two partners, free of all material interests. Love and nothing but love was to be the criterion for choosing a partner. This is what magazines, poems and novels taught the men and women of the upper middle classes. These, in turn, cultivated the language of love in bridal letters. The letter culture, which began to flourish in the eighteenth century, continued in the nineteenth century.[5] The Romantic writers, in particular, engaged in a war of words in opposition to marriages of convenience and in favour of love matches. In his 1796 work on natural law, the philosopher Johann Gottlieb Fichte (1762–1814) declared marriage to be a matter of the heart: 'For this reason the state need not pass laws governing the relationship between the two spouses, for their entire relationship is not juridical, but a natural and moral relation of the heart. The two are one soul.'[6]

But even if middle-class men and especially women read these texts with teary eyes, few of them actually took to heart the ideals praised therein. The bourgeois, naturally unspoken motto was, rather, marriage equals love *plus* reason. And even love here did not refer to a 'romantic love' that threw all conventions overboard, but to a well-tempered, 'rational' affection. For even when love was invoked, there were often practical considerations as well. Few middle-class women or men would have dreamt of tying the knot solely out of mutual affection. Family considerations carried a great deal of weight. Even in the middle classes, the right of parents to have a say in their children's marriages long went uncontested. Among the first and most common questions that middle-class fathers asked their potential sons-in-law related to the state of their finances and their professional prospects. Fathers not infrequently made detailed enquiries into the financial resources of their daughters' prospective spouses. For one thing was clear: the husband's secure professional existence was an essential prerequisite for maintaining bourgeois status. This was even truer of the economic bourgeoisie, which became stronger in the second half of the nineteenth century. After the pace of industrialisation quickened with the establishment of the German Empire, entrepreneurs, bankers and managers became ever more prominent as a segment of the bourgeoisie. If there was a solid family business in the background, practical considerations played a very open role alongside fondness. Marrying into a 'good family' was deemed a welcome opportunity to expand the circle of those with whom one not only did business, but also interacted privately. Particularly in the early years of industrialisation, which in Germany only truly began after 1850, 'systematic intermarriage' was a common means of strengthening and cementing ties between enterprises through family relationships. Apart from maximising business and social possibilities, the methodical founding of families also served to minimise possible risks. If business transactions took place in the framework of a widely ramified kinship circle, the actors operated within a network of mutual trust, which could help to reduce the density of contractual regulations and lower the costs of acquiring reliable information and supervising business relationships.[7]

The success of this reconciliation of the love match ideal with such economic criteria was connected with the places where future spouses usually met. Marriage markets filtered marriage circles. Thus the intended mainly met at family festivities, dinner parties, musicals and theatre premieres, the newly fashionable summer resorts and spa visits or on the tennis court or ice rink. Intimacy had to be demonstrated with polished manners, and wives and daughters also displayed the family's wealth with their gowns and jewellery. But regardless of whether young people met on the dance floor or the ice, on the spa promenade or the tennis court, all of the sites of growing acquaintance listed here kept social circles small. That true affection between individuals could grow out of such a limited range of choices was a result not least of this very fact. The apparently spontaneous elective affinities that emerged were based on shared preferences and notions of taste, a tableau of qualities that were deemed attractive, a similar habitus. Viewed from this perspective, the highly endogamous marriage circles in the German bourgeoisie are hardly surprising; choices of marriage partner rarely breached the boundaries of the upper middle class.

The culmination of the courtship and engagement phase was a glittering wedding party, traditionally at the expense of the father of the bride. One such father, Wilhelm Welber, a Berlin banker, noted in his house chronicle in 1895:

> The eve-of-the-wedding party was on Monday, the 6th of May, at our home. It was perfectly delightful, with splendid weather and we used the garden. Some 50 persons were present. The performances were printed as mementoes. The wedding was on Wednesday, the 8th of May. The civil ceremony in Steglitz, the church wedding in Berlin at the new church of our old friend, Pastor Richter from Mariendorf. The banquet was held in Berlin at the "English House", Mohrenstraße 49, elegant and excellent. It was attended by 85 persons and cost 2575 marks.[8]

'The newlyweds departed at 10 o'clock', reads the last entry; the honeymoon had become a common practice. As to the destinations of honeymoons, certain preferences emerged that accentuate the bourgeois complexion of these *tours d'amour*. A favourite locale was Italy, where the couple could spend their first longer period of time alone in the shadow of art and architecture, and thus on familiar terrain. During these journeys, the spouses also spent their first night together. Many young middle-class women were completely unprepared for their husbands' incomprehensible notions of marital relations, accustomed as they were to being treated with respectful distance. For young women in particular, this 'wedding-night trauma' (Peter Gay) hardly offered a positive basis for a fulfilling marital sex life.[9] While for most of them this night after the wedding represented their first sexual contact, husbands as a rule already had some instruction in the *ars amandi*.[10] Their teachers usually came from the lower classes. One can only imagine how these widely divergent experiences and expectations affected marital relationships. The otherwise so eloquent middle classes fell silent at the bedroom door.

We may know very little about activities after dark, but the flood of marriage manuals left no doubt as to who was to make the decisions in the daytime. The head of the family was the husband and father. His position was further fortified by the frequently large age difference between husband and wife. As a rule, upper middle-class German wives were ten or more years younger than their husbands. The reason for this age differential was that before they could court a woman, young bourgeois men first had to go through a lengthy period of professional education – whether after university studies and subsequent traineeships in the law, civil service or clergy, or after long practical training in business, frequently far from home. Their fiancées, in contrast, enjoyed a rather sparse, one-sided education that ended at a young age, when they were fourteen or fifteen.

But even before marriage, the horizons in which bourgeois women and men moved were quite different. Contemporary authors such as the ethnologist Wilhelm Heinrich Riehl, who dedicates a volume of his natural history of the people to the family, were less concerned with the early narrowing of women's sphere of influence to the family than with how to do justice to their position:

> Woman's influence is in the family, for the family; she sacrifices the best she has for it; she raises the children, and lives her husband's life alongside him ... If one does justice to the family, one does justice to women, for the hearth is after all the altar upon which they have laid down their silent and yet so decisive endeavours for society and the state.[11]

The special value of women's own familial sphere required promotion, and there was no shortage of literature dedicated to this end in the nineteenth century. Clergymen, journalists, educators and medical doctors tried to make middle-class women's 'vocation' more attractive by tirelessly reminding them of its great importance. And many middle-class women actually enjoyed their 'lofty' task, regarding the family as the site of their very own creativity. As custodians of the *Familiensinn* (sense of family), which ranked very high on the scale of bourgeois values, they set the rhythm and tone of family life, directed everyday family life and holidays, reared children as future citizens, managed their households on an often modest budget, represented themselves and the family at social affairs, supervised housemaids, cultivated contacts with closer and more distant kin and proved themselves as crisis managers. This was indeed a wide range of responsibilities. The diaries of upper middle-class women are accordingly a mix of pride and worry, as we can see from the journal of Helene Eyck, mother of six and wife of a Berlin merchant:

> The father of such a large family with all its demands upon life surely does not have an easy time of it, especially when he still has to support his family at an advanced age with less prospect than ever of a carefree future. ... And the grown children, in contrast! The full house – the desire to live well, to complete the children's education in every respect, all of this taken together and compared offers an example that is unfortunately not quite right. Where is the motive force here? Where can improvement be expected? Naturally with me; it is my arts that should allow us to live more simply and economically. And we are doing this, and I am quite conscious of truly restricting outlays for myself! I am also doing this with the children's clothing – but I do not deny that some things in the household might be simpler still, but I must add that it is extraordinarily difficult if one does not wish to shed certain life habits and demands, most notably the preservation of the status quo, that is the household economy. Yes, and I should like to offer the children and ourselves a pleasant home, I would also like to allow them to continue their friendships and sociability and not acquaint them too far with the cares and worries of life.[12]

The balancing act between bourgeois aspirations and reality indeed proved to be an 'art' in which middle-class women were compelled to prove themselves daily. This was heightened by the increased value attributed to motherhood; in the course of the nineteenth century, an ever-growing chorus of clergymen, social moralists, educators, female authors and medical doctors glorified it as a kind of sacred calling. They pondered maternal instincts, feelings and duties with tedious repetition, while fathers were largely absent from this primarily bourgeois discourse.

We know from diaries, letters and memoirs that matters looked rather different in real life. Here we encounter middle-class women and men who by no means allowed others to stop them leaving their assigned spheres. Just as bourgeois men could act irrationally from time to time and show their feelings – although, following the masculine idea of the second half of the nineteenth century, they were less demonstrative – their wives were also perfectly capable of public, farsighted and rational action. Most members of the middle classes proved themselves to be frequent border crossers who helped whittle away at the normative wall between private and public a bit every day. Wives offered professional advice, just as husbands spent time thinking about the feeding of their infants. In August 1856, Theodor Fontane wrote to his wife Emilie shortly after the birth of their daughter:

> Here I would do well to append a few remarks about George's little sister. I am extremely happy to hear that you are doing so well, touch wood. Take good care, but take moderate exercise, eat meat and drink coffee (according to George's instructions), and with God's help all will be well. As to a wet nurse, I really cannot offer any advice from here. All wet nurses are horrible but necessary. That is all of my advice, that is, take one and overcome your distaste in the knowledge that such a living source of milk is necessary. If you feel in advance that you cannot do it, it is better not to engage one. Otherwise there will be trouble, you will fall ill and so will the wet nurse and finally the child as well. Let me just say this much today, don't be dissuaded from taking a wet nurse by economic considerations. The money must be found, and I will surely be able to earn that much from here.[13]

The Fontanes's wet nurse remained a problem, but so did the couple's very different expectations of one another. The journalist and author believed that his wife's foremost duty was to keep him 'capable of swimming', and she was repeatedly compelled to adapt to the spontaneous decisions of her husband, which were not always conducive to the family budget. The marital correspondence of the Fontanes was not the only one to reveal the discrepancy between expectations and experience that overshadowed daily life in many marriages. Precisely because the bourgeoisie – unlike other classes and unlike previous periods – burdened marriage and married life with such high expectations, disappointments were inevitable.

After all, model spouses and model marriages were rare. In some cases – and this too was a popular motif for the critics of the bourgeoisie among writers and cartoonists – upper middle-class men had a penchant for straying from their marital vows. Even then, wives were frequently lenient enough towards their husbands' libertine ways and tolerated these adulterous affairs. What counted was to maintain the appearance of an intact marriage. The reigning double standard, which afforded men more scope to pursue their sexual needs, euphemistically dubbed this male behaviour a peccadillo, while adultresses were generally punished by expulsion from polite society, a fact skilfully criticised in Fontane's novels – *Effi Briest* was the most famous of these – which were frequently inspired by real-life cases.

Yet a comparatively large number of marriages in Imperial Germany ended in court. The relatively liberal guidelines in the 1794 Prussian Legal Code, which also allowed for the dissolution of marriages based on 'deep-rooted aversion' – a forerunner of the principle of irretrievable marital breakdown – led to a substantial number of divorces in comparison to other European countries. Between 1849 and 1860, 35,490 marriages ended in divorce, and in 1899 alone, 9,433 marriages were dissolved by legal verdict in Imperial Germany.[14]

This did not mean that people usually remained unmarried, however. The many widowers with young children who even in Imperial Germany still frequently lost their wives in *Kindbett* (childbed) frequently chose to remarry, often enough with another younger woman, and often from among the dead woman's family circle. This pattern underlines that the couple-centred family was increasingly accepted as the ultimate model in society. While unmarried adult men were stamped with the less than flattering title of 'confirmed old bachelor', they continued to enjoy more social respect than the unmarried aunts branded as 'old maids', of which every family had more than a few. They were, to be sure, useful as family helpers in an emergency, but received precious little thanks for their self-sacrifice. The fact that they became popular targets for contemporary caricature did little to raise unmarried women's sense of self-worth. 'Aunt arrives as is her way, unexpectedly to stay', rhymed the much loved painter and author Wilhelm Busch in 1877. The image of the wallflower was hard to shake.[15] Yet, with the brisk wind of the emerging middle-class women's movement behind them, young bourgeois women increasingly succeeded in making an independent future for themselves, far from the strictures of family, generally as teachers and governesses.[16] These often sophisticated young women, who returned with a wealth of experience, showed their nieces that a different way of life than that lived by their mothers was possible. Whether this went beyond the realm of the professional and included new forms of personal life is difficult to glean from the meagre sources. We do know that the pioneers of the German women's movement Helene Lange and Gertrud Bäumer lived together in a shared household in Berlin for several years. Whether this was more than a 'political life partnership' remains speculation.[17] In Imperial Germany with its rigid family ideal, homosexual partnerships did not find any acceptance. That unmarried women lived together was not seen as problematic for women were denied sexual needs. That single men lived together was considered unnatural with the exception of students who, for reasons of costs, shared rooms for some time during their studies. Because homosexuality was severely punished, it remained hidden from the public eye. Rumours like the Eulenburg Affair, which involved a close friend of the Emperor known to be homosexual, became veritable scandals still at the beginning of the twentieth century. With regard to homoerotic tendencies, it was therefore easier for women to live them, at least behind closed doors.

But although new possibilities opened up for young bourgeois women around 1900 beyond their traditional family role, middle-class childrearing remained extremely resistant to innovation. One of the reasons may be that the concentration on children and their upbringing as a central task for the family was rather new. The idea that children were people in their own right different from adults gained currency mainly among the middle classes, who could best afford the luxury of sentiment. The 'discovery of childhood' (Philippe Ariès) influenced the outfitting of nurseries, children's literature, children's clothing and not least a boom in toy manufacturing.[18] That husbands and wives now discussed their children's toys in some detail in their letters demonstrates their growing importance in the educational process.

Bourgeois family life increasingly revolved around the children. With admiration and amusement, parents listened to their little ones' first sounds and words, with patience and pathos they watched their first steps into life and took the opportunity to set them onto the right path. The bourgeoisie gladly took up the 'weapon of education', which Jean-Jacques Rousseau had already conceptualised in critique of the nobility, in order to stress their own superiority to aristocratic ways. Childrearing as an intentional affair directed by parents was observed with interest and invested with hopes. As a bridge between the worlds of children and adults, it was supposed to produce the character traits and personality structures deemed necessary and desirable in the bourgeoisie. The educator Friedrich Froebel brought the first kindergarten into life and thus paved the way for child-friendly environments.[19]

The more energy, emotionality and educational efforts parents devoted to children, the more they desired to offer them optimal mental and material opportunities. Since budgets were often tight, this meant restricting the number of children in the family. While up to the middle of the nineteenth century, middle-class German families had comprised five to seven children on average, the nurseries of Imperial Germany often had only two to four occupants. Educated middle-class families, with Jewish families taking the lead, played a pioneering role in reducing the number of children. That families from the economic bourgeoisie followed this trend significantly later reflects the specific function of the family among entrepreneurs – the larger the family, the greater the financial potential. A large number of 'good matches' for sons and daughters could strengthen the financial capacity of an enterprise, increase its creditworthiness, help to make new commercial and professional connections, turn competitors into business allies, further careers and ward off crises.

In the late nineteenth century, another reason for reducing the number of births was the growing chance of surviving childhood. Thanks to better hygiene, new knowledge about caring for infants and medical progress, from which the middle classes were the first to benefit, children survived illnesses that just a few years before had almost inevitably proved fatal. Yet the risk of losing the children was still traumatically entrenched in middle-class consciousness. The family size promoted by the ophthalmologist Emil Ludwig in the 1890s, 'two children and a spare', revealed the contemporary fear of losing beloved offspring.[20]

But despite the love between parents and children, there were also false notes in this middle-class family harmony. Even though bourgeois parents were prepared to go to great lengths to meet their children's age-specific needs, they never lost sight of boys' and girls' future social and above all gender-specific roles. From earliest childhood, bourgeois parents had very specific ideas about what boys must do and girls must not – and vice versa. Boys of the German middle classes could enjoy their early childhood years relatively unencumbered, but soon had to be trained to follow closely in their fathers' footsteps. With the father as a role model, and the glorification of his profession, in its combination of material acquisition and individual fulfilment as a maxim of the male life model, middle-class boys were confronted from a young age with high expectations of achievement. The Wilhelmine *Gymnasium*, the academic secondary school attended by most upper-middle-class boys, went one step further to make their lives difficult. To be sure, as recent research has shown, the military-style drill generally attributed to schools in Imperial Germany was not as universal as legions of childhood memoirs would have us believe.[21] Nevertheless, one topic gained sad relevance in German public discourse at the turn of the century, drastically reflecting the apparent damage done to many middle-class boys by the high expectations of parents and school. 'Like railway accidents and tourists coming a cropper, schoolboy suicides appear to have become a standard rubric in the newspapers', begins a 1908 treatise by a Berlin schoolmaster in which he laid much of the blame at the feet of his colleagues.[22] In general, as a large number of ego-documents reveal, many bourgeois parents in Imperial Germany were becoming increasingly wary of the state schools and their teaching staff.[23]

Even more than sons of the educated middle class, the sons of entrepreneurs had to bow to their predestined careers in business. If, as was common well into the nineteenth century, the family villa was located on the grounds of the factory, they literally always had their future destiny before their eyes. They gained early glimpses into the world of the family business, not only from their parents' conversations at the luncheon table, but also from regular visits to the firm with their fathers. Here they could observe the behaviour of a factory owner and develop a reverent admiration for their father's work, an attitude demanded by fathers and promoted by mothers.

Real life began for boys upon entry into academic secondary school, which by the Wilhelmine period, was considered the proper type of school for the sons of both the educated and the economic bourgeoisie. Their school schedule now dominated their everyday lives, which continued with a methodical division of their time after the school day ended. Family lunches played a central role. There were even clubs dedicated to cultivating 'eating lunch the proper German way'. In 1910, Georg Simmel wrote an article on the 'Sociology of the Meal', thus placing himself at the head of a whole phalanx of modern educators and sociologists who stressed the importance of shared meals as an instrument for cementing power structures within the family.[24] This ritual was able to persist in Germany for a relatively long time above all because here – unlike in the suburban societies of Britain and North America – the greater proximity of the paternal workplace to the family home made it possible for the father to return there for the midday meal.[25] How routine this everyday ritual remained even in the late nineteenth century is confirmed by a letter the student Max Weber wrote to his mother in 1886:

> One great advantage of being alone in this regard is the possibility of spending less time at meals. Otherwise one sits for quite a long time, and it is quite natural, on the other hand, since these are the only times when the entire family comes together, and the activity is one of the few in which adults and children and those of varying temperament can participate with equal interest.[26]

Midday meals did not simply promote exchange within the family, but also reaffirmed the familial hierarchy, regularly and repeatedly. Within a small and temporally condensed framework, the participants rehearsed the family hierarchy with its unequal distribution of power. That the head of the family served himself or was served by the maid first, that he also received the choicest and largest pieces, decided which topics would be discussed and also spoke first, were familiar conventions that became internalised precisely through daily repetition and helped to strengthen the patriarchal structure. Put to the test, children also had to confess to their marks and demonstrate that they had paid attention in school. Otherwise, the 'small folk' (*das 'kleine Volk'*) were expected to be quiet and eat in a civilised manner. Children experienced their mothers during meals largely as the managers of the outward process, running between kitchen and dining room and giving orders to the maid. Moreover, the children also had the rare opportunity to watch their parents interacting as a couple. It was these everyday rituals that generated the family traditions in which the family cultivated its own language and produced and handed down family (hi)stories. The father and founder of family studies, Wilhelm Heinrich Riehl, recommended the cultivation of family feeling: 'Each family must take an aristocratic pride in its own peculiarity. For that reason, it should carefully collect and preserve that which documents its special character.'[27]

The 'special character' of many bourgeois families also meant that their consciousness of education and achievement never slept. This ethos was upheld even on holiday. Middle-class fathers frequently packed their business files to take with them on their summer holidays, and children brought their schoolbooks. If a son seemed to be floundering at school, fathers resorted to drastic means. During the final week of the holidays, an architect in the civil service placed the following letter, along with instructions, on the desk of his son, whose scholastic achievements left something to be desired:

> Since Heinrich – as I have learnt to my great dismay from a fortnight's experience – persists in his irregular activities and careless obliviousness, and is utterly incapable of directing his industriousness in a rational and effective manner by his own free will, and can anticipate disgrace for his parents and the greatest disadvantage to himself as a result of this disorderliness, I should like hereby to remind him once again of his duty and admonish him to return to order, to regular hard work and to the rational apportionment of his time, so that he may become a useful member of society, and his parents may at least be justified in their expectation that he will not drown in the river of common everyday life. Fearing that this admonition may also not help, and with the firm intention that at least the impending final week of the holidays will not be spent in idle dawdling, I order the following schedule: 1) 20 minutes for washing and dressing. 2) Until coffee is served: practice the piano. 3) From 8–10 o'clock: drawing. 4) From 10 o'clock until luncheon: revision of Latin and Greek grammar. 5) From 2–4 o'clock: practice the piano. 6) From 4–7 o'clock: revision of German, French and English grammar. 7) From 7–9 o'clock: algebra. The hours of instruction with the pastor as well as in French and music are the only exceptions.[28]

The pressures of accomplishment and self-discipline mainly affected sons. Expectations of daughters were very different. They learned early on that the family was their destined place, and they had to begin preparing for it in girlhood, along with the attendant restrictions. Unlike their brothers, who were raised to be independent, middle-class girls were rarely allowed to leave the protective realm of the family. Mothers showed them what their 'vocation' looked like, and they practised with dolls, dolls' houses and miniature kitchen utensils. What they rehearsed in play as small children soon evolved into serious responsibilities for the family household. Until the turn of the century, they rarely had any further training, and professions for middle-class women were accepted only as stop-gap measures when no husband materialised, so that girls' formal education was correspondingly limited. In 1877, a former governess formulated the classic curriculum for the ideal education of girls of good family as follows:

> To one day speak three modern languages with fluency and elegance, to play the piano brilliantly, sing with expression, be at home in the literatures of three nations, be capable of writing ingenious letters, travel accounts and diaries, and also to have read edifying works in several languages. ... The skill to produce fine needlework and the pleasing talent to make original sketches from nature are considered activities that go without saying, among others.... The aim is eventually to be able to introduce a well-rounded, pleasing, piquant and graceful young woman into the world and society who knows how to captivate an independent wealthy man with the veneer of her knowledge, talents and charms of all kinds.[29]

But other young women also lived in the middle-class households of Imperial Germany alongside such well-bred young ladies. Without the obligatory housemaid, contemporaries and later historians agreed, the bourgeoisie could not claim their class status. In fact, it was these frequently very young, usually rural women whose hard work in bourgeois households afforded their mistresses the necessary leisure to help shape and pass on their bourgeois culture. If we speak of a 'bourgeois' nineteenth century, we can speak in the same breath of the 'century of the housemaid' (Jürgen Kocka).[30] The two histories were closely intertwined: If the middle classes needed at least a housemaid in order to be members of bourgeois society, maidservants looking for work knocked mainly on middle-class doors.

The position of maidservants in middle-class households once again reflects the Janus-faced quality of the bourgeoisie. When it came to their legal status, living and working conditions and position in the household, the housemaid embodied relics of a premodern world that the bourgeoisie had just declared outmoded. According to the sixty variants of German regulations governing servants (*Gesindeordnungen*), servants were legally integrated into their employers' households. These regulations, already criticised during the Enlightenment as 'leftovers from the legal Stone Age' or 'continuations of now abolished serfdom', would hold on until 1918.

Their socialisation had left these young women ill-equipped to resist. Practised as they were in frugality, trained to adapt and prepared to subordinate their needs, content with the occasional small treat and accustomed to hard work, the girls acquired a wealth of attributes and qualifications in their families of origin that proved much sought-after in their new positions in service. Scarcely more than children themselves, they shouldered various duties and responsibilities, managed the household and cared for younger siblings. Because of the proverbial diffidence attributed to girls from the rural lower classes in particular, middle-class households hardly expected servants to complain about their living conditions. It would have been perfectly understandable if they had, though. If they were lucky, the women moved into an unheated room under the eaves, but in most cases, they had only a bed that was set up every evening in the kitchen, an adjacent storeroom, a bathroom or hallway. Flats in nearly all large German cities also featured the (in)famous institution of the *Hängeboden*, a small structure created by building a platform over the pantry, the bathroom or the hallway. Families and their housemaids, in any case, lived at very close quarters. Sounds, smells and sentiments were difficult to conceal from one another. In this state of fragile privacy, singing housemaids and quarrelling employers were soon silenced.

Whether housemaids had much to sing about considering the huge amount of work they did is questionable. Until the end of the nineteenth century, middle-class households still produced a portion of their own basic foodstuffs and commodities. The advice on churning butter, pickling and candle dipping that fills contemporary housekeeping books is evidence of the wealth of tasks demanded of housemaids. The typical turn-of-the-century furnishings of fashionable bourgeois households with their dust-catching knickknacks and fringes everywhere made cleaning all the more difficult. All of this work also had to be done as unobtrusively as possible, as the common image of *dienstbare Geister* (literally subservient spirits) vividly invokes. The results were supposed to be not merely ghostly, but also perfect.[31] There was no special training for maidservants that might have justified such high expectations, however. The knowledge and skills the girls brought with them had been acquired from their own mothers or other female relations in the parental home; but many only learnt on the job from their mistresses or from experienced fellow servants.

The working relationship between the bourgeois housewife, daughters and servants was a precarious one. Contemporaries were already aware of the issue. They never tired of preaching obedience and gratitude to servants who had the opportunity to participate in middle-class life, and recommended that housewives regard themselves as the instructors of their servants. Apparently, many middle-class women showed themselves inclined to reinterpret the relationship as a pedagogical one. After all, as authors repeatedly emphasised, these women could serve as examples in an era of class divisions and grasp the opportunity to convey bourgeois values to the lower strata, more specifically to the future mothers of working-class and artisanal families. We know little about how servants received these educational efforts. They could only hope that a maternal willingness to take responsibility might counteract their employers' tendency to exploit them. On the other hand, however, the line between kind and patronising often proved very fine indeed. Misunderstandings were inevitable, and abuses of power common. In the long run, servants must have experienced the often petty commandments and prohibitions, which included limitations on when they could leave the house, instructions on how to address their superiors and what words to use, on hair style and clothing, on food and on how they were to spend their scarce free time, as serious restrictions of their personal freedom.

Oskar Stillich (1872–1945), a social economist from Berlin, who carried out a survey among maidservants and their employers at the turn of the century, confirmed this:

> The girl is viewed and treated as an under-age child who is to be educated as soon as she enters the domestic establishment, and must consent to the constant intervention of her employers in her conduct of life, supervision of her expenditures and income, her dress etc. The master and mistress are also concerned with the girl's morals. They forbid her to walk out with young men, to have a sweetheart, etc. In these and similar cases, our women believe it is not just their right but their moral duty to give their girl detailed prescriptions. They believe that if they purchase her labour power and allow her to live and eat in their homes, they have also acquired the right to dispose of her volition, her mental life and her right to her own sexual life. But another form of domination frequently lurks behind this backdrop of patronising concern ... Coercion appears here in the moral guise of education.[32]

But such enlightened voices came late and they were rare. They were drowned out by contemporary etiquette guides, household manuals and magazine articles, which unanimously warned against excessive intimacy. Their social origins, such texts opined, predestined maidservants to take an undesirably blatant approach to topics that the middle classes dared not touch, or only very gingerly. Middle-class children were especially endangered, since their penchant for spending time in the kitchen was legendary. They heartily sang along with the housemaids' melancholy kitchen songs, which touched upon bourgeois taboos such as seduction, unfaithfulness, infanticide and death, and they thrilled to the dramatic legends and horror stories. The world of children and the not-yet-disenchanted world from which the servants came harmonised here. The receptiveness of middle-class children to anything mysterious and inexplicable frequently took the housemaids back to their own world of values and beliefs whose dissolution the bourgeoisie deemed an accomplishment. It was precisely this that they invited back into their homes along with housemaids. If one did not wish to cast a shadow over the bourgeois system of values, it was necessary to keep a tight rein on the seemingly baleful influence of servants on the children, in particular. Master and mistress had no sympathy for 'too much' empathy for the situation of servants. Kathinka von Rosen offered a vigorous and harsh critique of Stillich:

> Now the girl uses the days or hours remaining until she enters service to make her own enquiries into master and mistress.... With their address in hand she visits a shop near their home; a dairy or bakery is especially welcome, she enters and asks for information about the home of her employers.... And now it begins, not the slightest trifle that occurs or might occur in the house is left out. The girl makes friends with all of the servants in the house, with all of the shop girls of the neighbourhood, and, incited and suspicious, enters her new position. Our straitened housing situation forces us into constant contact with servants. We live with them. ... All of us, whether we treat our servants well or badly, are in their hands and at the mercy of their mania for gossip and slander. Servants see and hear everything, misunderstand most of it and interpret it in their own way to our disadvantage. All day long we are under their scrutiny. Nothing goes unnoticed, and with the greatest of speed they make a mountain out of every molehill. How frequently rumours buzz through the air, a woman's good name is suddenly destroyed and a man's credit undermined.[33]

A housemaid peering through a keyhole or listening at the door became a popular motif of contemporary caricature. The German term *Gerüchteküche* (literally rumour kitchen) may well have emerged from this cliché. The closer the quarters, the more opportunities maidservants had to look behind the scenes. The initial admiration that a young country girl may have felt for the distinguished lifestyle of her bourgeois master and mistress could soon turn into mocking contempt. Domestic servants were all too familiar with the daily efforts of middle-class households to save money. Carefully guarded family secrets, feuds and indiscretions could not be kept hidden from them, and provided them with trump cards that the fewest actually played, fearful of endangering their positions.

Farewell to the bourgeois value system? The feudalisation of the middle classes

After the founding of the Empire and the increasingly rapid pace of industrialisation, the number of bourgeois families that had made great fortunes and put their wealth on display grew alongside the educated middle class, with their rather spartan way of life. While the aspiring middle classes of the early nineteenth century had still propagated values such as achievement, moderation and modesty, thereby explicitly setting themselves apart from the aristocracy, there was now a tendency – viewed critically by contemporaries – to emulate the nobility and their way of life. The alleged 'feudalisation' of the upper middle classes was generally understood by many of those who engaged in this debate not only as a political alliance with the nobility, but also as an imitation and adaptation of the aristocratic lifestyle, including dreams of palaces rather than simple middle-class dwellings, sending daughters to distinguished finishing schools, generally abroad, replacing the usual 'maid of all work' with a veritable staff of servants, delegating most of the childrearing to nannies hired for the purpose and a habitus orientated towards outward prestige more than inner values. These developments were regarded as signs of a gradual abandonment of specifically middle-class values in favour of aristocratic worldviews and modes of existence.

If one studies the memoirs of bourgeois childhoods, it becomes clear that while this phenomenon existed, it applied only to a minority. Thus, for example, the daughter of a Hamburg entrepreneur, recalled:

> In 1878 we gave up city life altogether. My father had an enormous house built to his specifications – with comforts rare for that era – at Sofienterasse 11 in the suburb of Harvesthude. It was surrounded by a large garden with splendid old trees. A greenhouse and stables for horses and carriage, as well as a [flower] bed for each of the five siblings to plant was their delight.[34]

Not least the reference to a bed for each child to plant shows that for all their aristocratic trappings, the upper middle classes still prized work and accomplishment. Feudal habits exerted the greatest influence in the realm of sociability. In Imperial Germany, many housewives complained, the simple and informal cosiness of circles of friends and family meeting regularly had given way to elaborate, costly and highly ritualised dinner parties. The glamorous evening parties with their long and careful planning, judiciously composed guest lists, rigidly hierarchical seating plans, the variety and sophistication of menus and the standardised sequence of events more generally bore little resemblance to relaxed family gatherings. 'The days of tea and sandwiches are over, nowadays, in high finance circles, but also among scholars and artists, one encounters exclusive culinary pleasures', wrote one German author in 1898 in a critique of the new spirit of the age.[35] Aristocratic guests also frequently attended such soirées, which also went some way towards changing the composition of marriage circles. Nevertheless, such matches between the bourgeoisie and the nobility remained so uncommon that, as someone familiar with these circles noted with amusement, a bourgeois daughter- or son-in-law 'kicked up a good deal of dust in the aristocratic world'.[36]

One institution, however, that had existed since the Wars of Liberation but experienced a boom in Imperial Germany was that of the 'one-year volunteer'. It offered middle-class sons the opportunity to enter the world of the military, the upper ranks of which were still dominated by the nobility. The fact that the long-awaited German Empire was founded in the course of a victorious war contributed enormously to the status of all things military after 1871, and this new status also extended to middle-class families. Dressing little boys by preference in sailor suits was just one aspect, while the middle-class run on the ranks of reserve officers was the far less harmless one. They also paid dearly for this position. Middle-class fathers had to lay out 300–400 marks for their sons' uniforms and equipment in order to buy them an officer's title.

Enthusiasm for the military doubtless also left its traces in family life. Nurseries were populated by tin soldiers, boys' rooms were papered with battle scenes, soldiers were the heroes of picture books and, in keeping with the spirit of the age, even the *Nesthäkchen* book series, so loved by girls in particular, which depicted the life of the daughter of a Berlin doctor in rosy tones, dedicated one of its volumes, in 1915, to the First World War. 'My dear child, in this challenging time you do not need to be a grownup and do great things in order to support Germany. Children also can make sacrifices that can help,' Grandmother informs Nesthäkchen, who would happily have gone off to war herself.[37] By the time the war broke out in 1914, such chauvinistic attitudes had presumably penetrated not just German families. The differences likely related more to class than to nationality.[38]

Working-class families: Variants of a community of survival

Working-class families in Imperial Germany were less infected by enthusiasm for the military and war. To be sure, caricatures on postcards of the period often show housemaids giving a farewell kiss to a soldier dressed in field grey. But farm labourers were more interested in tilling fields than in losing their lives on the field of honour, and working-class women tended to watch their husbands and family breadwinners march off to war with more dismay than excitement. This shows once again how greatly family values and rhythms were influenced by material starting conditions.

It is hardly astonishing that working-class families had a very different way of life from middle-class ones. It is all the more surprising, then, that the bourgeois ideal nevertheless proved so attractive to proletarian families. This attraction meant that even around 1900, rural working-class families preferred their young daughters to enter the service of an urban bourgeois family until they married, where they could engage in the female duties they had learnt by watching their mothers or grandmothers. While from the 1880s these young girls, who left home at fourteen, increasingly would have preferred what they saw as more attractive factory jobs, with more regular wages and working hours, their parents' choices reveal how widely accepted the notion was throughout society that women – regardless of their class – belonged in the kitchen.

In any case, it became more common from the 1890s for daughters to move to the nearest town or even big city for a place as a 'maid-of-all-work'. The families of rural labourers from which they came had become more diverse over the course of the nineteenth century. The 'sub-peasant' strata, in particular, grew with the rapid rise in population since the middle of the century in combination with different types of legal succession. Rural family life was already extraordinarily varied in this period.

A not insignificant proportion of the lowest social strata never married, or did so only later in life. This was also true of journeyman artisans, who lived with their masters or other families as subtenants or bed lodgers. All of them shared the unit of production, consumption and reproduction under one roof, however. Kin and non-kin lived and worked together and frequently also shared their few moments of leisure. This community was dedicated less to profit than to subsistence, and formed a sort of community of survival with little scope for agency. At the head of the household were the farming couple, with servants and day labourers under the supervision of the farmer, while the wife instructed the female labourers and housemaids. We know little about the lives of the children in these households. Naturally, they worked from an early age. This was especially true of families engaged in cottage industry, whose activities were less differentiated by age and gender.

What about the atmosphere within the family and what of parental affection? Since child mortality remained high for a long time, scholars suspected that people became inured to such deaths and were less prone to emotional expression. But can we really equate contemporary silence with coldness? We do at any rate find evidence that great importance was placed on the act of baptism. And even stillborn children were honoured with a funeral cortège, eulogy and tolling of the bells. This does not suggest an absence of love.

Urban working-class families experienced the largest growth in Imperial Germany. But here, too, we cannot speak of *the* family, since the variations were substantial. They ranged from the widespread lack of a family of one's own, with or without integration into the households of others, to the productive family unit in cottage industry, which also still existed in the cities, and the nuclear family as a community of survival among workshop and factory workers of various kinds. Despite all these differences, there were also certain analogies that allow us to regard the working-class family as one variant of family forms in Imperial Germany. Above all, it was the actual and mental proximity to work in the sense of wage labour that determined the communal life of all family members. The type of work and the place where it was done defined the structure, patterns and rhythm of life and shaped the habitus of family members. And it was generally *dependent* work, and labour power was the family's sole 'asset'. As a rule, there was no property to be passed down. The work also set the pace of family life; its beginning and end also determined the beginning and end of family life. In these circles, free evenings or holidays were foreign concepts, and leisure was limited to a few hours during the week. Since this work was increasingly done outside the family, it severely restricted the time families spent together.

Unlike middle-class families, the majority of working-class families at the end of the nineteenth century depended on the earnings of both parents. But the mothers usually worked in different spheres than the fathers. While in the second half of the nineteenth century more than 60 per cent of male breadwinners worked in the industrial sector, only five per cent of their wives worked as industrial workers. Instead, most earned money in housework or as maids.[39] Frequently this also applied to older children, unless they were designated as caretakers for their younger siblings. The few working-class autobiographies we have paint an ambivalent picture. On the one hand, the authors lament their curtailed playtime and the lack of consideration for children's needs. On the other, however, they had an early self-awareness of contributing to family survival.

What all of them share, however, is a more or less implicit comparison with the bourgeois family ideal. Around the turn of the century, even Social Democrats began vociferously promoting the father as sole family breadwinner and proclaiming that the proper place of working-class women was in the family, not the factory. Middle-class critics, too, regarded the circumstance that proletarian women were hindered from fulfilling their 'maternal duties' as the core of the 'social question', which increasingly became the key question in the social discourse of Imperial Germany.

During this period, well-meaning and charitably minded citizens launched a number of social surveys. A few of the most dedicated among them mingled with the working class incognito in order to experience their situation personally. They included the former cleric Paul Göhre, who spent three months living as a factory worker in Chemnitz and wrote about his experiences. He complained above all of the close quarters at which families were forced to live, and the fragile privacy, which was rendered impossible by the frequent strangers who lodged with families.[40] At the same time, he underlined the great efforts made by women in particular to make clean and comfortable homes.

Less benevolent contemporaries judged the working class harshly. The economist Werner Sombart, for example, wrote that 'a generation is growing up within the proletariat for which familial relationships have become virtually non-existent'.[41] Such critiques in turn related to the narrow, middle-class definition of family. In fact, the classic nuclear family consisting of father, mother and usually two children, was difficult to find in the working class of Imperial Germany. In cramped quarters and frequently catastrophic hygienic conditions, the nuclear family lived with additional relations and non-family members, often in a single room. There was no question of a separate bed for each family member. Around 1900, a deliberate restriction of the number of children was scarcely possible, given the absence of modes of contraception as well as knowledge about them. Coitus interruptus, popularly known as *Vorortgeschäft* (literally doing business in the suburbs), was one of the few practices passed on in whispers. Figures on abortion in working-class families before the First World War are not available for Imperial Germany. It was common for families to have five to ten children, and thus many hungry mouths to feed. Many children meant more hardship, but also a continuing high rate of infant and child mortality. It is thus hardly surprising that many people became stoic under the circumstances, and artists such as Heinrich Zille approached the death of children with black humour.

The fact that working-class women frequently worked outside the home apparently did not serve to level the gender hierarchy. Women's frequently far lower wages were considered additional earnings, a necessary evil that did not however diminish their family responsibilities. The working-class marriage, too, remained a largely patriarchal one, although, in contrast to the bourgeoisie, the little time husbands and wives spent together had less impact in cementing it. This pattern had little effect on large segments of the Social Democrats, who were just consolidating as a party. To be sure, in his widely distributed book *Woman and Socialism*, August Bebel offered suggestions such as communal kitchens to reduce family duties by centralising them.[42] But the fact that he was concerned with partial relief for mothers, not the more equitable distribution of family work to include men, shows how half-hearted and non-emancipatory this idea ultimately was. It was no coincidence that a Social Democratic women's movement developed parallel to the middle-class women's movement, which, despite statements issued by their own party, attested to the Social Democrats' lukewarm approach to the question of equal rights for women. From the few working-class autobiographies available, we know that it was mainly mothers who formed the bulwark of the family in their children's eyes, upholding family life with frequently 'heroic' efforts and offering emotional stability. Fathers, in contrast, often appear in these works as violent alcoholics who did more to encumber than to enrich family life. A male lodger from outside the family might be experienced as more approachable, however.

Overall – and this was a significant difference to the bourgeois model – a strict distinction between the family and others was neither possible nor opportune. Even in the cities of Imperial Germany, the important role of neighbours as helpers in distress, the street as a living space for children and work colleagues as advisors persisted, if in altered form, and thus also to some extent adapted practices from traditional rural family life, the 'whole household' projected as romantic retro-fiction by the ethnologist and bestselling author Wilhelm Heinrich Riehl. Despite all restrictions, though, precisely because many members of the lower classes could not afford a family of their own, belonging to a family, preferably their own, was the preferred way of life for most of the working class. There is good reason to believe that family was understood, and ideally also experienced, as a community of survival.

The eternal decline: The crisis of the family as a long-burning issue

From the very inception of debates about families, the discourses were dominated by talk of crisis. Societal developments around 1900 fuelled visions of doom for the family. The disruption of the gender order by the bourgeois and proletarian women's movements since the 1870s played a part in this. The growing number of middle-class women going out to work – frequently as teachers, if they came from the upper middle class, or as part of the army of shop girls or typists, if they came from the lower middle class – challenged the notion that women were destined to be housewives and mothers alone. To be sure, German universities only began to admit female students between 1903 and 1911, but this was a response not least to long and energetic pressure from bourgeois daughters and increasingly their fathers as well. Mothers, we know from memoirs, frequently opposed the emancipation of their daughters, since they saw their own life paths called into question.

Middle-class sons also rebelled. The youth movement that began in Berlin at a Gymnasium in Steglitz in the late nineteenth century saw itself as a counter-movement to the values of Wilhelminism. Its members, middle-class pupils and students, defined themselves as apolitical, and the *Wandervogel* movement invoked escape from grey city walls and a return to nature and – last but not least – suspended the absolute authority of the father, the very heart of the family ideal.[43] A new tendency in pedagogy offered scientific support for these ideas. The reform pedagogues of the early twentieth century brought new tones into the family debate, propagating values such as trust, self-confidence and autonomy over obedience and subordination.

It is difficult to judge to what extent such societal and scientific developments actually penetrated to families. We occasionally read in diaries, letters and autobiographies, above all by later protagonists of the women's movement, that the authors had in late Imperial Germany argued with their parents over divergent notions about their future. In the meantime, the young women had new role models in the form of employed aunts, and thus alternatives to the lives of their mothers. Now they could compare and wanted to make their own choices.

The most momentous impact was exerted by the First World War, from which sons, husbands and fathers returned weakened, if they returned at all. During the war, as we know from the billions of forces letters sent back and forth between the front and the home front, the family served the important function of offering the emotional support that made the war bearable. Soldiers were very deliberately allowed daily hours for letter-writing in order to let their loved ones know that they were still alive. Letters from home, often written by the wives and mothers left behind, described everyday family life and thus suggested a bit of normality in a world out of joint. The often very young sons, who not infrequently went directly from the schoolroom to the battlefield, grew up very fast, as the changing tenor of the letters made clear.

At home, it was wives and mothers who now kept 'operations' running in many places outside the family. Women in men's positions, such as driving trams and in heavy industry, now supported the family on their own, surely with consequences for their position in the family structure. The fact that German women were allowed to vote for the first time after 1918 was at once a result and a recognition of their accomplishments during the war. Additional challenges that touched the family more or less directly would follow in the course of the twentieth century. The result was a further pluralisation of family forms, although, as we have seen, the forms of family life had already been quite varied in the nineteenth century. But despite all disruptions, changes and incursions, the bourgeois family ideal proved very resilient. Down to our present-day debates – one need only think of the discussion surrounding the so-called *Herdprämie* (bonus for mothers who stay at home to take care of the children and not send them to the kindergarten), it is clear how powerful it remains and how quickly its value system can be revived.[44] Whether this represents another German *Sonderweg* remains to be discussed.

Notes

1 Jacob and Wilhelm Grimm, in *Deutsches Wörterbuch*, 33 vols. (Leipzig, 1853–1971).
2 C. Rotteck and C. Welcker, *Staats-Lexikon* (1837), p. 386.
3 J. Kocka (ed.), *Bürgertum im 19. Jahrhundert. Deutschland im europäischen Vergleich*. 3 vols. (Munich, 1988).
4 K. Hausen, 'Die Polarisierung der "Geschlechtscharaktere". Eine Spiegelung der Dissoziation von Erwerbs- und Familienleben', in W. Conze (ed.), *Strukturwandel der Familie im industriellen Modernisierungsprozess – Historische Begründung einer aktuellen Fragen* (Dortmund, 1979), pp. 363–93.
5 E. Saurer and C. Hämmerle (eds), *Briefkulturen und ihr Geschlecht. Zur Geschichte der privaten Korrespondenz vom 16. Jahrhundert bis heute*

(Vienna, 2003); I. Bauer and C. Hämmerle (eds), *Liebe schreiben. Paarkorrespondenzen im Kontext des 19. und 20. Jahrhunderts* (Göttingen, 2017).
6   J. Fichte, *Naturrecht. 2. Teil*. Paragraph 15 (Jena, 1796–7). J. Fichte (2000), *Foundations of Natural Right*, translated by M. Baur (Cambridge, 2000), p. 281.
7   G. Budde, 'Das wechselvolle Kapital der Familie', in G. Budde (ed.), *Kapitalismus. Historische Annäherungen* (Göttingen, 2011), pp. 97–115.
8   I. Weber-Kellermann, *Vom Handwerkersohn zum Millionär. Eine Berliner Karriere des 19. Jahrhunderts* (Munich, 1990), p. 131.
9   P. Gay, *Erziehung der Sinne. Sexualität im bürgerlichen Zeitalter* (München, 1986).
10 Ibid.
11 W. H. Riehl, *Die Familie* (Stuttgart, 1854), p. 101.
12 H. Eyck, *Tagebuch*. Entry of 26 November 1897. Eyck Private Archive, Calgary, Canada.
13 T. Fontane, *Dichterfrauen sind immer so. Der Ehebriefwechsel 1844–1857* (Berlin, 1998), p. 372.
14 D. Blasius, *Ehescheidungen in Deutschland 1794–45. Scheidung und Scheidungsrecht in historischer Perspektive* (Göttingen, 1997).
15 G. Budde, *Auf dem Weg ins Bürgerleben. Kindheit und Erziehung in deutschen und englischen Bürgerfamilien 1840–1914* (Göttingen, 1994), pp. 262–70.
16 G. Budde, 'Als Erzieherinnen in Europa unterwegs: Gouvernanten, governesses und gouvernantes', *Europäische Geschichte Online*, published by the Institut für Europäische Geschichte (Mainz, 2011).
17 A. Schaser, *Helene Lange und Gertrud Bäumer. Eine politische Lebensgemeinschaft* (Cologne, 2000).
18 P. Ariès, *Geschichte der Kindheit* (München, 1998).
19 G. Budde, *Histoire des jardins d'enfants en Allemagne*, in: Jean-Noel Luc (ed.), *L'école maternelle en Europe XIXe–XX siècles* (Paris, 1999), pp. 43–72.
20 E. Ludwig, *Geschenke des Lebens* (Berlin, 1931), p. 44.
21 C. Grone, 'Schulen der Nation? Nationale Bildung und Erziehung an höheren Schulen des Deutschen Kaiserreichs von 1871 bis 1914', PhD University of Bielefeld (2007); G. Budde, 'From the "Zwergschule" to the comprehensive school: German elementary schools in Imperial Germany and the Weimar Republic, 1870–1930', in L. Brockliss and N. Sheldon (eds), *Mass Education and the Limit of State Building, c. 1870–1930* (London, 2012), pp. 95–117.

22 L. Gurlitt, *Schülerselbstmorde* (Berlin, 1908), p. 5.
23 G. Budde, 'Familienvertrauen – Selbstvertrauen – Gesellschaftsvertrauen. Pädagogische Ideale und Praxis im 19. Jahrhundert', in U. Frevert (ed.), *Vertrauen. Historische Annäherungen* (Göttingen, 2003), pp. 152–84.
24 G. Simmel, 'Soziologie der Mahlzeit', *Der Zeitgeist. Beiblatt zum Berliner Tageblatt 41,* 10.10.1910. Engl. translation, 'The Sociology of the Meal', in D. Frisby and M. Featherstone (eds), *Simmel on Culture: Selected Writings* (London, 1997), pp. 130–6.
25 Budde, *Auf dem Weg ins Bürgerleben*, pp. 82–4.
26 M. Weber, *Jugendbriefe* (Tübingen, 1936), p. 159. Letter of 16 June 1885 to his mother Helene Weber, in *Jugendbriefe*, p. 159.
27 Riehl, *Die Familie*, p. 115.
28 H. Hoffmann, *Lebenserinnerungen* (Frankfurt am Main, 1985), pp. 37–8.
29 M. Wellmer, *Deutsche Erzieherinnen und deren Wirkungskreis* (Leipzig, 1877), pp. 55 and 58.
30 J. Kocka, *Arbeitsverhältnisse und Arbeiterexistenzen. Grundlagen der Klassenbildung im 19. Jahrhundert* (Berlin and Bonn, 1990), p. 109.
31 G. Budde, 'Der Alltag von Dienstmädchen im 19. Jahrhundert', *Damals. Das Magazin für Geschichte* (2013), p. 10.
32 O. Stillich, *Die Lage der weiblichen Dienstboten in Berlin* (Berlin, 1902), pp. 243–4.
33 K. von Rosen, *Zur Dienstbotenfrage. Eine Erwiderung an Dr. Oskar Stillich* (Leipzig, 1903), pp. 29–30.
34 L. G. Heymann, cited in M. Twellmann (ed.), *Erlebtes – Erschautes. Deutsche Frauen kämpfen für Freiheit, Recht und Frieden 1850–1940* (Meisenheim am Glan, 1972), p. 26.
35 G. Steinhausen, *Häusliches und gesellschaftliches Leben im 19. Jahrhundert* (Berlin, 1898), p. 160.
36 F. von Zobeltitz, 'Die beiden Geschlechter innerhalb der Aristokratie', in R. Koßmann and J. Weiß (eds), *Mann und Weib. Ihre Beziehungen zueinander und zum Kulturleben der Gegenwart* (Stuttgart, 1908), p. 268.
37 E. Ury, *Nesthäkchen und der Weltkrieg* (Berlin, 2015/1915), p. 6. English translation S. Lehrer (ed.), *Nesthäkchen and the World War* (Lincoln, Nebraska, 2006), p. 2.
38 D. Wierling, *Eine Familie im Krieg. Leben, Sterben und Schreiben 1914–1918* (Göttingen, 2013); G. Budde, *Elsbeth und ihre Jungs. Krieg und Frieden in Briefen einer Familie im Ersten Weltkrieg* (Göttingen, 2019).

39 J. Kocka, *Arbeiterleben und Arbeiterkultur. Die Entstehung einer sozialen Klasse* (Bonn, 2015), pp. 57 and 158.
40 P. Göhre, *Drei Monate Fabrikarbeiter und Handwerksbursche – eine praktische Studie* (Leipzig, 1891), pp. 21–3.
41 W. Sombart, *Das Proletariat. Bilder und Studien* (Frankfurt am Main, 1906), p. 20.
42 A. Bebel, *Die Frau und der Sozialismus* (Berlin, 1985/1899), p. 268 ff.
43 J. Reulecke, *„Ich möchte werden so wie die . . .": Männerbünde im 20. Jahrhundert* (Frankfurt am Main, 2001).
44 Critics used the slogan *Herdprämie*, literally stove or hearth bonus, to refer to the 2012 introduction of a childrearing bonus paid to families in Germany who kept their two- and three-year-old children at home rather than availing themselves of public childcare services.

2

Rejuvenating the family: The struggle between tradition and modernity in Weimar Germany

Michelle Mouton

The Weimar Republic, Germany's first parliamentary democracy, was characterised by political chaos and economic turbulence. At its outset in 1919, with the nation reeling from military defeat and the birth rate at an all-time low, general consensus existed that the German nation was in crisis. The family was believed to be critical to the nation's future and women were anticipated to play a central role in rebuilding families. Despite this general agreement, there were stark divisions between the Right, which saw the re-establishment of traditional gender roles and patriarchal families as key, and the Left, which advocated governmental support of families through scientifically based welfare and modern gender roles. As a result, throughout the era, politicians, clergy, nationalists, feminists, and many other Germans all of whom supported the general aim of *Bevölkerungspolitik* (population policy), debated how best to rejuvenate families. These debates transpired against a backdrop of cultural vibrancy, social change and sexual experimentation. This chapter surveys how support and policy towards families changed during the Weimar era as economic exigencies arose, political and ideological worldviews shifted, and society modernised. The chapter begins with an overview of the Weimar context and attitudes towards families. It then examines three areas in which the state tried to support families: marriage, divorce and motherhood.

The Weimar debate over families

When the First World War ended, the trauma of defeat and revolution created a sense that the German nation's very survival stood in peril. The death of more than 1.6 million men in the war permanently disrupted the lives of many German families. The birth rate plummeted and together with war casualties, induced fears among some Germans of the *Volkstod* (death of the nation). The war casualties left in their wake close to 600,000 widows and almost 1.2 million war orphans, whose standard of living deteriorated sharply as they became dependent on limited widows' pensions and/or single mothers' meagre earnings from low-paid work.[1] Even more ominous for the future of the nation, because 15 per cent of men aged twenty to forty had been killed, a 'surplus' of more than 2 million women had dim prospects for marriage.[2] There was a dramatic upsurge in the marriage rate immediately after the war, up from 4.2 per 1,000 in 1915–16 to 14.5 per 1,000 in 1920. This was a result of both the wartime postponement of marriage and the desire of many men and women to re-establish 'home' after the war ended. But widespread fears of societal crisis were not quelled – in part because the divorce rate rose simultaneously. Illegitimacy rates too, were on the rise, underscoring for many, how far societal morality had strayed from pre-war standards. As one Christian Conservative delegate to the Prussian *Landtag* (state parliament) put it, the most important task facing the new regime was to heal 'the corrosive, nearly incurable ills' that had befallen the German people, which were those 'predominantly caused by the fact that our *Volk* no longer has a healthy family life'.[3]

In light of this, it is perhaps not surprising that many Germans, including politicians from all parties, feared that the German family, the only institution they deemed capable of stabilising and restoring German society, might not be equal to the task without substantial help from the state. In particular, paternal authority, widely viewed as the essential core of families, needed to be shored up. In some families, women had grown restless in their roles as traditional wives and mothers and thus resisted the re-establishment of paternal authority. In others, men fortunate enough to survive the war returned with physical and psychological trauma – shell shock – that prevented them from reasserting themselves as patriarchs. Many Germans associated the absence of paternal authority with rising juvenile crime rates and the proliferation of antisocial youth gangs. Although the concern that the war had destroyed the patriarchy was exaggerated, there is no doubt that many families had been shaken to the core. Re-establishing families and the father's place in them thus assumed a position of primary importance in the post-war period. Chief among the perceived obstacles was the matter of women's work. More than 2 million women had entered the labour market to boost the war economy, many of whom resisted returning to their domestic roles after 1918. Returning soldiers complained that women's continued employment made it more difficult for them to find work and prevented a restoration of the pre-war patriarchal family structure. The effort to save German families thus began with a demobilisation policy that removed women from paid war work.

But if politicians across the political spectrum envisioned a 'peaceful and harmonious society' based on the 'patriarchal principle' – with soldiers and 'women of the war' returning to their roles as providers and mothers, respectively – this did not easily translate into agreement on how to formulate policy.[4] The Weimar era was characterised by tremendous political conflict and legislative turmoil that greatly affected the debates about how to fix the problems facing families. Politicians confidently enshrined the preservation of marriage and public support for the family into the constitution. They unanimously agreed that the state had a responsibility to protect and strengthen families. Despite this unanimity, great disparities existed in the way politicians conceptualised the family itself, the problems facing families and the appropriate role for the state in helping families. At the heart of the matter lay a fundamental disagreement about what caused families distress: theories ranged from women's rejection of domesticity, to rising immorality, decreasing influence of the church, and industrialisation. Nor did politicians hold a monopoly on explanations of what troubled families. Throughout the Weimar era, myriad interest groups, including feminists, churches, and morality leagues, entered the debates, sometimes siding with specific political parties and at other times straddling political lines in support of specific platforms. Because each interpretation of what troubled the family reflected a particular vision of Germany, debates over many legislative proposals were characterised by bitter conflict. Attempts to formulate and implement family policy during the Weimar era failed repeatedly because of the lack of consensus on what to do about benefits for large families, contraception, abortion, counselling for engaged couples, and a variety of other issues.

Three overarching themes ran throughout the debates about the German family during the Weimar era. First, there was the question of gender roles. Traditional gender roles had been severely disrupted during the war as women entered the labour force both as part of the war effort and to support themselves and their families in the absence of men. Lawmakers on the political right believed that the high mortality rate during the war, the low birth rate, and what they saw as the spread of immorality at all levels of society undermined national rejuvenation and threatened the German race. They rejected arguments about the benefits of modernity, which they believed reflected women's egoism, and advocated instead that women should return to the home and resume their domestic duties while men again assumed the patriarchal role. Because they generally maintained that only the restoration of traditional gender roles could rejuvenate the family, they supported legislation to increase penalties for abortion and prostitution, forbid contraception and restrict the accessibility of divorce.

Liberal lawmakers opposed this legislation because they interpreted the problems facing German families differently. Most left-wing parties believed that women and men had interests and needs that were fundamentally different, but that the sexes were nonetheless to be regarded as equal. As a result, they fought for sexual equality before the law, women's access to higher education and to many professions. Despite this, left-wing lawmakers' views were not uniform. While some worried that divorce reform and legal abortion would discourage women from becoming mothers, Social Democratic Party (SPD) delegates single-mindedly rejected arguments that attributed the German families' woes to faltering morality. They instead asserted that the disruption of families and the falling birth rate stemmed primarily from the social upheaval caused by the war combined with the bitter hardships that industrialisation caused the working classes. The SPD advocated greater support for mothers and infants, provision of adequate housing, and improvement in health care for all Germans – measures they claimed would give women the strength and confidence to choose motherhood. Like their more conservative colleagues, the SPD also promoted pronatalism, but they consistently supported women's equality and voluntary motherhood. Only the Communist delegates fundamentally rejected the notion that women's primary role was as mothers. They believed that the only way to support families was to give women the right to work and equal wages.

A second theme that complicated family policy was a fundamental disagreement about the state's right to intervene in families. As the application of science, medicine, and technology to social policy expanded the hope for benefits of state intervention, Social Democrats and Communists eagerly advocated applying this new knowledge. They envisioned a comprehensive social welfare programme that went well beyond providing material support and involved intervention 'in all aspects of family life including health, sexuality, childrearing, and education to help create an "orderly family".[5] They envisioned welfare and youth departments monitoring families and intervening before problems ever arose. In contrast, conservative lawmakers and religious leaders argued that extensive state intervention would ultimately destroy the very families it sought to help. They worried that state benefits would erode masculine independence; that child welfare interventions would threaten a father's authority over his children; and that state intervention would diminish parental responsibility.

Because individual families tended to avoid state-sponsored efforts at social discipline even when they were designed with an eye to social benefit, resistance to a policy of intervention was not limited to conservative politicians and the churches. To be sure, the burgeoning ranks of social workers increased individualised scrutiny of families, and social workers' own middle-class backgrounds not infrequently caused them to see working-class families in a negative light. As a result, many families found the state's increased supervision invasive, making the relationship between state agents and the families they sought to assist volatile. Families sometimes resented even education and preventive care when it occurred in combination with disciplinary efforts. As historian Eric Weitz has demonstrated, 'Often, the "clients" defiantly rejected such interventions.'[6]

A third powerful theme within family policy was the 'new science' of eugenics. In the context of post-war social chaos, a broad coalition – including both left and right public administrators, health officials, welfare advocates, the Catholic and Protestant churches, Social Democrats, Communists and ultra-right wing nationalists – joined together 'to promote "valuable" and discourage "valueless" life'.[7] New organisations like the *Deutscher Bund für Volksaufklärung und Erbkunde* (German League for Regeneration and Heredity) flourished and promoted public eugenic education. Before the war, government officials had largely ignored the eugenics movement, but the social disruption associated with military defeat prompted many politicians to believe that 'they could no longer afford to exclude eugenics from official policy'. But while supporters of racial hygiene generally agreed that there was a 'hierarchy of human worth' and that restoring Germany 'demanded the subordination of the individual to the community or the *Volk*', they often vehemently disagreed about how to translate this belief into policy.[8] Some advocates of eugenics believed that by allowing people with weaker constitutions to live, medical progress had destroyed the natural Darwinian struggle for survival. They worried that so-called 'inferior' people's faster reproduction rate underlay the genetic deterioration of the German population. They argued that eugenics, including compulsory sterilisation, differential medical care, and, in extreme cases, euthanasia, would purge 'alien socialist, democrat and racial elements so that a truly Germanic social order could be realised'.[9] But these advocates of so-called negative eugenics met stiff resistance from other supporters of eugenics who rejected compulsory eugenics as contradictory to the democratic principles of the Weimar Republic. They attributed social degeneration to deteriorating social conditions and advocated welfare-oriented measures, including improved public housing, state supported maternal and infant health care, and readily accessible contraception to improve individual lives and national health.

Weimar was a tumultuous era for German families.[10] It began as families struggled to rebuild amid the destruction of the lost war. Even after the Kaiser had abdicated and a liberal democracy had been established, Weimar politics remained turbulent. Weimar politicians' failure to agree on diplomacy, economics or how to help German families led to fraught debates that often played out in the public arena. The economic turmoil at the beginning and end of the era also rocked the financial foundation of many German families. Hyperinflation in 1923 destroyed middle-class savings and caused many Germans to question whether marriage could provide a stable base. With the onset of the Great Depression in 1929, unemployment skyrocketed so quickly and so extensively that the government was unable to provide the social services needed to sustain families. Throughout the Weimar era, Germany also witnessed a modernisation of social relations and a burst of unprecedented cultural creativity. Especially during the stable middle years of the Republic, the rich offerings of cities drew many people away from traditional family structures. Cities offered a haven for homosexual women and men whose very existence challenged tradition. For many young women, employment in cities granted them a freedom from family constraints and at least temporarily allowed them to postpone marriage. These 'New Women' seemed to many contemporaries to symbolise both Germany's chance to return to 'normalcy' and the improbability of such a return.

Building the foundation for families: Marriage

Many Germans viewed marriage not only as the foundation of the German family, but also as a key to the nation's health. As a result, politicians enshrined the preservation of marriage and 'the maintenance of the purity and health of family, and public support for the family' in the constitution (Article 119). Although Germany witnessed a veritable *Heiratsflut* ('flood of marriages') during the Weimar era and the married proportion of the population increased from 36.1 per cent in 1910 to 40.1 per cent in 1925, marriage itself was in flux. The post-war 'surplus' of women meant that many women could not marry and by 1926 one-third fewer women between the ages of twenty and twenty-five were married than in 1910. Even once married, German couples seemed not to be acting 'responsibly'. Low birth rates magnified fears that even women who did marry were failing to fulfil their 'natural' roles. As information about contraception spread, many German adults sought to limit their family size, and the two-child family became the norm. Indeed, as Lisa Pine summed it up: 'Birth control was part of the way of life of Weimar society.'[11]

Beyond the recognition of the centrality of marriage to rebuilding Germany, however, no consensus existed about how to encourage Germans to marry and found families.[12] Conservative politicians and nationalists advocated public eugenic education and mandatory marriage counselling to ensure that only healthy, well-matched couples married. The right-wing German National People's Party (DNVP) petitioned the Prussian Assembly to have the science of heredity taught in medical schools. A prominent textbook on hereditary health asserted that improving national health depended on parents, doctors, teachers, and priests all working together to teach children that they 'were a subordinate part of a great racial organism'.[13] For these conservative politicians, nationalists and some doctors, the strong healthy marriage was so important to public health that it took precedence over the interests of the individual. Although racism and anti-Semitism began to appear in the right wing of the Weimar eugenic movement, the primary focus remained on personal and societal health. Most who advocated the application of eugenics within government policies emphasised that so-called genetically unhealthy people should be prevented from reproducing. Some went even further and advocated the compulsory sterilisation of those who could not be trusted to behave responsibly. Although discussions of eugenics became widespread during the Weimar era, no mandatory eugenic policies were enacted.

Far from agreeing with this right-wing interpretation, many left-wing politicians opposed the traditional bourgeois marriage itself, which they believed was too integrally bound to civil registration, economic connections and financial dependence to result in healthy relationships.

Instead, they advocated a companionate marriage grounded in 'love, respect and trust' between two people.[14] The Social Democratic politicians believed that expanding the grounds for divorce so that unhappy partners could separate would actually strengthen marriage. They also advocated contraception to ensure that married couples could control their reproduction. More broadly, they hoped that creating a more open and just society, making women equal to men, and allowing people a greater freedom of lifestyle would improve marital health. Alfred Grotjahn, spokesman for the SPD, petitioned to create a Reich Ministry of Health in 1918 that would oversee education and health care and teach about heredity. Although the ministry never came to be, the state did begin to seek out and assist families in need.

Women also worried about the viability and health of marriage. The Federation of German Women's Organisations (BDF), an umbrella group for women's associations firmly believed that only the 'undivided trinity [of] love, marriage and motherhood' would 'guarantee women's self-realisation, the protection of their children and the preservation of the national culture'. But their leaders also argued that marriage needed to become more advantageous to women. They pointed out that if women had to forfeit their rights and become imprisoned in marriage, they would inevitably avoid it. BDF members thus campaigned to enhance married women's legal status and to establish their right to own property. Though the BDF held no firm position on contraception and scorned 'free love', they acknowledged that a 'temporary and infertile union' outside of marriage might sometimes be a 'reasonable way out of the "modern marriage crisis"'.[15] They agreed with the SPD that marriage would be stronger if unhappy couples were allowed to divorce.

If lawmakers could not reach an accord over state intervention into marriage, one point on which they could agree was that more education about health issues was essential. In 1920, the Reich government produced a pamphlet to be distributed to all couples when they registered their engagements at the civil registry. Couples were explicitly encouraged to notify their parents or guardians before they finalised their engagements, since 'those who refuse [to notify their parents] commit a serious wrong, which can take bitter revenge'. Individual *Länder* (states) had the legal right to declare a marriage invalid if the bride's or groom's parents had not been informed about their child's future spouse (BGB, German Civil Code, Paragraphs 1333, 1334). Health was deemed 'the cornerstone of marital happiness' and couples were encouraged to consult a physician before marriage, since 'some people are sick without ever being aware of it'.[16] Couples were further advised that it was their 'holy duty to themselves, their future partner and their desired children, as well as to the fatherland, which desperately needs healthy offspring' to avoid marriages that would create unhealthy couples and burden the state with inferior, even useless children. Unhealthy partners or partners who abused alcohol or drugs were told that they endangered not only their marriages but also their future children – and, as a result, the *Volkskörper* (body of the nation). Though it lacked any legal force, the pamphlet appealed to couples' common sense and their desire to gain the state's blessing to marry. By means of the marriage pamphlet, the Weimar state set new health-based guidelines for 'proper' marriage and imbued marriage with national significance without directly embracing interventional eugenics.

Perhaps unsurprisingly, the pamphlet had at best a modest impact on couples' behaviour. Not all couples paid attention to the pamphlet and authorities debated what to do when couples ignored its advice. Members of the German Society for Racial Hygiene argued that marital health should be taught in school before young people began seriously considering marriage.[17] Physicians worried that they could not reconcile patient confidentiality and the desire to report a spouse with a health problem.[18] For example, officials in Schaumberg-Lippe expressed concern that strengthening the state's premarital counselling would lead to a decrease in the number of marriages, encourage men to have extramarital affairs, spread venereal disease and increase the number of illegitimate children.[19] While some authorities continued to argue that mandatory medical examinations would increase the health of marriage, neither local authorities nor most Weimar lawmakers believed that the state had a right to demand compulsory marriage examinations.

Given the decidedly limited impact of the pamphlets, lawmakers sought other means to increase marital health. The Social Democrats and Communists advocated legalising contraception in order to free couples from the constant fear of unwanted pregnancy. Since conservative lawmakers' resistance to contraception led to government inaction, it was left to various non-governmental groups to meet the real reproductive needs of working-class families. Members of the sex reform movement opened lay clinics to educate couples about contraception under the motto that sexuality was better regulated than repressed.[20] With an emphasis on public education, the staff in these clinics – doctors, feminists and social workers – led the charge for inexpensive, safe, effective and accessible contraception. The Federation for the Protection of Mothers also opened clinics to provide advice about contraception, abortion, and sexuality. It skirted the anti-obscenity regulations of the BGB (German Civil Code) and conservative objections by referring women to doctors for the fitting of diaphragms.[21]

While many German families welcomed the reproductive health clinics, right-wing politicians, the churches, and much of the medical profession allied against them. Members of the DNVP and the Catholic Centre Party opposed the lay clinics because they believed that contraception and abortion distracted women from their roles as mothers and permitted – even encouraged – a loosening of societal morals. August Mayer, a Catholic gynaecologist, was not alone in feeling that the clinics were contributing to the 'dissolution of the family [and] the state'.[22] Members of the Centre Party argued that preserving and shoring up traditional bourgeois marriage represented the only way to save Germany, and the Catholic Church established its own marriage clinics 'to promote the Christian ideal of large families'.[23] The Church vehemently opposed the decriminalisation of abortion and any reform of the obscenity clause that banned the advertisement, display or publication of 'obscene' material, including contraceptives.

In response to the ongoing wrangling by the political parties and the pleas of the medical profession, Prussian Minister of Welfare Heinrich Hirtsiefer issued a decree on 19 February 1926, encouraging local authorities throughout Germany to establish *Eheberatungsstellen* (marriage-counselling clinics). His decree caused a veritable boom of state-supported marriage clinics, and by the beginning of the 1930s, more than 200 new marriage clinics had opened in Prussia to provide eugenic and health advice – rather than contraceptive information – and to control the lay movement for birth control that had grown among the working classes.[24] State social workers, who collected general and social information, and doctors, who conducted detailed medical examinations and issued health certificates to engaged couples, staffed the clinics. In many towns, marriage counselling took place in the office of the district doctor, who generally believed his primary responsibility was to educate the public about hereditary health.[25]

Because practising birth control inside marriage had become a reality for many couples, many women shunned the marriage counselling centres and continued to visit the lay clinics that provided contraceptive information. As a result, doctors in state clinics who largely obeyed their mandate and refused to distribute (or discuss) contraceptives had difficulty attracting women. By 1930, the competition from lay clinics had become so intense that many doctors in state marriage counselling clinics were forced to provide contraceptive information in order to build a clientele. This led to new conflicts between doctors and private organisations over providing contraceptives.[26] Once the state marriage clinics began to discuss contraception, it fostered the sense among Germans that contraception was the norm and that traditional rules were loosening.[27]

Many German couples viewed contraception as correct, but resisted the application of eugenic criteria to their reproductive lives. This meant that 'healthy' couples were as likely to limit family size as were so-called unhealthy couples. Contrary to popular belief, the majority of requests for birth control came from married or engaged women who wanted to control their family size, not from 'immoral' single women.[28] As Atina Grossmann has pointed out: 'In a context where the average working-class family size had shrunk to about four, and the "two-child system" had become the norm, women were redefining the meaning of "need" or "hardship" requiring prevention or termination of pregnancy.'[29] Especially during difficult economic times, women sought medical help with contraception, not genetic advice, and people across the political and social spectrum rallied together against Paragraph 218, which criminalised abortion. As Cornelie Usborne has argued, in view of the apparent rise in abortions, 'members of the medical and legal professions and the law enforcement authorities reluctantly came to tolerate, sometimes even support, abortion law reform.' In 1926, the 'draconian penalties prescribed by the Wilhelmine criminal code were substantially modified . . . in favour of the aborting woman; the new law scapegoated professional abortionists instead; this was followed in 1927 by the permission of therapeutic abortion by decree'.[30]

During the Depression, increased misery among German families led to a renewed debate over abortion that further politicised both sex advice clinics and state marriage counselling centres. The Depression necessitated cutbacks in social welfare programmes and sparked discussions about the potential benefit of a 'differentiated welfare' system that would distribute state aid only to those deemed genetically worthy. In this context, contraception was seen as weakening the nation when genetically healthy Germans used it, but as a necessity for those deemed unhealthy. Already hard-pressed to feed their children, many working-class families were devastated by unwanted pregnancies. Speaking for such families, the German Communist Party (KPD) declared Paragraph 218, which criminalised abortion, 'a particularly brutal and immediately personal form of sex-specific class oppression'.[31] At the same time, the right-wing Reich Health Education Council, the Protestant Union for Health, and the League for Child Rich Families preached against contraception. They held up moral duty and restraint as the solutions to the 'catastrophe' that had befallen the German family.[32] The Catholic position was reinforced on New Year's Eve 1930, when Pope Pius XI issued an encyclical entitled 'On Christian Marriage', which denounced sexual intercourse without procreative intention and called on the state to protect the weak and unborn. The encyclical was viewed by the KPD as a reflection of the Reich government's willingness to forsake working-class women. On International Women's Day, 8 March 1931, demonstrations and rallies took place throughout Germany to protest Paragraph 218, and by June a broad coalition had developed that included the Communist women's movement, sex reformers, independent feminists and pacifist groups, all of whom called for the immediate revocation of Paragraph 218.[33] In the end, Paragraph 218 remained and the debates over its removal fell victim to the larger parliamentary stalemate that rendered the Reichstag unable to function, a dysfunction that threatened the Republic's very survival.

Divorce as individual freedom or a sign of moral decline

Although the number of divorces fell during the war, by 1920 it had risen to a record high. The apparent impermanence of marriage shocked many Germans and reinforced the feeling that the German family was in a state of crisis. In Prussia, the number of divorces rose from 9,277 in 1910 to 22,524 in 1920, suggesting to many that Germany was experiencing a divorce epidemic.[34] The factors leading to divorce were also changing with fewer normal causes (adultery, failure to provide and abuse) and more war-related causes. Some pre-war couples realised after the war that they could not live together; other hastily arranged war marriages proved unsustainable. Still others found that women's financial independence during the war had undermined marriage. In considering whether to allow a couple to divorce, lawmakers and judges were concerned not only about the morality of dissolving a marriage, but also about protecting children stemming from the marriage.

The growing number of couples wishing to divorce led lawmakers to debate whether to make it easier for couples to leave unhappy marriages. At the heart of the issue lay one question: could a reformed divorce law increase individual happiness without undermining the state's effort to bolster families and shore up the German nation? In the Reichstag, left-wing advocates of divorce reform asserted that freeing spouses from unhappy marriages would illustrate the state's commitment to equal democratic gender roles, ensure greater personal freedom and make Germany a more just place for men, women and families. They argued that many couples suffered unnecessarily in socially worthless marriages while waiting for their relationships to deteriorate sufficiently to give them grounds to file for divorce. In contrast, opponents of divorce reform feared that any change in the divorce code would lower moral standards, overburden the state with unsupported wives and children, and discourage responsible male behaviour. Moreover, they believed that any departure from traditional law would lead to the destruction of the family and the ruin of German civilisation. As a result of this political chasm, divorce remained an intractable domestic issue in the struggle between maintaining traditional values, modernising families, and society at large.[35]

At the centre of the divorce debate was the issue of whether to introduce an 'irreconcilable differences' clause to replace mandatory guilt clauses (adultery, culpable marital breakdown, desertion, mental illness and death threats). In April 1922, the liberal German Organisation of Law advocated such a change to allow the 'thousands in the Reich who still currently must remain in the deepest of mental anguish in socially utterly worthless marriages to become useful members of the state again'.[36] Marie Elisabeth Luders, a German Democratic Party (DDP) delegate and an early champion of divorce reform, was the first to raise the issue in the Reichstag. Gustav Radbruch, the SPD justice minister from October 1921 until November 1923 and a strong proponent of reform, proposed adding a sub-clause that would separate guilt from alimony by making one spouse (usually the man) responsible for economic support regardless of guilt. Radbruch argued that this would eliminate the humiliating situation in which a spouse who wanted to divorce had to engage in adultery or abuse in order to create the grounds for divorce. Radbruch hoped his proposal would secure women's economic stability after divorce while preserving their dignity.

Conservative lawmakers passionately disagreed with the liberals' divorce reform proposals and thus ensured that divorce reform debates were hyperbolic from the outset. DNVP, DVP and Centre Party politicians who defended the traditional divorce law claimed that nothing less than German civilisation was at stake. In January 1922, Cardinal Adolf Bertram, Furstbischof of Breslau, wrote to the justice minister, the leader of the Centre Party and the Reichstag to oppose the reform of the 'culpable marital breakdown' clause. In his letter, he explained: 'Marriage and the family are the basis of the whole of human society, the holy cell of the nation's life, and the nation's strength. . . Making divorce easier is a concession to that kind of cowardice, which will not wait and suffer, will not make sacrifices, but rather allows itself to be guided by mood, passion, and fickleness.'[37] Centre Party delegates used this letter from the cardinal to bolster their refusal to discuss divorce reform.

Nonetheless, in 1922 three DDP delegates brought a proposal for divorce reform to the floor of the Reichstag for debate. They emphasised that their intention was not to increase the number of divorces, but rather to make the entire process more just. They argued that deleting the guilt clause would enhance the position of the weaker partner (usually the woman) and they claimed that alimony should be firmly connected to equality and need, not marital circumstances and guilt. To this, Johannes Bell, future Reich Minister of Justice, retorted: 'From our religious and moral perspective we maintain the unshakeable conviction that marriage is insoluble, and thus we will decisively resist all bills and all petitions that seek to expand the grounds for divorce.'[38] The political success of the Communist Party in 1925 complicated the landscape for divorce reform further. Communist lawmakers believed that the matter of both divorce reform and abortion laid bare 'all the lies and hypocrisy of bourgeois society'.[39] While the SPD delegates agreed with Communist policy suggestions on divorce, they feared the Communists' wider revolutionary goals. The precarious nature of the Weimar governing coalition forced the SPD to scale back its goals with regard to divorce. As a result, divorce reform legislation efforts, like the effort to repeal Paragraph 218, proved unsuccessful.

Although there was no legislative change to divorce law during the Weimar era, this did not mean that nothing changed. Responsibility for assessing the viability of existing marriages fell to judges. While technically the judiciary was independent, during the Weimar era the courts themselves became political institutions, and the political context of the day strongly influenced judges' verdicts. As conservative, upper-class representatives of the state, Weimar judges viewed preserving marriage and sustaining families as beneficial to the public interest and as one of their most important responsibilities. Many judges believed that it was their duty to use their position on the bench to help stabilise post-war society. As the battle lines between liberal lawmakers – especially the SPD – and judges became entrenched, many judges explicitly sought to re-establish the status quo ante with their verdicts. They resisted all legislation that they believed eroded patriarchal authority or undermined women's roles as wives and mothers, as defined by the German Civil Code of 1900.

Nineteenth-century divorce law had been written in gender-neutral language and men's greater earning potential had made them responsible for supporting their ex-wives financially. After Weimar lawmakers wrote sexual equality into the constitution, however, many judges assumed that women could support themselves and began to hand down decisions that did not compensate for men's greater earnings. They increasingly assigned guilt also to women, even when men were clearly the guilty parties. Frau R. and her husband, for example, were both declared guilty even though his adultery could be proven and hers was inconclusive.[40] This had a profound impact on Frau R.'s future well-being since only innocent spouses received alimony. For women who earned, on average, 20 to 40 per cent less than men, the loss of alimony was a strong economic disincentive to divorce, even when the divorce itself promised to free them from undesirable marriages. Judges also shifted the meaning and impact of divorce through their interpretation of 'culpable marital breakdown'. After the war 'culpable marital breakdown' – defined as an instance in which one partner violated the marital duties through shameful, immoral, or abusive behaviour to such a degree that the marriage was no longer sustainable – surpassed adultery as the number one cause of divorce.[41] By interpreting women's behaviour that lay outside the traditional nurturing role as grounds for divorce, judges altered the meaning of the law without the law having been changed.

As judges reinterpreted guilt and the grounds for ending marriage, they necessarily contended with issues of alimony and child support. In December 1920, the chief magistrate of the high court in Hamm wrote to the Bielefeld *Landgericht* president to express his concern that especially in cases in which parents led 'a dissolute way of life', their children were 'alarmingly endangered morally and physically and that this danger often escalated after the spouses separated'.[42] He suggested that the state bypass parents to collect information about children in troubled marriages and alert the guardianship courts as soon as they found children in trouble.[43] Many judges, however, resisted alerting guardianship courts because they believed it decreased the odds that couples would reconcile. After couples separated, most children stayed with their mothers and were supported by their fathers up to the time of the divorce trial. Following the trial, the 'innocent' parent uniformly received child custody. When both parents shared the guilt, courts awarded mothers custody of all daughters and sons under the age of six, while granting fathers custody of older sons (Paragraph 1635).

Even when the courts granted women alimony and child support, this did not guarantee their income since many men refused to cooperate and stalled in making payments. As Dr. Georg Guggemoos, director of the city youth department in Freising, pointed out: 'Anyone active in practical welfare work knows only too well that in the majority of cases in which marriages deteriorate, and especially if divorce follows and children stay with their mothers, fathers neglect their obligation to support their children.'[44] Youth departments, which often acted as mediators between mothers and fathers in cases of alimony and child support also did not always receive or turn over the money to mothers punctually. When fathers remarried, the likelihood that they would support their prior families declined precipitously. In many cases, the financial burden of supporting the child fell to state youth departments.

In a further effort to maintain societal morality, German law also regulated marriage after divorce. German women were forbidden from remarrying sooner than ten months after a divorce, since doing so might raise confusion about the paternity of a child born immediately after divorce. The law also prevented adulterous couples from marrying. Not all couples felt compelled to have their new relationships sanctioned by the state. Many divorcees, who were declared guilty of the breakup of their marriages, ignored the state's prohibition of their relationships and lived together without state sanction. Couples in these 'wild marriages' often felt the censure of their neighbours, became the targets of gossip, and were 'a favourite research subject for snooping police'.[45] As a result, some couples felt pressured to try to remarry. Other couples waited until they had improved their chances of attaining a judge's sympathy, for example by bearing a child whose legitimacy stood in peril.[46] Judges waived the prohibition only if a new marriage promised to be morally sound and economically viable, and if it reflected the best interests of the ex-spouse, the potential future spouse, any children involved and German society itself.

Motherhood

For many Germans, the clearest sign that German families were in trouble during the Weimar era lay in the low birth rate. The birth rate, which was 28.6 per 1000 in 1911, fell by half to 14.3 in 1918. A brief post-war baby boom brought the birth rate up to a high of 25.8 in 1920, but this did little to calm fears, since it declined thereafter to 23.2 in 1922, 20.9 in 1925 and 17.5 in 1930.[47] Though the declining birth rate represented the continuation of a trend that had begun at the turn of the century, lawmakers across the political spectrum regarded it as a new problem. The seeming prevalence of abortion during the Weimar era exacerbated fears about the low birth rate, as did high infant mortality rates among the children of unmarried mothers. Although the rhetoric of *Bevölkerungspolitik* (population policy) 'gained enormous force from the German defeat, the precise form and extent of government involvement in encouraging higher birth rates produced fierce and enduring disagreements.'[48] At the centre of the debate lay the question of the appropriate role for women. Politicians on both the Right and Left attributed the low birth rate first to women's labour force participation, lamenting women's entrance into paid labour during the war – and frequent reluctance to leave it. Later politicians also bemoaned the fact that throughout the Weimar era more than a quarter of married women held non-household employment.[49] The connection between women's work and the low birth rate was 'proven' by means of many narrow and unbalanced studies that ignored other critical factors that affected the birth rate, including poverty levels and the home environment. Much of the perceived increase in the number of female workers can in fact be attributed to more accurate counting – for the first time, both family helpers and domestic workers were taken into account – but contemporaries believed that the number reflected a drastic and detrimental shift in women's attitudes and behaviour.[50]

When the war ended, politicians across the political spectrum, clergy, feminists and doctors were united in the belief that the promotion of motherhood was necessary to boost the birth rate and improve national health.[51] The question they faced, however, was how best to promote motherhood. Immediately after the war, many people argued that mothers needed material support especially since infant mortality and maternal morbidity and mortality were integrally connected. The infant mortality rate was so alarmingly high that immediately after the war an atmosphere prevailed in which any 'resistance to the creation of a public child welfare system might have seemed vaguely unpatriotic'.[52] As we have seen in other contexts, however, although lawmakers across the political spectrum agreed that something should be done to help mothers and their infants, they disagreed both about what was causing the problem and its solution. While politicians on the Right blamed abortion for maternal mortality and morbidity, those on the Left blamed poverty, poor housing and ill health. In light of this insoluble difference of opinion, politicians agreed to target the financial woes that forced many pregnant women and nursing mothers to work until late in their pregnancies and then to resume work too soon after they gave birth. In 1919, the Law for Maternity Benefits and Maternity Welfare extended the wartime maternity welfare benefits to women with incomes of less than 2,500 marks per year.[53] Eligible women received food and medical care before, during and after delivery, money for delivery and additional financial aid to compensate a midwife or doctor if necessary. To ensure that women had a respite from employment, the law also offered daily subsidies to new mothers for up to ten weeks after delivery. New mothers could also qualify for an additional breast-feeding bonus.[54]

As impressive as these maternity benefits were on paper, however, the success of the maternity welfare law was limited. The law excluded many needy women, since only women covered by insurance (or who had been covered by their husbands' insurance for six months prior to delivery) were eligible for state maternity benefits. The unstable economic situation during the Weimar era meant that despite adjustments for inflation – and especially hyperinflation in 1923 – the payments fell far short of meeting women's needs. Many pregnant women were forced to continue to work until just before they delivered their babies and to resume work very soon afterwards. Lawmakers recognised the inadequacy of the benefits to protect women, and in 1925 they ratified the Washington Convention of 1919, which called for paid maternity leave before and after delivery. From July 1927, all female factory workers were supposed to receive maternity leave of eight to twelve weeks and two half-hour periods per day for breast-feeding.[55] The 1927 law was the most far-reaching maternity benefit passed during the Weimar Republic, but it still left many women, particularly agricultural and household workers, outside its scope.

It soon became evident that maternity benefits alone would not reverse the demographic decline in Germany. Because Weimar lawmakers believed that 'the business of procreation was politically far too important to be left to the individual', on 20 August 1920 the Minister of Welfare, Heinrich Hirtsiefer proposed the creation of mother advice centres.[56] He emphasised that although 'the shortage of apartments, clothing and food affected the entire population, [it was] mothers, limited by employment before and after delivery and their infants [who] were the first victims of the sad economic conditions'.[57] The new mother advice centres would aim to 'grasp the entire realm of welfare questions and find solutions' and coordinate the efforts of doctors, midwives, social workers, the labour office, and private organisations. By 1921, 2,600 advice centres existed and the number doubled by 1928.[58]

Mother advice centres stood at the crossroads of the expanding state welfare programme and an older private system of social aid. As such, the mother advice centres put the question of the state's willingness to intervene in families – and whether it had the right to do so – into stark relief. By granting both social workers and doctors greater contact with mothers and children, mother advice centres allowed for the development of a state standard by which to assess whether mothers were raising their children 'properly'. Among the pertinent questions was whether mothers were spending their maternity benefits appropriately.[59] Although many social workers continued to emphasise the importance of relationships with clients and the traditional advisory nature of their work, others became more receptive to the application of racial and eugenic thought to their practices. An unusual set of service instructions for social workers in the district of Brake from 1925, for example, suggested that children and mothers should receive different treatment based on their 'worth'. These instructions declared that the purpose of the mother advice centre was 'to provide information and advice about infant care and nutrition for mothers whose children were not hereditarily ill'. Children who were 'hereditarily ill' were to be sent to the doctor's office.[60] Although the distinction may well have been intended to ensure that children with serious health problems received extra care, the chosen terminology hinted at a more sinister reason for the differential treatment. Eugenics was not yet widespread (or state mandated as it would become after 1933), but it is evident here and elsewhere that eugenic concepts had begun to creep subtly into public discourse.

Even as they sought to support mothers, many Germans including politicians, clergy and nationalists worried that they faced an attitude problem: young women demonstrated less interest in becoming wives and mothers than they once had. Throughout the 1920s, more German women than ever before appeared to reject an exclusively domestic role in favour of gainful employment outside the home, study at university, and the postponement of marriage. Simultaneously, consumerism, leisure and mass entertainment significantly reshaped unmarried women's lives. The 'New Woman', according to her contemporaries, discarded traditional values in favour of self-indulgence and luxury. Fashion and cosmetics sales skyrocketed; young women cut their hair short and wore their skirts shorter. Some even actively rebelled against marriage. Frau Dewald (b. 1910), interviewed by the author, who grew up in Detmold, emphasised that when she received her first marriage proposal, marriage itself held no appeal for her. She enjoyed interacting collegially with both men and women and took pleasure in a previously unknown level of personal freedom. In her view, marriage would have brought everything she was enjoying to an end.[61] Many young working-class women, familiar with the burdens of married life and the loss of freedom it brought, similarly put off marriage for as long as possible.

Attitudes towards sexuality changed dramatically during the Weimar era. For some young women, the financial turmoil of the 1920s undermined their confidence in marriage and 'destroyed the whole idea of remaining chaste until marriage'.⁶² Although the Reich Youth Welfare Law of 1922 declared illegitimate children wards of the state and infant mortality among these children fell, single motherhood still brought shame and scandal.⁶³ Furthermore, the availability of contraception made sex outside of marriage far less dangerous. Single women 'knew about contraception or, more likely, had access to abortion', which led to a decline in the number of children born outside marriage.⁶⁴ Young women's freer lifestyles drew women out onto the streets and into nightclubs, and caused the line between respectable women and prostitutes to blur in some cities. Some scholars have argued that especially in urban areas Germans 'embraced, rather than rejected, changes in gender roles and a more audacious expression of sexuality'.⁶⁵ Furthermore in 1927 the Law for Combatting Venereal Diseases decriminalised prostitution and transferred efforts to control venereal disease from the police to health and welfare authorities. The law distinguished between 'women who did discreet sex work [and] were free to conduct business' and those 'morally endangered' women, who were subjected to policies of surveillance and compulsory treatment.⁶⁶ The law also legalised displays of contraception and 1,300 condom-dispensing machines were installed in public lavatories by 1932.⁶⁷ Julia Roos has argued that 'for women, improved access to certain contraceptives after 1927 marked an important gain in reproductive rights'.⁶⁸

Shifts in attitudes towards sexuality went beyond opening the city streets to respectable women and helping prostitutes, however. As Marti Lybeck has argued, the 'sexualized metropolitan spaces [were] ... based on pleasure and desire rather than judgment, cultivation and critique'.⁶⁹ This atmosphere also allowed for a rich homosexual culture to flourish in clubs, dance halls, and in print. Though issues regarding sexuality were highly divisive among politicians, they managed to pass several important pieces of legislation that profoundly affected sexuality. In addition to decriminalising prostitution, in 1931 the penal code reform committee cut Paragraph 175, the law that criminalised sodomy, from the criminal code.⁷⁰ Not only did this open the path to a more public homosexual lifestyle, but also it drew discussions of sexuality into the public realm, a reality that in itself reinforced the sense that sexuality was modernising.

As Laurie Marhoefer has demonstrated, however, Paragraph 297, the replacement for Paragraph 175, raised the age of consent to twenty-one and explicitly criminalised homosexual prostitution. The question of whether this law represented progress caused bitter debate among the leaders of the German homo emancipation movement.[71]

In the face of such substantial societal changes, many Germans believed that advice centres and maternity benefits together were insufficient to reverse the low birth rate or to restore traditional gender roles. Instead, with the strong support of the churches, state officials increasingly recognised mothers' crucial contribution to society. The near-unanimous support for motherhood found expression in the creation of Mother's Day. In 1922 Dr. Rudolf Knauer, the head of the Association of German Florists and the first vocal advocate of Mother's Day in Germany, cited 'the inner conflict of our *Volk* and the loosening of the family' as his inspiration for introducing Mother's Day in 'our fatherland'.[72] He hoped that Mother's Day would unite the politically divided and economically troubled Germany. As one observer noted: 'Mother's Day should bring about a spiritual unification of the *Volk* on neutral ground.'[73] When, in 1925, Knauer's Reich Committee for Mother's Day joined the independent Taskforce for the Recovery of the *Volk*, the movement became firmly connected to population concerns.[74] The Taskforce strongly believed that the moral crisis besetting the German *Volk* could only be cured by drawing women back to their responsibility as mothers. Nationalism also became intertwined with Mother's Day, since motherhood was celebrated as a means of rejuvenating the nation. Beyond the celebration of Mother's Day lay the hope shared by all that the holiday would inspire more young women to bear children.

Although many progressive forces saw Mother's Day as a reaction against women's equality and especially against the 'New Woman', whose independent lifestyle allegedly threatened families, it was not merely symbolic. Many local city authorities viewed it both as a day to honour all mothers symbolically, and as an opportunity to provide material support for mothers with large families. In 1925, local officials in Westphalia began honouring mothers with many children with a cup of coffee and small monetary awards. In 1927, Prussian state officials expanded their awards for prolific mothers with a child welfare programme that provided large families – those with more than twelve children – a bonus for education and an honorary gift for the mothers: either an honorary cup or 100 marks.[75]

Many Germans viewed honouring mothers as insufficient to help society recover from the war. Social Democrats, bourgeois feminists, religious groups and organised housewives agreed that educating girls to be efficient housewives and 'modern' mothers would strengthen the nation. Training young women – especially from a working-class background, where girls' lack of knowledge of home economics was believed to be particularly severe – promised to rectify the perceived deterioration of morals, make motherhood and housework seem more attractive, and ensure the future of the race.[76] As a result, religious and secular vocational schools for mothers proliferated. In Westphalia, the curriculum varied, but all courses emphasised infant care, health care for the sick, and national birth and population policy. Some large companies also sponsored mother courses for their employees' wives, trusting that better wives and mothers would in turn make better workers.[77]

Household and motherhood training could not alter the fact that many German girls and women worked outside the home or that the nature of women's work was changing. After the First World War, the number of women employed in agriculture and domestic service dropped significantly and the number of women in white-collar jobs rose. The rationalisation and mechanisation of business led to the creation of many new jobs in such fields as typing and bookkeeping, while the consumer boom created myriad positions for women as sales clerks. Even within heavy industry, mechanisation opened up to women some previously male fields in the electrical, iron and metal industries. Although women earned less than half as much as their male counterparts, many families depended on female contributions for financial survival. For working women, household responsibilities constituted a double burden. Bourgeois feminists, Social Democrats and especially doctors stressed that even in the aggregate, maternity benefits, medical care and education could not eradicate the exhausting reality of motherhood for many women. As a result, Weimar authorities, religious and secular, designed two other programmes for mothers of small children: recuperation homes for fatigued or ill mothers and kindergartens for the children of working mothers.

Concerns about the burden of housework and childcare and the worry that 'mothers and housewives... suffer the most' led a variety of organisations, including both the Catholic and Protestant churches and city welfare offices to sponsor *Muttererholung* ('mother recuperation') programmes.[78] Women typically stayed at the recuperation homes for ten to forty days, during which time the sponsoring organisation made arrangements for their children at home. Even as late as 1931, when Germany's economy was at its worst, mother recuperation programmes continued. As the economy faltered, rather than discontinue programmes, authorities screened applicants more carefully and reduced the length of stay. The Protestant Women's Aid Society advertised its programme as providing essential help in difficult times: 'When the work never stops, when the money never stretches to the end of the week. When the children never cease to ask questions, when the unemployed husband's complaints never subside, when the mending basket needs attention, when during the washing the back hurts so badly – then hundreds of thousands of German mothers of all classes think: "Oh how wonderful – a day just to lie peacefully in the sun with nothing to do but think about beautiful, sunny rest!"'[79]

In addition to mother rest homes, kindergartens provided an invaluable safe haven for the children of working mothers. They were not without contention, however. In 1919, the Social Democrats argued that kindergartens should be public and universally available on a voluntary basis. Religious and political conservatives, who outnumbered the Social Democrats, opposed expanding public kindergartens because they believed that 'the right and duty of raising preschool children belongs basically to the family'.[80] As a result, the capacity of kindergartens did not rise during Weimar and many working mothers continued to depend on relatives, friends or neighbours to care for their children when they worked. Even so, Weimar kindergartens constituted an increasingly essential part of a multi-layered welfare system designed to further the national goals of lowering infant mortality and raising the birth rate. Those children who attended kindergartens could be observed by social workers and given health examinations. Kindergarten teachers also visited children at home to check on home environments, had parent and child evenings, and met individually with parents. Many mothers saw in their children's kindergarten teacher someone who could support and advise them about their children. At the same time, the observations and contacts with families allowed teachers to be more helpful to mothers and to intervene 'when a mother neglects childrearing'.[81]

Conclusion

In the end, the family underwent distinct shifts during the Weimar era. On the one hand, the Constitution enshrined women's equality with men, and women enjoyed far greater opportunities in education, work and entertainment. In contrast to earlier generations, when women worked outside the home only out of necessity, during the Weimar era, the expansion of white-collar service work and the opening of many professions to women drew middle- and upper- class women into the job market as never before. For most women, this foray into employment proved a delay rather than an outright rejection of marriage. The percentage of single women steadily fell, while the percentage of married women rose. On the other hand, as we have seen, in spite of the rising number of marriages, the number of births fell as Germans of all classes took advantage of the availability of birth control, and the two-child family became the norm. Moreover, young women's hesitation to follow in their mothers' footsteps as wives and mothers caused widespread concern. Weimar lawmakers adopted the rhetoric of *Bevölkerungspolitik* across the political spectrum, agreed that families and women needed help. Though they disagreed about what kind of support to provide, they did manage to create a broad array of state programmes for families. Most provided material support or emphasised education and none became compulsory or eugenically based.

The ultimate crisis for Weimar family policy occurred in 1929, when the worldwide economic depression overwhelmed the government's fragile welfare system. When unemployment skyrocketed to nearly

25 per cent, the economic foundation and security of many German families was destroyed. Middle-class daughters joined working-class women in the workforce, male heads of household lost their jobs and wives with unemployed husbands began working to sustain their families. Weimar politicians, local government leaders and welfare agencies all sought ways to decrease state expenditures at exactly the moment when more German families were applying for help. Ironically, in the face of such upheaval, many blamed women for overstepping their domestic roles, and the anti-feminist backlash fuelled right-wing critiques of modernisation. New legislative alliances led to support for laws against double-earners, 'modern' marriage, birth control, liberalised abortion and divorce reform. The economic crisis also opened the door for the political ascendance of the National Socialists who, together with other right-wing politicians, criticised the failure of parliamentary democracy to save the German family from peril.

Notes

1 R. Bessel, *Germany after the First World War* (Oxford, 1993), pp. 225–7.
2 These figures come from the 1925 census and are cited in A. Grossmann, *Reforming Sex: The German Movement for Birth Control and Abortion Reform 1920–1950* (Oxford, 1995), p. 6.
3 Bronisch, *Verhandlungen des Preussischen Landtags* 51, Sitzung 10 September 1919, cols. 4098–100, cited in Y. Hong, *Welfare, Modernity, and the Modern State 1919–1933* (Princeton, 1998) p. 56.
4 S. Rouette, *Sozialpolitik als Geschlechterpolitik: die Regulierung der Frauenarbeit nach dem Ersten Weltkrieg* (Frankfurt am Main, 1993), p. 41.
5 E. Weitz, *Creating German Communism, 1890–1990: From Popular Protests to Socialist State* (Princeton, 1997), p. 110.
6 Ibid., p. 114.
7 C. Usborne, *Politics of the Body: Women's Reproductive Rights and Duties* (Ann Arbor, 1992), p. 134.
8 Ibid., p. 134.
9 P. Weindling, *Health, Race and German Politics between Unification and Nazism, 1870–1945* (Cambridge, 1997), p. 341.

10 For a more in-depth analysis of Weimar family policy, see M. Mouton, *From Nurturing the Nation to Purifying the Volk: Weimar and Nazi Family Policy 1918–1945* (Cambridge, 2007).
11 L. Pine, *Nazi Family Policy 1933–1945* (Oxford, 1997), p. 90.
12 For a broader discussion of marriage policy during the Weimar Republic, see Mouton, *From Nurturing the Nation*, Chapter 1.
13 Weindling, *Health, Race and German Politics,* p. 330.
14 K. Hagemann, *Frauenalltag und Männerpolitik: Alltagsleben und gesellschaftliches Handeln von Arbeiterfrauen in der Weimarer Republik* (Bonn, 1990), p. 331.
15 Usborne, *Politics of the Body*, p. 92.
16 'Merkblatt für Eheschließende', 'Familienstammbuch' (Gießen, 1924), Staatsarchiv Detmold (hereafter StaD), L80 IA, Gruppe 26, Titel 6, 15.
17 Deutsche Gesellschaft für Rassenhygiene to Lippische Regierung, Detmold, received 30 April 1923, StaD, L 80 IA, Gruppe 26, Titel 1,1, Bd. 16.
18 Gesundheitsamt Charlottenburg to the Reichsministerium des Innern, 30 June 1921, Bundesarchiv Berlin (hereafter BAB), R 15.01, 9379.
19 Rundschreiben der Gesundheitsamt Berlin to Reichsminister des Innern, 27 December 1921and Schaumberg-Lippische Landesregierung to Reichsminister des Innern, 5 May 1921, BAB R 15.01, 9379.
20 Grossmann, *Reforming Sex*, p. 15.
21 K. von Soden, *Die Sexualberatungsstellen der Weimarer Republic, 1919–1933* (Berlin, 1988), p. 65.
22 Grossmann, *Reforming Sex*, p. 60.
23 Usborne, *Politics of the Body*, p. 96.
24 For more information on debates around Prussian marriage counselling see A. Timm, *The Politics of Fertility in Twentieth-Century Berlin* (Cambridge, 2010), pp. 103–15.
25 Jahresgesundheitsbericht, Siegen 1931, Staatsarchiv Münster (hereafter SAM), Kreis Siegen Kreis Wohlfahrtsamt, 8, Bd. 3.
26 M. Blank, '"Die Schutzmittel wurden meistens unreifen Burschen und Mädels vorgeführt": Sexualaufklärung, Verhütung und §218 während der Weimarer Republik und in den ersten Jahren des Nationalsozialismus in Herford', *Historisches Jahrbuch für den Kreis Herford* (1995), pp. 66–71.
27 Grossmann, *Reforming Sex*, p. 11.
28 Ibid., p. 55.
29 Ibid., p. 99.

30 C. Usborne, *Cultures of Abortion in Weimar Germany* (New York, 2007), p. 215.
31 A. Grossmann, 'Abortion and Economic Crisis: The 1931 Campaign against Paragraph 218', in R. Bridenthal, A. Grossmann and M. Kaplan (eds), *When Biology Became Destiny: Women in Weimar and Nazi Germany* (New York, 1984), p. 74.
32 Weindling, *Health, Race and German Politics*, p. 422.
33 For discussion of earlier protests against Paragraph 218 see C. Usborne, 'Body Biological to Body Politic', in G. Eley and J. Palmowski (eds), *Citizenship and National Identity in Twentieth Century Germany* (Stanford, 2008), pp. 139–41.
34 Georg Guggemoos, 'Schutz der Kinder aus zerrütteten Ehen', *Caritas* 10 (1927), p. 307, StaD, L 80 IC, Gruppe 28, Fach 25,5.
35 For a broader discussion of divorce policy during the Weimar Republic, see Mouton, *From Nurturing the Nation*, Chapter 2.
36 Entschließung einer Versammlung des 'deutschen Rechtsbundes' vom 4 April 1922, quoted in D. Blasius, *Ehescheidung in Deutschland im 19. Und 20. Jahrhundert* (Frankfurt am Main, 1992), p. 165.
37 Blasius, *Ehescheidung in Deutschland*, p. 169.
38 Ibid., p. 170.
39 Ibid., pp. 173–4.
40 SAM, Landgericht Dortmund, 9.8.R.238/31.
41 *Statistisches Jahrbuch* 21 (1925), p. 27; *Statistisches Jahrbuch* 27 (1931), p. 111.
42 Preußisches Minister für Volkswohlfahrt, Oberpräsidium, 26 November 1927, SAM, Oberpräsidium 5916.
43 In November 1927, the Prussian Minister of Welfare recommended that other courts follow Hamburg's example and bring children to the youth department's attention.
44 Guggemoos, 'Schutz der Kinder', p. 308.
45 Hagemann, *Frauenalltag und Männerpolitik*, p. 173.
46 SAM, Landgericht Arnsberg, 712.
47 *Statistisches Jahrbuch fur Preußen*, 30 (1934).
48 Timm, *The Politics of Fertility*, p. 81.
49 For further discussion of women's work during the Weimar era, see H. Boak, *Women in the Weimar Republic* (Manchester, 2013), Chapter 3.
50 Usborne, *Politics of the Body*, p. 109.
51 For further discussion of policy towards mothers, see Mouton, *From Nurturing the Nation*, Chapters 3 and 4.

52 E. Dickinson, 'State, Family and Society in Modern Germany: Child Welfare Policy from the Empire to the Federal Republic.' Ph.D. diss., University of California, Berkeley (1991), p. 615.
53 Usborne, *Politics of the Body*, p. 47.
54 Reichstag Gesetz 26 September 1919 and 30 April 1920 (*Reichgesetzblatt* 1920, p. 1069). BAB, Tape 36218, 9407.
55 For further information about the maternity benefits and maternity welfare, see Usborne, *Politics of the Body*, Chapter 1.
56 Ibid., p. 35.
57 Der Minister für Volkswohlfahrt Berlin, Runderlass über Mütter und Säuglingsfürsorge, 20 August 1920, Stadtarchiv Paderborn (hereafter StaP), Amt Neuhaus G2, 844.
58 Mouton, *From Nurturing the Nation*, p. 157ff.
59 Magistrate der Fürsorge Amt Detmold, 16 August 1926, StaD, D 106 Detmold, 277.
60 Dienstanweisung für Fürsorgerinnen in Verwaltungsamtbezirk Brake, Lippische Verwaltungsamt Bezirksfürsorgestelle, 28 April 1925, StaD, D 102 Lemgo, 30.
61 Interview Frau Dewald, conducted by the author, tape recording, Detmold, 25 February 1995.
62 Boak, *Women in the Weimar Republic*, p. 219.
63 Mouton, *From Nurturing the Nation*, p. 198ff.
64 Usborne, *Cultures of Abortion*, p. 208.
65 J. Smith, *Berlin Coquette: Prostitution and the New German Woman 1890–1933* (Ithaca, 2013), p. 152.
66 L. Marhoefer, *Sex and the Weimar Republic: German Homosexual Emancipation and the Rise of the Nazis* (Toronto, 2015), pp. 110–11.
67 Boak, *Women in the Weimar Republic*, p. 207.
68 J. Roos, *Through the Lens of Gender: Prostitution Reform, Women's Emancipation, and German Democracy, 1919–1933* (Ann Arbor, 2010), p. 113.
69 M. Lybeck, *Desiring Emancipation: New Women and Homosexuality in Germany, 1890–1933* (Albany, 2014), p. 157.
70 Marhoefer, *Sex and the Weimar Republic*, p. 120ff.
71 L. Marhoefer, 'Degeneration, Sexual Freedom, and the Politics of the Weimar Republic, 1918–1933', *German Studies Review* Vol. 34, No. 3 (2011), p. 538.
72 Rudolf Knauer, 'Die Entwicklung des deutschen Muttertages', Bundesarchiv Koblenz (hereafter BaK), R36, 1028.

73 Archiv für Wohlfahrtspflege, 5 July 1924, BaK, R36, 1028.
74 Rudolf Knauer, 'Die Entwicklung des deutschen Muttertages', BaK, R36, 1028.
75 Regierungspräsident Münster to Oberbürgermeister Roxel, 28 March 1928, Stadtarchiv Münster (hereafter StaM) Amt Roxel A Fach 33, 5. See also letters from Oberbürgermeisters of Recklinghausen, Gladbeck, Bochum and Hagen, StaM, Armenkommission, 864.
76 E. Harvey, *Youth and the Welfare State in Weimar Germany* (Oxford, 1993), p. 33.
77 M. Nolan, *Visions of Modernity: American Business and the Modernization of Germany* (Oxford, 1994), p. 218.
78 Regierungspräsident Minden, 27 May 1932, StaD, M1 IM, 842.
79 'Ferien für unsere Müttern!', Archiv Evangelische Frauenhilfe, 118.
80 Die Reichschulkonferenz, 1921, 692 quoted in A. Taylor Allen, 'Children between Public and Private Worlds: The Kindergarten and Public Policy in Germany, 1840-Present', in R. Wollons (ed.), *Kindergartens and Cultures: The Global Diffusion of an Idea* (New Haven, 2000), p. 31.
81 Niederschrift über die Verhandlung des Fürsorgeausschusses des Landkreises Münster, 19 November 1922, StaM, Kreisarchiv B, 298.

3

'The germ cell of the nation':
The family in the Third Reich

Lisa Pine

Introduction

The family, extolled in National Socialist ideology and propaganda as 'the germ cell of the nation', played a very important part in the *Volksgemeinschaft* ('national community'). However, Nazi family policy did not always accurately reflect Nazi ideology. This chapter examines the impact of Nazi policies upon the German family between 1933 and 1945. Based on original primary sources, including Nazi policy documents and legislation, it analyses the policies implemented by the Nazi regime to redress both the 'crisis of the family' and the decline in the nation's birth rate. Its significance lies in its distillation of the essence of Nazi family policy in terms of *Auslese* (selection) and *Ausmerze* (eradication). It clearly shows the extremes of Nazi policy towards those families regarded as 'desirable' or 'valuable' to the nation, and those which were 'undesirable' on grounds of racial, social, mental or physical 'inferiority'. It examines a whole series of measures and incentives designed to achieve the goal of increasing the birth rate, which had fallen dramatically from almost forty-two births per 1,000 inhabitants in 1874 to fewer than fifteen in 1933.[1] These included: the Marriage Loan Scheme; the Cross of Honour of the German Mother; the introduction of a new divorce law in 1938; the banning of contraceptives and the closure of family planning centres; the tightening up of abortion laws; welfare for mothers and children; and the *Lebensborn* organisation. This chapter also explores the more sinister side of Nazi family and population policy, including the introduction of legal measures designed to prevent marriages between Jews and 'Aryans' and to prevent marriages between healthy 'Aryans' and those deemed 'unfit' for marriage due to physical or mental illness, as well as the sterilisation law. It analyses Nazi policy towards families that did not fit into the 'national community', especially Jewish families, regarded as 'racially inferior' and expendable. The chapter examines Nazi policy towards homosexuals and lesbians. It ends with an analysis of the impact of the Second World War upon the German family.

Nazi family policies

Point 21 of the NSDAP's Programme declared that 'The state has to care for the raising of the nation's health through the protection of mother and child'. Once in power, the National Socialist regime introduced an array of measures and incentives to achieve its goal of increasing the birth rate. By 1936, the number of births per 1,000 inhabitants had risen – from just under fifteen in 1933 – to nineteen.[2] Indeed, Paul Ginsborg notes the 'extraordinary combination of strategies' that the Hitler government directed at German families.[3] French historian Johann Chapoutot convincingly argues that procreation was central to the Nazis' overall aims and ambitions: 'The Aryan race had to be fertile and to produce as many children as possible, especially as a defense against the Slavic enemy; it also had to be attentive to the quality of the biological substance it produced, which was to be free of all foreign and degenerate elements.'[4] Indeed, recent research by Amy Carney has highlighted the importance of family, in particular, in the SS, the Nazi elite formation led by Heinrich Himmler.[5]

The Minister of the Interior Wilhelm Frick claimed in 1934: 'The family is the primordial cell of the *Volk*, that is why the National Socialist state places it at the centre of its policy.'[6] This statement encapsulated the impression that the Nazi regime wished to portray publicly, namely, a firm and solid commitment to family life. With very few exceptions, the Nazi leadership publicly exalted the ideological status of the family throughout the Nazi era. The Nazis attacked the Weimar lifestyle, in which the extravagant enjoyment of the individual had taken precedence over collective moral and national obligations. They argued that the sense of 'duty' towards the community and nation had been lost and called for German people to show a renewed sense of obligation to the *Volksgemeinschaft* ('national community'). They further claimed that the Weimar governments had encouraged egocentricity. Bachelorhood and childless marriages had been acceptable in Weimar society. The 'two-child family' had become accepted, while large families had been scorned and derided. From 1933 onwards, there was a reversal in attitudes. There was a call for women to become valuable mothers of large families. The Nazi ideal family was termed *kinderreich* ('rich in children') and comprised of four or more children. In the Third Reich, parents of large families were to be proud. However, there was a qualitative aspect to this concept and the regime was careful to promote only 'hereditarily healthy', 'racially valuable', politically reliable and socially responsible families as *kinderreich*. 'Racially inferior' or 'asocial' large families were pejoratively labelled *Großfamilien* ('big families').[7]

In June 1933, the Marriage Loan Scheme was set up to promote marriages between healthy 'Aryan' partners. A loan of RM. 1000 was made to a German couple in the form of vouchers for the purchase of furniture and household equipment. The loan was given to a couple only if the wife agreed to give up her job. In addition, the loan was made only if the political affiliation and 'way of life' of the couple were considered acceptable. It was denied to couples if either or both partners had connections with the German Communist Party (KPD), or had had such connections in the past, and it was denied to prostitutes and the 'workshy'. The repayment of the loan was reduced by one quarter for each child born, and was completely cancelled out with the birth of the fourth child. Between August 1933 and January 1937, some 700,000 marriages were assisted by marriage loans.[8] In 1937, the prerequisite that women had to give up paid employment was revoked and this instigated a large increase in applications. In 1939, 42 per cent of all marriages were loan-assisted.[9] However, couples granted a marriage loan had, on average, only one child.

The Nazi regime also attempted to raise the status of motherhood. A woman's 'most glorious duty', according to Joseph Goebbels, Minister for Propaganda and Popular Enlightenment, was 'to present her people and her country with a child'. A classic example of a symbolic tribute to mothers with large families was the Cross of Honour of the German Mother. This was awarded to prolific mothers, in bronze, silver and gold, for four, six and eight children, respectively. There was a slight increase in the nation's birth rate in the period 1934–9 as compared with the years 1930–3. But this was not necessarily attributable to Nazi incentives to promote procreation. Many couples felt more secure about getting married and having children because the economic climate had improved. Hence, the number of marriages increased, but the number of children per marriage did not. In addition, Nazi incentives and propaganda were not sufficient on their own to redress the long-term trend in low birth rates.

A new divorce law was introduced in 1938 that allowed for a divorce if a couple had lived apart for three years or more, and if the marriage had effectively broken down. On the surface, this appeared quite liberal. However, the reasoning behind it lay more in perceived benefits to the state than in benefits to private individuals. The objective was to dissolve marriages that were of no value to the 'national community'. The National Socialists believed that once a divorce had been granted, the two partners involved might then re-marry and provide the nation with more children. Premature infertility became a ground for divorce, as did either partner's refusal to have a child.[10]

Many other measures were taken to encourage marriages between healthy 'Aryan' partners that would result in large families and to increase the nation's birth rate. Contraceptives were banned and family planning centres were dissolved. In 1941, Himmler's Public Ordinance prohibited the production and distribution of contraceptives.[11] In addition, the abortion laws were tightened up by the re-introduction of Paragraphs 219 and 220 of the Criminal Code, which made provisions for harsher punishments for abortion.[12] Eventually, in 1943, the death penalty was introduced for anyone performing an abortion to terminate a 'valuable' pregnancy, as this was considered an act of 'racial sabotage' during the crisis of the war.[13]

The regime employed an existent organisation, the *Reichsbund der Kinderreichen* (RdK or National League of Large Families) to put an end to lax sexual and marital morals and to promote the ideal large family as a model for emulation. The RdK offered advice to *kinderreich* families, on issues such as rent, housing and employment. It was also involved in propaganda work. Its leader Wilhelm Stüwe, claimed that 'the more hereditarily healthy families a nation possesses, the more certain its future is'.[14] There was some concern that the organisation had 'asocial' or 'hereditarily unfit' families among its members, and in 1940, under a new leader, Robert Kaiser, the organisation was renamed the *Reichsbund Deutsche Familie, Kampfbund für erbtüchtigen Kinderreichtum* (National Association of the German Family, Combat League for Large Families of Sound Heredity). The organisation redoubled its efforts to attain a larger membership of 'valuable' *kinderreich* families and to expound the correct ideals for German families to emulate. The Cross of Honour of the German Mother and the Honour Books awarded to large families exemplified the symbolic significance of *kinderreich* families.

Yet, despite the honour and status accorded to *kinderreich* families, the regime was unwilling to undertake major financial expenditure to assist them. While some measures were put in place to redress the inequalities between *kinderreich* families and single people or couples with no children or few children, such as tax reforms and child supplements, these remained insufficient to convince people to have large families. Furthermore, the Nazi administration failed to make adequate housing provision for *kinderreich* families. Propaganda and piecemeal initiatives did not change the inclination of German couples to limit the size of their families. Hence, the promotion of *kinderreich* families was not successful. Indeed, the proportion of married women with four or more children decreased from 25 per cent in 1933 to 21 per cent in 1939.[15] Much to the dissatisfaction of the Nazi leadership, the 'two-child family' was perpetuated throughout the Third Reich.

The *Hilfswerk 'Mutter und Kind'*

The *Hilfswerk 'Mutter und Kind'* (Mother and Child Relief Agency) was a special agency of the *Nationalsozialistiche Volkswohlfahrt* (NSV or National Socialist People's Welfare), established on 28 February 1934. The agency's central concern was with the health of mothers and children, in order to preserve 'the immortality of the nation'. Four of the most significant aspects of its work were: welfare for mothers; recuperation for mothers; advice centres for mothers; and welfare for small children. The Nazi regime utilised welfare as an instrument to educate the German nation in the spirit of National Socialism. Welfare, understood in population policy terms, was directed at the promotion of the 'racially pure' and 'fit'. Instructors, social workers and staff in the advice centres and in the recuperation homes were trained in the Nazi *Weltanschauung* ('worldview') so that they could provide German women not only with material, practical and educational support, but also with ideological guidance.

Welfare for mothers who had recently given birth had existed in Germany since the end of the First World War. However, it was only in the Third Reich that this sphere of welfare became a central element of state policy. Self-mobilisation of the family through Nazi social work benefited millions of families. Welfare for mothers entailed help in the home. However, this did not usually take the form of direct financial aid. It consisted of material help, such as the provision of beds, linen, children's clothes or food allowances. In addition, home helps were assigned to pregnant women or those who had recently given birth to assist with household chores. Welfare workers and/or nurses made home visits to pregnant women in order to help prevent miscarriage, premature birth and illness. They educated and cared for expectant mothers. After the birth of the child, regular visits continued and welfare workers gave advice on breast-feeding and childcare. They also observed the general behaviour of the family. It is significant to note that welfare visits to 'hereditarily ill' or 'abnormal' children were restricted 'to a minimum'.[16]

The *Hilfswerk 'Mutter und Kind'* helped single mothers too, as long as they were 'racially valuable' and 'hereditarily healthy'. Hence, a distinction was not made on the basis of marital status, as all German children were 'valuable' to the nation, but on eugenic and racial grounds. The *Hilfswerk 'Mutter und Kind'* was involved in the organisation of foster care and adoptions and in the struggle against abortion. The *Hilfswerk 'Mutter und Kind'* helped single mothers by trying to procure their marriages to their babies' fathers or to seek other solutions if this was not successful or possible, including the recommendation of single mothers to *Lebensborn* homes to give birth discreetly and then give up the baby for adoption.

Welfare for mothers also took the form of recuperation measures. While there had been some moves towards recuperation for mothers during the Weimar era, under National Socialism, mother recuperation became ideologically motivated and fundamental to state family policy. Recuperation for mothers took a variety of forms – going to stay with relatives, visiting local convalescence centres or being sent away to recuperation homes. The homes were located in the mountains or by the sea, or at natural springs and spas. The average stay was for 26 days. The type of recuperation for each mother was determined by her medical condition, 'state of mind' and social status. The practice of ascertaining the 'hereditary-biological' worth of each mother was a dominant feature of this area of work. Recuperation or convalescence was not made available to the 'hereditarily inferior'. For example, in the period up to the end of October 1941, one-third of applications for entry to recuperation homes in the Hamburg area were rejected on the grounds that the women were 'hereditarily inferior' or behaved in a manner that was 'adverse to the community'.[17]

Other than 'hereditary health', the main prerequisite for convalescence was that a mother did not have enough financial means of her own for this purpose. Mothers weakened through childbirth, those with two or more children and those whose husbands had been long-term unemployed were given priority for recuperation measures. During a mother's absence from home, a relative, neighbour or household help stepped in. Mothers received a 50 per cent reduction on train travel to and from the recuperation homes. Official NSV statistics stated that 40,340 women went to the recuperation homes in 1934, the number rising to 77,723 in 1938.[18]

The homes had a strong educational aspect to them. Copies of the educational pamphlet *Guidelines for the Practical Housewife* were made accessible to mothers. Along with recuperation in the form of good wholesome food, rest and exercise, mothers learned about Nazi ideology, their place in the Nazi worldview and their role in the 'national community'.

Indeed, the aim of mothers' rest care was 'to toughen up German women for their tasks in the house and family'. Staff observed the mothers carefully and made reports about their conduct and attitudes. If they behaved in a 'cantankerous' or 'contrary' way, they were required to leave the rest homes. The work of the recuperation homes ensured that mothers returned home with renewed vigour and spirit in order to undertake their familial tasks and duties. If, on their return home, mothers were still not quite ready to undertake all their household duties, home helps were sent to assist them for up to four weeks.

Letters from mothers expressing their gratitude to the NSV and the *Führer* were proudly used by the *Hilfswerk 'Mutter und Kind'* to demonstrate the success of its work. 'We live as in fairy tales … It is overwhelmingly beautiful here. I cannot put it into words … This trip, this experience will certainly count as the most beautiful memory of my life.'[19] Another stated: 'I would like to thank the *Führer* heartily with the assurance that I am aware as a German woman and mother of my responsibility to look after my children … and to educate them into fit, useful people.' Men also wrote letters to the organisation on behalf of their wives: 'She has put on 14 pounds, and the strength she was lacking before her trip has considerably come back again … March forward, NSV, flourish, prosper, and the nation will be healthy.'[20]

Many women, exhausted physically by the demands of motherhood, enjoyed their time away. Yet others were reluctant to go to recuperation homes or even outright refused to go because they had no desire to have a 'strange woman' run their household and 'snoop', because they would not leave their children, or in rural areas because they refused to leave their land. Hence, the impact of Nazi welfare policies on women was not uniform. Furthermore, despite the intentions of the regime, the ideological atmosphere in the homes did not always meet the requirements of inspectors, where staff in recuperation homes either did not introduce politics into rest care or did not pressurise mothers to participate in ideological training if they preferred to sit in a garden chair and relax.

A network of help and advice centres was established throughout Germany to offer advice to mothers. A total of 25,552 centres had been set up by 1935. This number increased to 28,936 in 1941.[21] These centres were an important focus of *Hilfswerk 'Mutter und Kind'* work. They offered advice about all aspects of household management, nutrition, health, baby and childcare. The medical profession approved of the work of the advice centres as valuable aspects of state welfare. Educational work was of paramount significance in the advice centres as the staff had direct contact with members of the population. This point illustrates that National Socialist welfare measures were, as Michelle Mouton argues 'from the outset ... intended to be interventionist'.[22] To be sure, in addition to the material, financial and medical advice offered at these centres, 'the Nazis also viewed the centres as agents for inculcating Nazi ideology and infused racial hygienic thought into all aspects of clinic life'.[23] They advocated *kinderreich* ('child-rich') families, of four or more children, claiming that children did not thrive in 'small families' with no or too few siblings.

In terms of health policy, special attention was devoted to the prevention of infant mortality by means of wider public education in childcare. The infant mortality rate of 7.7 per cent in 1933 was reduced to 6.58 per cent by 1936. Prevention of childhood disease was also a central aim of *NSV* work – 'what is prevented in childhood is prevented for life'. It was considered dangerous for the future of the nation for infants and small children to be negatively affected by factors such as lack of care and bad nutrition, hence the promotion of their health was a key function of the *Hilfswerk 'Mutter und Kind'*. Advice and consultation centres were essential in contributing both to the population policy objectives of the regime and to a heightened awareness of issues such as prevention of illness, the importance of breast-feeding and correct nutrition. For example, nutritional information was given to mothers, especially the need for fresh fruit and vegetables in the diet, as well as supplementary vitamin and mineral preparations. General health education was also served by a pamphlet entitled 'The Adviser for Mothers', of which almost 1.2 million copies were distributed in 1937. Former healthcare provisions were frowned upon by the *NSV*, which described the lack of monitoring of the health of small children as 'completely unacceptable'. The continual healthcare of growing children was expanded by means of regular medical examinations and more medical advice being made available to mothers.

Childcare was an important aspect of the work of the *Hilfswerk 'Mutter und Kind'*. Children under the age of six were sent to day nurseries or kindergartens, where they could be looked after properly, especially if their mothers had jobs outside the home. The day nurseries were clean, spacious, bright and airy, ensuring a 'healthy environment' for the children. Each day, on arrival, the children washed and cleaned their teeth, and then were separated into different age groups and supervised by nurses and welfare workers, as they played, exercised, ate, sang and slept. The 'Guidelines for Day Nurseries' in 1936 set out the following among its tasks: to sponsor the physical, mental and spiritual development of the children, to educate them in National Socialism and service to the *Volksgemeinschaft*, and to instil in them a sense of care for the German nation. Hence, the nurseries clearly had the function of socialising small children in the spirit of National Socialism. *NSV* kindergartens were considered 'essential bases . . . for the education of young German people'. According to official *NSV* statistics, the number of day nurseries rose from approximately 1,000 in 1935 to 15,000 in 1941, although no indication is given about their size and quality.

In addition to ordinary nurseries, 'Harvest kindergartens' were set up in rural areas. These had a special function. They freed agricultural women from their familial responsibilities during the day, allowing them to carry out their harvesting. The necessity for these kindergartens was demonstrated by the lack of available, satisfactory supervision for children during harvest time. The care for children during the harvest period by the oldest, frailest – and often ill – village inhabitants was considered completely inadequate and unsuitable. 'Harvest Kindergartens' were first set up in the summer of 1934, to take in healthy, unsupervised children from the age of two upwards. They consisted of one or two large rooms, simply furnished with tables, benches and chairs, and equipped with wash basins and good sanitation. There was also a play area outside. Milk was supplied by local farmers. The kindergartens were run by trained kindergarten workers, who were helped by older school girls and *BDM* (League of German Girls) girls, provided that they were not needed for harvest work. The children were medically examined and a health questionnaire was filled out for each child. Both oral hygiene and general health were regularly monitored. The number of 'harvest kindergartens' increased from 600 in 1934, to 8,700 in 1941 and to 11,000 in 1943. They promoted the physical, mental and spiritual development of the children and educated them in the ideas of National Socialism.

Lebensborn

The *Lebensborn* agency, established in December 1935, set up maternity homes in which single women could give birth to illegitimate children, in a comfortable environment, distant from their own homes, and thus without the knowledge of their neighbours, relatives and priests. These homes were, according to Himmler, 'primarily . . . for the brides and wives of our young *SS* men, and secondarily for illegitimate mothers of good blood'. The aims of the organisation were to support 'hereditarily-biologically valuable, *kinderreich* families', to care for 'racially valuable and hereditarily healthy mothers-to-be', to care for the children born from such mothers and to care for the mothers after the delivery of their babies. The prerequisite for such care was, of course, fulfilment of the *SS*'s criteria regarding race and hereditary health. The *Lebensborn* did not serve mothers who had been involved in 'indiscriminate relationships' that would lead to the birth of 'racially inferior' or 'hereditarily ill' children. Indeed, of nearly 3,000 applications by unmarried mothers-to-be, less than half were accepted.

The *Lebensborn* organisation was run from its headquarters in Munich, under the personal chairmanship of Himmler. By the end of 1937, it had 13,300 members, of whom 12,500 were from the *SS* and 500 were from the German police. The organisation saw its chief task as 'the support . . . of mothers-to-be of good blood'. It played a part in the struggle against abortions, by providing discreet delivery homes for illegitimate births and thereby preventing a number of pregnant girls and women from feeling the necessity to terminate their pregnancies. For if the mother and the father of the baby were both 'hereditarily healthy', the child would be 'valuable'. Hence, the *Lebensborn* provided practical protection for such mothers-to-be in its delivery homes, of which six were established in the first two years of its existence. By 31 December 1938, 653 mothers had used the *Lebensborn* delivery homes. The infant mortality rate in the homes was 3 per cent, which was half that of the national average.

Himmler took a personal interest in the running of the *Lebensborn* homes. For example, he advised the homes about the correct diet for the women, promoting the importance of porridge and wholemeal bread. He also ensured that the homes received priority treatment during the war, in terms of rations of luxury items such as fresh fruit. To prepare the mothers for their future responsibilities, Himmler ensured that *RMD* (National Mothers' Service) courses were held in each *Lebensborn* home, to train mothers in all aspects of household management and childcare. In addition, the SS was responsible for the 'ideological education' of the women, which it achieved by holding lectures, film screenings and discussion evenings.

In the homes, mothers had the chance to relax during their free time and to form friendships with the other women. According to a *Lebensborn* pamphlet, a sense of camaraderie developed between the mothers as each was giving a German baby a life. Once she had given birth, a mother who could not take her baby with her could leave it to be looked after in the home for one year. If, after that time, the mother was still unmarried or not in a position to take care of the child, it was given out to foster parents, usually to SS leaders who were childless or who had just one or two children. The *Lebensborn* organisation accepted that marriage was the best possible situation in which a man and woman could have children, but it also stated that it recognised that many young men and women engaged in extra-marital sexual relationships for a number of reasons. In such cases, it was the 'hereditary health' and 'blood' of the parents that were important. In this sense, the *Lebensborn* organisation claimed to protect Germany's future.

The *Lebensborn* statistics for its home 'Pommern' provide an interesting account of the activities of the organisation. Between 23 May 1938 and 1 September 1941, 541 mothers gave birth at this home. Of these, 245 were married and 296 were single – that is, 45 per cent were married. According to the *Lebensborn* statistics, 71 per cent of those having their first child were unmarried, but only 26 per cent of those having their second child were unmarried, and of those having their third or more child, none were unmarried. Forty-two of the single mothers subsequently got married, thirty-seven of them to their child's father. In total, only seven babies were stillborn or died within twenty-four hours of birth. Hence, the mortality rate was exceptionally low compared with the national average. The length of stay in the homes was on average seventy-one days, forty-three and a half days for married mothers and ninety-four and a half days for single mothers. The longest stay was 256 days and the shortest was nine days.

The *Lebensborn* and its activities have courted a considerable amount of controversy. At the time, the *Lebensborn* homes were unpopular with many ordinary German citizens, especially in rural, Catholic areas, where people were disgruntled with the official condonement and even encouragement of the birth of children out of wedlock. As a result, all sorts of rumours were perpetuated about the *Lebensborn* homes. These included allegations that the *Lebensborn* homes employed permanent 'procreation helpers' or that they were 'stud farms' for the SS. The fact that the homes were set up in secluded areas and shrouded in secrecy served to fuel such rumours. However, although the *Lebensborn* homes were not 'stud farms' for the SS, their ethics came into question for a different reason. During the war, they played a significant role in the SS's abduction and Germanisation of children from the territories occupied by the *Reich*. In the *Lebensborn* homes, such children were subjected to racial examinations. Those that passed the tests were either reared in the *Lebensborn* homes or sent to live with German foster parents. Their role in this kind of activity is another major reason for the controversy surrounding the *Lebensborn* homes, quite separate from that of their original purpose. The Nazi regime also attempted to establish its *Lebensborn* homes in lands it occupied during the war in western and northern Europe, achieving most success in Norway.[24]

'Inferior' families

'More happiness, more relaxation, healthier mothers and children – that is the aim!' The *Hilfswerk 'Mutter und Kind'* emphasised its welfare work for mothers and children very strongly. However, as we have seen, welfare was applicable only to those mothers and children who were deemed to be 'hereditarily healthy', racially pure and whose behaviour and lifestyles accorded with the dictates of the regime. Ginsborg rightly notes: "The Nazis laboriously developed the most systematic typology, from the early legislation against the "hereditarily unfit," to the discrimination against "asocial families," to the gathering crescendo against all members of racially inferior families."[25] At the same time as the positive population policies directed towards fit members of the 'national community' occurred, another side of Nazi population policy was taking place. Legal measures were introduced to prevent marriages between Jews and 'Aryans' (Nuremberg Laws, September 1935); and to prevent marriages between healthy 'Aryans' and those deemed 'unfit' for marriage due to physical or mental illness (Marriage Health Law, October 1935). In order to marry, it was necessary to undergo a medical examination first. On passing this, the local health authorities issued a 'certificate of fitness to marry'. The regime was very strict about the implementation of these laws, for the children from 'undesirable' marriages would be 'inferior'. Sterilisation was the principal method used by the Nazi regime to prevent people it considered 'undesirable' from having children. On 1 January 1934, a compulsory sterilisation edict, the Law for the Prevention of Hereditarily Diseased Offspring, came into effect. It called for the mandatory sterilisation of anyone that suffered from 'congenital feeble-mindedness, schizophrenia, manic depression, hereditary epilepsy, Huntington's chorea, hereditary blindness, hereditary deafness, serious physical deformities' and 'chronic alcoholism'. Between January 1934 and September 1939, approximately 320,000 people (0.5 per cent of the population), were forcibly sterilised under the terms of this law.[26] The majority of them were of German ethnicity; however, they were considered to be 'hereditarily ill' or simply 'feeble-minded' by the regime and its eugenic experts. The 'feeble-minded' made up two-thirds of all those sterilised, of which about two-thirds of these were women. Sterilised women became the objects of sexual abuse, especially in the cities, where soldiers or factory workers asked their colleagues on Mondays: 'Did you not find a sterilised woman for the weekend?'[27]

Nazi discrimination against 'asocials' spanned a whole array of actions, from the symbolic, such as excluding the mothers of 'asocial' families from the Cross of Honour of the German Mother, through forced sterilisation, compulsory accommodation in 'asocial colonies', to internment in concentration camps, hard labour and physical annihilation. The social policy of the regime reacted against all kinds of non-conformist behaviour, by the implementation of force and terror, and in many cases, ultimately, death. What was new in the Nazi state was the penetrating biological argument that proposed the 'elimination' of 'asocials' for the future. In this respect, the families of 'asocials' were directly affected, for, in 'asocial clans', negative traits of every kind – from speech defects to the suicide of distant relatives – were used to purport and to demonstrate that 'asociality' was hereditary. This was justification enough for members of 'asocial' families to be institutionalised and sterilised for 'congenital feeble-mindedness' or 'annihilated' just for existing at all. 'Gypsy' clans were doubly excoriated by the Nazi regime on account of their 'asociality' and their 'racial inferiority'. Germany's Sinti and Roma ('Gypsy') population experienced wide-ranging discrimination and harassment during the Nazi era, culminating in their annihilation during the war.[28] These families were considered not to belong to the German nation and were therefore expendable.

Germany's Jews were excluded from the 'national community' and were categorised as 'racially alien' and 'racially inferior'. Jewish families were subjected to a wide range of discriminatory policies throughout the Nazi period, culminating in the 'Final Solution'. There is no clear-cut correlation of the effects of persecution upon Jewish families and their responses to it in the period up to 1939.[29] In many cases, there is evidence to suggest that families pulled together, and that in particular, the Jewish home provided a shelter against the discrimination and growing problems that individual family members had to face outside it. Yet, in other cases, the Jewish home seemed unable to shield its members from the situation, and tensions between spouses and between parents and children arose. Parents often felt unable to maintain their position as protectors of and providers for their offspring, and children sometimes experienced a loss of respect for their parents for not fulfilling this role.[30] Such feelings presented themselves even more strikingly in the transit camps, concentration camps and death camps, where children saw their parents in a different light imposed by the abnormal circumstances and by those in charge.[31]

Contrary to traditional norms of not harming women and children, women's fertility and ability to reproduce became the ultimate aim of Nazi extermination policy. Pregnant women were searched out and killed in many camps. Rochelle Saidel notes that 'being female was a significant factor that influenced life and death during the Holocaust in general and in concentration camps in particular'.[32] Physiological considerations – particularly pregnancy – made women 'especially vulnerable in concentration camps'.[33] For example, from the start, Himmler had insisted that no births were to take place at Ravensbrück. And so, at Ravensbrück concentration camp, until 1942, pregnant prisoners were sent to local hospitals in order to give birth. The new babies were then taken from their mothers, who returned to the camp. In 1943, pregnant women were pressurised to have abortions and many were performed in the camp – some of them up to the eighth month of pregnancy. It is, of course, extremely important to note that this policy was very different from that for 'Aryan' German women, for whom abortion was illegal.[34]

From the autumn of 1944, however, with many pregnant women arriving at the camp, the SS allowed most of them to give birth to their babies at Ravensbrück. A maternity ward was established at the end of 1944, with a prisoner nurse, named Hanka Houskova, acting as midwife there. This was the only concession made by the SS to the mothers and their babies. Shortly after giving birth, the new mothers were expected to return to work and roll calls, which meant that the babies remained unfed for many hours at a time. However, most of the mothers were very malnourished in any case and unable to produce much milk. Between 19 September 1944 and 22 April 1945, 551 children were born at Ravensbrück.[35] In many cases, it appears that the new-born babies survived for only a few days. Eliska Valentova, one of the nurses at the infirmary, who tried to look after the new-born babies described her efforts to help them with no success, because of their malnutrition. She recalled: 'And yet there was nothing more that we could do except to watch as the babies lost their appetites, became thin and weak and eventually, but slowly, died.'[36] The dead bodies of the babies were then taken to the crematorium. As Sarah Helm explains, 'the deliberate starving of babies was a long-established Nazi technique of killing'.[37] In February and March 1945, orders were received to transport all children and pregnant women out of Ravensbrück. Hundreds of children were sent away, mainly to Bergen-Belsen, and almost none of them survived. They died of extreme cold on the train journey or shortly afterwards from starvation.

In the death camps, the Nazis linked the destiny of women and children, as mothers holding the hands of their young children were among the first to be selected for the gas chambers. In addition, women were the targets of sexual assault and rape by their persecutors, even though this contravened Nazi racial policy. Myrna Goldenberg has explored the physical vulnerability of women, both as mothers and as objects of sexual assault.[38] This was partly a response to patriarchal assumptions about the characteristics of women and the capacity of men to appropriate their bodies and reproductive power.[39]

Homosexuals and lesbians

Sexual outsiders were also persecuted by the Nazi government and homosexuals remained the 'forgotten victims' of the Nazi regime for many decades. Almost nothing was written about the fate of homosexuals under National Socialism after 1945. In addition, prejudice against homosexuals continued and the legal position of homosexuals in both the German Democratic Republic and the Federal Republic of Germany remained unchanged from that of the Nazi era until 1968 and 1969 respectively. For these reasons, it was only in the 1970s that the taboo status of the subject was broken, and only since the 1980s that the subject began to be more adequately researched by historians and other scholars.[40] In addition, many homosexual victims were reluctant to relate their experiences.[41] The Nazi position towards lesbianism was not investigated until the 1990s.[42]

Homosexuals were persecuted by the Nazi regime on grounds of their 'deviant' sexual behaviour. In 1935, the Nazis amended the law in relation to homosexuality. In addition to Paragraph 175, Paragraph 175a stated that:

Confinement in a penitentiary not to exceed ten years and, under extenuating circumstances, imprisonment for not less than three months shall be imposed: (1) Upon a male who, with force or with threat of imminent danger to life and limb, compels another male to commit lewd and lascivious acts with him or compels the other party to submit to abuse for lewd and lascivious acts; (2) Upon a male who, by abuse of a relationship of dependence upon him, in consequence of service, employment, or subordination, induces another male to commit lewd and lascivious acts with him or to submit to being abused for such acts; (3) Upon a male who being over 21 years of age induces another male under 21 years of age to commit lewd and lascivious acts with him or to submit to being abused for such acts; (4) Upon a male who professionally engages in lewd and lascivious acts with other men, or submits to such abuse by other men, or offers himself for lewd and lascivious acts with other men.[43]

Paragraph 175b stated that: 'Lewd and lascivious acts contrary to nature between human beings and animals shall be punished by imprisonment; loss of civil rights may also be imposed.'[44] Penalties for homosexual acts were made harsher.

In October 1936, the Reich Central Office for the Combating of Homosexuality and Abortion, headed by Josef Meisinger, was assigned the task of registering homosexuals. By 1940, this office stored the personal details of some 41,000 men convicted or suspected of homosexuality.[45] Special card indexes were compiled on 'rent boys' and 'corrupters of youth', who were regarded as 'incorrigible' and 'especially dangerous'. The number of prosecutions increased during this time and the period between 1936 and 1939 marked the high point in terms of the numbers of homosexuals convicted. The number of convictions rose steeply from 948 in 1934, to 5,320 in 1936, 8,271 in 1937 and 8,562 in 1938.[46]

In contrast to their strong revulsion of homosexual men, Nazi ideologues were largely indifferent to lesbian women and most jurists were disinterested in extending Paragraph 175 to apply to them. There were four main reasons for this. First, homosexual men were excluded from the reproductive process, but this did not apply to the same degree to lesbian women. Second, homosexual activity was considered to be less widespread and more unobtrusive in women, and hence less likely to set a corrupting example. Third, intimate forms of friendship between women made lesbianism much more difficult to detect. Fourth, women played a comparatively smaller role in public life.[47] Claudia Schoppmann has argued that there was 'no systematic persecution of lesbian women comparable to that of male homosexuals'.[48] The Nazis did, however, destroy the beginnings of a collective lesbian lifestyle and identity, which had been developing over the previous two decades.[49] Lesbian meeting places, such as the Dorian Gray, one of the oldest women's bars in Berlin, and lesbian magazines, such as *Frauenliebe* – established in 1926 and renamed *Garçonne* in 1930 – that had flourished during the Weimar years, were destroyed. This led to the withdrawal of lesbian women into private circles among their friends.

The impact of the Second World War on family life

As Ginsborg notes, 'even for German Aryan families', the Nazi regime 'entailed their gradual splitting-up and maiming'.[50] The Second World War had profound implications and consequences for the German family. As fathers and sons were conscripted into the armed services, women were encouraged back into the workforce to replace them.[51] The war created almost impossible circumstances for intimate and stable family life to be conducted. Many women who were accustomed to their husbands making decisions and dealing with family finances had to manage unaided. In rural areas, women had to cope with both their sources of livelihood and their families on their own, as farmers and male farm labourers were conscripted. In urban and industrial areas, women had to bear the strain of industrial work and maintain their families single-handed. Female relatives, neighbours and friends helped each other, providing mutual support and relief. Food rationing, bombings and the destruction of gas and water supplies, were among the difficulties experienced in daily life. Air raids disrupted life and many families were made homeless and dispossessed. Many women and children were evacuated from the cities to the countryside, and families became separated in the process. Hence, the ultimate legacy of the Nazi regime and of the war to German family life was disastrous.

Hester Vaizey has examined the ways in which family members communicated with each other during periods of lengthy separation, using letters and diaries to find out how families stayed in touch. Letters helped to bridge the gap of enforced separation in wartime. Of course, it was in the interests of the Nazi regime to maintain popular morale and so it facilitated letter exchanges, although this process was subjected to heavy censorship. Vaizey maintains that despite the obstacles that confronted family members, they did maintain communication, which was 'crucial to family cohesion'.[52] Through letter-writing, spouses could convey to each other their own separate experiences of the war. Soldiers on the front gained comfort from the letters of their wives. Vaizey argues that even if emotional intensity in letters was not necessarily to be replicated in person, that couples which communicated by letter 'had good reason to feel optimistic and committed to working on their marriage post-reunion'.[53]

However, Ginsborg notes how 'service to the state engulfed and destroyed families' in the war years.[54] Spouses worried about how their loved ones were faring under the conditions of the war. Women feared for the lives of their husbands on the front; men were concerned about how their wives were managing at home without them, especially as they faced food shortages and air raids. Long periods of separation and scanty communication inevitably meant that some husbands and wives questioned each other's fidelity or were unfaithful. Others were looking forward to a time when they could be together again. Wartime letters show how couples were able to keep their relationships alive and provide an insight into the private world of their marriages. While many letters were nostalgic about the past and painted a rosy picture of the future, some couples were very realistic about their situation. Vaizey notes that 'As people learned to cope with less, they adjusted their outlooks accordingly'.[55]

Without their men, women had to make decisions and engage in all sorts of different types of work and activities than before. Their independence affected their subsequent reunions with their husbands. The concept of women 'standing alone' on the Home Front during the war and the 'Hour of the Woman' after the war, meant a new situation for married couples once men returned from the front. Despite the prevalent image in the historical literature of strong women, who dealt with the realities of war and subsequently cleared up the rubble, many women did feel vulnerable or were physically exhausted by the strains of life. Vaizey argues that ultimately they 'wanted to return to a sense of normality'.[56] In the end, she maintains, changes in gender roles engendered by the circumstances of the war were not permanent ones, and power dynamics between spouses adjusted back to how they had been previously.

Years of separation took their toll on family life. Both men and women were confronted with changes in the physical appearance of their partners. Feelings of reserve and alienation made it hard for many married couples to communicate with each other. In addition, it was difficult for them to recount painful experiences to one another. Other problems also contributed to the destabilisation of families, such as sexual distance between spouses and difficulties in the relationships between children and their recently returned fathers. Many children were unable to recognise their fathers on their return home. Younger children, in particular, had often had no knowledge of their fathers, sometimes having only seen photographs of them. Elder sons, in the absence of their fathers, had become the confidants of their mothers and ersatz fathers to their siblings. With the homecoming of their fathers, there inevitably ensued a conflict about the recognition and maintenance of this status. Many fathers were unwilling to accept it and many sons were reluctant to give it up. Older children, in general, resented their fathers for treating them still as children, when they had been forced to grow up faster as a consequence of the war. They rebelled against and felt alienated from their fathers, which put mothers in the difficult position of trying to maintain some element of harmony and balance within the family.

Conclusion

While Nazi welfare measures were comparable to those introduced in other countries at around the same time, they differed in terms of their application within German society, as certain sections of the population were excluded from welfare measures on racial or eugenic grounds. As Ginsborg notes, the starting point for Nazi family policy was 'a profound distinction between approved and non-approved families'.[57] The goal, as Goebbels put it, was not 'children at any cost', but 'racially worthy, physically and mentally unaffected children of German families'.[58] Nazi policies spanned an array of initiatives from positive population policies, such as incentives aimed at encouraging early marriages between 'healthy' German couples, to the sterilisation of the 'unfit' and the extermination of the 'undesirable'. As Gisela Bock has argued, 'with respect to the "inferior", National Socialism pursued a policy not of family welfare but of family destruction.'[59]

The Nazis' aims of an increased birth rate, racial homogeneity and a regimented social life invaded the private domain of the family deeply. As Mary Nolan has explained: 'Few regimes have made as extensive an effort to penetrate, politicise and restructure the private, be it in terms of sociability, reproductive behavior, family life, or attitudes toward the relationship of individual to state and society.'[60] Hence, the home was not a safe haven insulated from National Socialism. In the end, the Nazis' recognition of the importance of the family was as a vehicle for their own aims. Marriage and childbirth became racial duties, instead of personal decisions, as the Nazi regime systematically reduced the functions of the family to the single task of reproduction. As Ingeborg Weber-Kellermann has noted: 'In the name of restoring tradition, the Nazi state did more than any other regime to break down parental autonomy and to make the family simply a vehicle of state policy.'[61] Quite contrary to their rhetoric about the restoration of the family, the National Socialists atomised family units, allowing for intrusion and intervention in everyday life. The Nazi administration undermined the family in an unprecedented way. Privacy, intimacy and leisure were greatly threatened by the intervention of the Nazi regime into family life. The family under National Socialism became an institution for breeding and rearing children, with its relationships largely emptied of their emotional content. The Hitler government subjected the family to intervention and control, reduced its socialisation function, attempted to remove its capacity to shelter emotionally its members and subjected it to racial ideology. The undermining of the family through racial policies and the policing of families' daily lives ultimately destroyed the private sphere, in both physical and practical terms. The legacy of the Second World War and of the Nazi regime meant that it was only in the 1950s that everyday family life began to regain any true sense of unity, as we shall see in the following chapter.

Notes

1. A. Carney, *Marriage and Fatherhood in the Nazi SS* (Toronto, 2018), p. 170.
2. Ibid., p. 175.
3. P. Ginsborg, 'The Family Politics of the Great Dictators', in D. Kertzer and M. Barbagli (eds), *Family Life in the Twentieth Century* (New Haven and London, 2003), p. 175.
4. J. Chapoutot, *The Law of Blood: Thinking and Acting as a Nazi* (Cambridge, MA, 2018), p. 19.
5. Carney, *Marriage and Fatherhood in the Nazi SS*.
6. Cited in L. Pine, *Nazi Family Policy, 1933–1945* (Oxford, 1997), p. 8.
7. Ibid., p. 88.
8. Ibid., p. 18.
9. Ibid., p. 18.
10. Ibid., p. 18.
11. P. Ginsborg, *Family Politics: Domestic Life, Devastation and Survival 1900 to 1950* (New Haven and London, 2014), p. 380.
12. Pine, *Nazi Family Policy*, p. 20. See also, C. Usborne, *Cultures of Abortion in Weimar Germany* (Oxford and New York, 2007), pp. 216–18.
13. J. Stephenson, *Women in Nazi Society* (London, 1975), p. 69.
14. Bundesarchiv (hereafter BA) NSD 64/3, *Der RDK: Was ist er? Was will er?*.
15. G. Bock, 'Antinatalism, maternity and paternity in National Socialist racism', in G. Bock and P. Thane (eds), *Maternity and Gender Policies: Women and the Rise of the European Welfare States 1880s–1950s* (London, 1994), p. 245.
16. BA NS 37/1010, 'Arbeitsanweisung für die offene Fürsorge für werdende Mütter, Wöchnerinnen, Säuglinge und Kleinkinder', 20 January 1943, p. 7.
17. Pine, *Nazi Family Policy*, p. 27.
18. Ibid., p. 27.
19. BA NS 37/1035, 'Aus Mütterbriefen'.
20. Ibid.
21. Pine, *Nazi Family Policy*, p. 34.

22 M. Mouton, *From Nurturing the Nation to Purifying the Volk: Weimar and Nazi Family Policy, 1918–1945* (Cambridge and New York, 2007), p. 170.
23 Ibid., p. 171.
24 On this, see K. Olsen, 'Under the Care of Lebensborn: Norwegian War Children and their Mothers' in K. Ericsson and E. Simonsen (eds), *Children of World War II: The Hidden Enemy Legacy* (Oxford and New York, 2005), pp. 15–34.
25 Ginsborg, 'The Family Politics of the Great Dictators', p. 181.
26 G. Bock, 'Racism and Sexism in Nazi Germany', in R. Bridenthal, A. Grossmann and M. Kaplan (eds), *When Biology Became Destiny: Women in Weimar and Nazi Germany* (New York, 1984), p. 279.
27 Bock, 'Antinatalism, maternity and paternity in National Socialist racism', p. 238.
28 On the persecution and destruction of the Sinti and Roma, see M. Zimmermann, *Rassenutopie und Genozid. Die nationalsozialistische "Lösung der Zigeunerfrage"* (Hamburg, 1996); M. Zimmermann, 'From Discrimination to the "Family Camp" at Auschwitz', in W. Benz and B. Distel (eds), *Dachau Review 2. History of Nazi Concentration Camps: Studies, Reports, Documents.* (Dachau, 1990), pp. 87–113.
29 Pine, *Nazi Family Policy*, p. 178. See also, J. Michlic (ed.), *Jewish Families in Europe, 1939-Present: History, Representation, and Memory* (Waltham, MA, 2017).
30 For example, on the experiences of Jewish men, see M. Carey, *Jewish Masculinity in the Holocaust* (London, 2017).
31 Pine, *Nazi Family Policy*, p. 178.
32 R. Saidel, *The Jewish Women of Ravensbrück Concentration Camp* (Madison, 2004), p. 204.
33 Ibid., p. 210. On pregnancy and birth in the Gross-Rosen camps, see B. Gutterman, *A Narrow Bridge to Life: Jewish Forced Labor and Survival in the Gross-Rosen Camp System, 1940–1945* (New York and Oxford, 2008), pp. 170–2.
34 On this, see G. Czarnowski, 'Women's crimes, state crimes: abortion in Nazi Germany', in M. Arnot and C. Usborne (eds), *Gender and Crime in Modern Europe* (London, 1999), pp. 238–57.
35 J. Morrison, *Ravensbrück: Everyday Life in a Women's Concentration Camp* (Princeton, 2000), p. 271.
36 Cited in ibid., p. 273.

37 S. Helm, *Ravensbrück: Life and Death in Hitler's Concentration Camp for Women* (New York, 2014), p. 416.

38 M. Goldenberg, 'From a World Beyond: Women and the Holocaust' *Feminist Studies* 22 (Fall 1996), pp. 667–87.

39 R. Smith, 'Women and Genocide: Notes on an Unwritten History', *Holocaust and Genocide Studies*, Vol. 8, No. 3 (1994), p. 316. For a greater discussion of patriarchy and patriarchal assumptions, see G. Lerner, *The Creation of Patriarchy* (New York, 1986).

40 The most significant works include: B. Jellonnek, *Homosexuelle unter dem Hakenkreuz. Die Verfolgung von Homosexuellen im Dritten Reich* (Paderborn, 1990); R. Plant, *The Pink Triangle: The Nazi War against Homosexuals* (New York, 1986); H.-G. Stümke, *Homosexuelle in Deutschland. Eine politische Geschichte* (Munich, 1989); H.-G. Stümke and R. Finkler, *Rosa Winkel, Rosa Listen. Homosexuelle und 'Gesundes Volksempfinden' von Auschwitz bis heute* (Reinbek, 1981); G. Grau, *Hidden Holocaust? Gay and Lesbian Persecution in Germany, 1933–1945* (London, 1995); J. Müller and A. Sternweiler, *Homosexuelle Männer im KZ Sachsenhausen* (Berlin, 2000); B. Jellonnek and R. Lautmann, *Nationalsozialistischer Terror gegen Homosexuelle: verdrängt und ungesühnt* (Paderborn, 2002); T. Bastian, *Homosexuelle im Dritten Reich. Geschichte einer Verfolgung* (Munich, 2000); H. Diercks, *Verfolgung Homosexueller im Nationalsozialismus* (Bremen, 1999); F. Rector, *The Nazi Extermination of Homosexuals* (New York, 1981); W. Spurlin, *Lost Intimacies: Rethinking Homosexuality under National Socialism* (New York, 2009).

41 H. Heger, *The Men with the Pink Triangle* (London, 1980); P. Seel, *I, Pierre Seel, Deported Homosexual: A Memoir of Nazi Terror* (New York, 1995); L. van Dijk, *Ein erfülltes Leben – trotzdem: Erinnerungen Homosexueller 1933–1945* (Hamburg, 1992).

42 C. Schoppmann, *Nationalsozialistische Sexualpolitik und weibliche Homosexualität* (Pfannenweiler, 1997) was the first serious study on lesbianism in the Third Reich. See also C. Schoppmann, *Verbotene Verhältnisse. Frauenliebe 1938–1945* (Berlin, 1999).

43 Cited in W. Johansson and W. Percy, 'Homosexuals in Nazi Germany', *Simon Wiesenthal Center Annual* Vol. 7 (1990), p. 235.

44 Cited in ibid., p. 236.

45 Grau (ed.), *Hidden Holocaust?* p. 104.

46 H.-G. Stümke, 'From the "People's Consciousness of Right and Wrong" to "The Healthy Instincts of the Nation": The Persecution of Homosexuals in

Nazi Germany', in M. Burleigh (ed.), *Confronting the Nazi Past: New Debates in Modern German History* (London, 1996), p. 160.
47 Johansson and Percy, 'Homosexuals in Nazi Germany', pp. 236–7.
48 C. Schoppmann, 'The Position of Lesbian Women in the Nazi Period', in G. Grau (ed.), *Hidden Holocaust? Gay and Lesbian Persecution in Germany, 1933-1945* (London, 1995), p. 15.
49 Schoppmann, 'National Socialist policies towards female homosexuality', in L. Abrams and E. Harvey (eds), *Gender Relations in German History: Power, Agency and Experience from the Sixteenth to the Twentieth Century* (London, 1996), p. 179.
50 Ginsborg, 'The Family Politics of the Great Dictators', p. 179.
51 On this, see B. Kundrus, *Kriegerfrauen: Familienpolitik und Geschlechterverhältnisse im Ersten und Zweiten Weltkrieg* (Hamburg, 1995), pp. 322–47.
52 H. Vaizey, *Surviving Hitler's War: Family Life in Germany, 1939–48* (Basingstoke, 2010), p. 61.
53 Ibid., p. 59.
54 Ginsborg, 'The Family Politics of the Great Dictators', p. 196.
55 Vaizey, *Surviving Hitler's War*, p. 92.
56 Ibid., p. 109.
57 Ginsborg, *Family Politics*, p. 354.
58 Ibid., p. 359.
59 Bock, 'Antinatalism, maternity and paternity in National Socialist racism', p. 247.
60 M. Nolan, 'Work, gender and everyday life: reflections on continuity, normality and agency in twentieth-century Germany', in I. Kershaw and M. Lewin (eds), *Stalinism and Nazism: Dictatorships in Comparison* (Cambridge, 1997), p. 337.
61 I. Weber-Kellermann, 'The German Family between Private Life and Politics', in A. Prost and G. Vincent (eds), *A History of Private Life. V: Riddles of Identity in Modern Times* (Harvard, 1991), p. 517.

4

Post-war paternalism and modern mothers: Changing families in 1950s West Germany

Alexandria N. Ruble

In 1946, as occupied Germany slowly began to recover from the destruction of the Second World War, German newspaper columnist and radio host Walther von Hollander stated: 'Since the turn of the century, there has been repeated talk about a general marriage crisis; the complete downfall of marriage has been prophesied, and with it – indeed, brought on by it – the decline of the West.'[1] He attributed the failure of marriage and the 'crisis of the family' in Germany after 1945 to women's liberation during the war, the fragility of masculinity in the wake of defeat, and the appearance of young, strong Allied soldiers in Germany.[2] This chapter explores the crises that Hollander described in his book. To be sure, his remarks were not prescient to a population that had already endured many of the preceding crises of marriage and the family after the First World War. For middle-aged Germans who had been in their teenage years or their twenties during and right after the war, for instance, similar crises had defined their early adult years and left them with vivid memories of the period. They remembered, for instance, the significant increases in out-of-wedlock births and divorce rates during and immediately following the First World War.[3]

Nevertheless, Hollander captured a critical element of contemporary discussions on the role of marriage and the family as stabilising forces in a destroyed society. Scholars dating back to the period itself have trod this ground extensively. Sociologist Helmut Schelsky, for example, published his well-known study *Changes in the German Family in the Present Day* to critical acclaim in 1953.[4] Later on, in the 1970s and 1980s, historians began to publish volumes of primary sources documenting women's experiences after the war, which necessarily touched on the family and marriage as core topics of contemporary significance. The subject gained new interest in the late 1980s and the 1990s, especially in the context of the fall of the Berlin Wall and the reunification of East and West Germany. Historians such as Robert G. Moeller, Merith Niehuss and Elizabeth D. Heineman, for instance, published monographs that uncovered the importance of the family to post-war West German debates over reconstructing German society.[5] Although more loosely related thematically, Dagmar Herzog's *Sex after Fascism* offered critical insights on the role of sexuality in the divided, post-fascist Germanys.[6] In 2007, historian Donna Harsch published a study of women and the family in East Germany, complementing the existing scholarship on the family in West Germany by adding the critical perspective of the former German Democratic Republic (GDR).[7]

At their core, these studies emphasised the dual post-war project of simultaneously rejecting the Nazi visions of the family and reconstructing a new version of the family. More recently, scholarship on the history of the family has shifted in two main directions. First, scholars such as James Chappel have become more interested in how pre-Nazi conceptions of the family resurfaced after 1945 and took hold in this critical, post-fascist moment.[8] Second, other historians such as Carola Sachse, Leonie Treber and Jane Freeland have taken a greater interest in comparative and entangled histories that illuminate the significance of gender and the family in the Cold War context and the divergence of East and West Germany after 1945 and again after 1961.[9]

This chapter draws from these studies – as well as select primary sources – to analyse the history of the family in West Germany in the 1950s on a few different levels. First, it compares demographic trends with the discourse on the perceived 'crisis of the family' and points to evident gaps between trends and the hysteria surrounding them. Second, this chapter suggests a critical reframing of West German debates and legislation in the 1950s not only as post-fascist and anti-Communist, but also as the result of a long history of rethinking the family in Germany. Sociological surveys, parliamentary debates, articles in the mass media and personal letters all pointed to a contemporary obsession with restoring the 'traditional' German family, typically imagined as a nuclear family with a male breadwinner, female homemaker and children. At the same time, the family remained a highly contested and fluid subject from the late 1940s to the early 1960s. Politicians and legal experts may have aimed to use legislation and policies to create an idealised image of the family, but they hardly accomplished this goal in day-to-day life. As a result, attitudes about marriage and the family in West Germany began liberalising in the late 1950s and early 1960s. This essay is structured into three main parts. The first section explores the changing demographics of the family in West Germany between 1945 and 1961. The second part explores the centrality of the family in political and legal debates in West Germany in the 1950s and 1960s. The third section examines discourses about 'outliers' – homosexuals, 'incomplete' and 'non-traditional' families – in West Germany in the 1950s.

The changing demographics of the family, 1945–61

Between 1945 and 1961, the demographics of the family in the Western occupation zones and the subsequent Federal Republic of Germany changed dramatically. After the war ended, contemporary observers identified a 'crisis of the family'. They cited, for instance, the rising numbers of out-of-wedlock children, increasing rates of divorce and the gender imbalance in Germany caused by the Second World War. Despite panic in society, however, demographic changes fell into longer patterns in German history. Furthermore, the shifting gender roles and changes in the general population did not necessarily alter patterns in marriage. Finally, post-war opinion polls indicated that West Germans were slowly accepting that these changes were permanent.

One of the subjects that concerned contemporaries was the rising out-of-wedlock birth rate. Right after the war, non-marital births rose and fell significantly. In 1946, out-of-wedlock births hit an all-time high of 16.4 per cent – even surpassing the post-First World War average rate of 11 per cent.[10] The raw numbers dropped dramatically, however, in the first four years after the war, from 116,310 in 1946 to 74,506 in 1950.[11] The average rate of illegitimacy then dropped to 9.6 per cent in 1950.[12] By 1961, the rate in West Germany hovered at around 60 non-marital births per thousand residents.[13] Between 1949 and 1970, the numbers dropped by nearly half, from 9.7 per cent to 5.46 per cent.[14]

Another topic that captured contemporaries' attention was the rising divorce rate. For instance, the number of divorces in 1948 – 87,013 total – was ten times the pre-1914 divorce rate.[15] Considering the total population and the percentage of marriage at the time, this number was relatively small. Furthermore, the raw number of divorces hit its second all-time lowest point in 1956, at 69,450.[16] Although divorce rates were effectively shrinking, the divorce boom after the war made contemporaries anxious about the future state of the institution of marriage.

Moreover, contemporaries noted the severe gender imbalance after the end of the Second World War. A post-war census, conducted in 1946, identified an estimated 'surplus' of 7 million more women than men.[17] In some ways, this was new – the female percentage had actually decreased in the late *Kaiserreich*.[18] But the discursive panic was quite similar. According to popular belief, which stretched back several decades, the 'surplus of women' endangered (West) German society. In magazines and academic texts, authors expressed dismay that a generation of young women had missed the opportunity to marry. In addition, politicians became obsessed with the matter. For instance, in September 1949, while giving his inaugural address to the Bundestag, the new Chancellor Konrad Adenauer, a Christian Democrat and devout Catholic, promised job training for women facing 'unavoidable spinsterhood'.[19] Across the board, in West Germany, there was an obsession with the status and future of so many unmarried women.

Contemporary concerns with single women had a long history in Germany. In the late nineteenth century, historian Catherine Dollard argues, there was an imagined demographic crisis – for which no demographic surveys offer conclusive evidence – centred on the perceived problem of a 'surplus' of unmarried women in Imperial Germany. After the First World War, this imagined gap turned into reality, when wartime destruction left roughly 2 million more women than men in Germany. The decimation of men in the Second World War further widened this gap between the genders. Approximately 5 million men, or around 30 per cent of the 18 million who had gone to the front, were killed. At its height in 1946, the gap reached 7 million, although it decreased significantly over the following years. By 1950, there were 5 million more women than men in East and West Germany combined. The 'surplus' of women caused politicians, members of society and media pundits to panic about the future of unmarried women.

Contrary to popular belief at the time, the imbalance of the sexes did not fundamentally change patterns in marriage after 1945, nor in the long run. Between 1871 and 1910, for instance, marriage rates hovered around 50 per cent.[20] According to Heineman, the imbalance after the Second World War 'did not condemn a generation of women to singlehood', nor did it alter 'the next generation's desire to marry'.[21] In fact, many Germans in the West after 1945 wanted to marry. In 1950, 45.6 per cent of the population (47,695,672 at the time) was married.[22] By 1960, 41.9 per cent of the population was unmarried; 48.7 per cent was married; and 9.5 per cent was widowed or divorced.[23] Notably, these numbers were not far off percentages of earlier eras. While the gender imbalance did not reduce the desire to marry among young people, marriage nevertheless remained a much easier prospect for men in the 1950s. By 1960, the male percentage had increased to 51.2 per cent, while the female percentage increased to 46.4 per cent.[24]

Post-war opinion polls point to a society ambivalent about the changing status of marriage and the family.[25] Several surveys indicate strong feelings about the importance of marriage, especially 'traditional' marriages where men had more rights and obligations. In September 1949, for instance, 87 per cent of men and 90 per cent of women reported that they found marriage to be necessary.[26] While most Germans agreed that marriage was necessary, clear differences between men and women emerged. In 1949, 62 per cent of men thought it was necessary for a woman to be married, though this number decreased to 46 per cent by 1963. Meanwhile, 47 per cent of women thought it was necessary for a woman to marry, but this number dropped to 40 per cent in 1963.[27] For many men, the post-war 'crisis' of the family cemented their beliefs in 'traditional' marriage. Many women, however, had survived the war and the immediate post-war years without male support. They therefore began to invest less stock in marriage as an institution.

As much as post-war polls indicated that Germans believed strongly in marriage, polls also point to an increasing openness towards divorce. In 1949, 78 per cent of men and 79 per cent of women, when asked about whether they approved of divorce, responded: 'Yes, absolutely.'[28] The experiences of war and of difficult homecomings had convinced many Germans that divorce, for the right reasons, was a healthier option than remaining in a bad marriage. Furthermore, the war had opened up Germans to other social changes, such as the increased numbers of out-of-wedlock children. In September 1949, when asked if they approved of unwed women becoming mothers, 39 per cent of men and 43 per cent of women replied that it depended (although they did not specify on what conditions). Interestingly, 54 per cent of men and 52 per cent of women responded that they approved of unmarried women purposefully becoming mothers.[29] In either case, the Germans polled took into account the conditions under which an unwed mother became pregnant and chose to care for a child. They shied away from stigmatising unwed mothers, indicating that West Germans were becoming more open to alternative family models in practice (even if the ideal remained the heteronormative marriage).

Immediately after the end of the Second World War, contemporaries spoke of a 'crisis of the family'. To some degree, this was an imagined crisis. While divorce rates and out-of-wedlock births rose dramatically, they were coupled with rising marriage rates and large numbers of couples who decided to work through the crises. Furthermore, post-war polls suggest that Germans' attitudes towards marriage, divorce and illegitimacy were changing and becoming more open to alternative family models. As the next section shows, the Christian Democratic-controlled government and its counterpart in the Bundestag had different ideas about the role of the 'traditional' family in West Germany, which they attempted to put into legislation in the 1950s.

The family as a cornerstone of West Germany, 1948–61

Between 1948 and 1961, the post-war 'crisis of the family' loomed large in the minds of female activists, legal experts and future legislators. After the first post-war national election in West Germany in 1949, politicians from the Christian Democratic Union (CDU) and its Bavarian sister party, the Christian Social Union (CSU), took control of the Bundestag and federal government. From the beginning, Christian Democrats (aided by the German Party, the Centre Party and some Free Democrats) set out to implement a 'traditional' family model consisting of a male breadwinner and a female homemaker (and later female part-time worker). They found mass support among Protestants and Catholics. Meanwhile, they faced opposition from the Social Democrats (SPD), the Communist Party (KPD), some Free Democrats (FDP), several independent women's associations and the major trade unions. By the end of the 1950s, after much struggle, the Bundestag passed several different forms of legislation that simultaneously reinforced the 'traditional' family model desired by the CDU/CSU and expanded rights for married women and working mothers. In their debates over these new laws and policies, all politicians in West Germany had to take into account the historical legacies of the German Empire and the Weimar Republic; the reconstruction of Germany after the Third Reich; and the burgeoning Cold War.

Debates over the future of the family, especially its legal definitions, had already begun in the four occupation zones. Right after the war ended on 8 May 1945, women's committees across Germany began debating the future of women's rights in marriage and the family. Still, they could not formally advocate any reforms until the Western and Soviet Allies settled the broader 'German question', which was further complicated by the start of the Cold War. In 1947, American President Harry S. Truman announced the Truman Doctrine and then introduced the Marshall Plan and currency reform in the Western zones in 1948. Furthermore, the Western Allies excluded the Soviets from the Six-Power Conference in February 1948, leading the Soviets to pull out entirely from the Allied Control Council. Shortly thereafter, they cooperated with members of the

Socialist Unity Party (SED) to initiate constitutional reforms in the Eastern zone. Six months later, the Western zones set up the Parliamentary Council and began creating their own provisional constitution, the *Grundgesetz* (Basic Law), for the future Federal Republic of Germany (FRG).

In September 1948, sixty-five delegates assembled in Bonn to construct the new Basic Law. The four female representatives fought to expand rights for women in the new constitution, eventually introducing a new version of the equality clause in Article 3 that read: 'Men and women have equal rights.'[30] The 'equality clause' was not new; the 1919 Weimar Constitution had had a version of it that partly expanded women's political and economic rights, but continued to limit their rights in marriage and the family. Using the 1919 Weimar constitution as a model, the four female delegates worked together to persuade their male colleagues in the Parliamentary Council to include a more expansive equality clause in the Basic Law.[31] After intense struggle against Christian conservatives, the female activists successfully convinced the Council to adopt the more expansive version of the clause, which became Article 3. In exchange, they adopted a new family and marriage protection clause as part of Article 6, which declared that, 'Marriage and the family stand under the special protection of the state' and pledged state aid for mothers and children. Furthermore, they added Article 117, which stated that the Bundestag had to alter all existing legislation to include equality by 31 March 1953.

The Parliamentary Council's political compromise over Articles 3 and 6 was a temporary solution that left future legislators with conflicting guidelines for gender and family policies and laws. As lawmakers began their terms in September 1949, they found that the divisions from the Parliamentary Council had not disappeared. In the 14 August 1949 election, voters gave neither of the leading parties a clear majority: 31 per cent of the vote favoured the CDU/CSU and 29.2 per cent stood behind the SPD. Among the smaller parties, the FDP took 11 per cent of the vote, the KPD had 5.7 per cent and others, such as the German Party and the Centre Party, registered around 4 per cent.[32] In the early years of the FRG, West German politics were divided almost evenly down the centre.

These divisions were evident in the politics concerning gender and the family. In September 1949, Konrad Adenauer – a pro-Western Catholic CDU member and the new Chancellor of the FRG – laid out his agenda for social policy to the Bundestag. Adenauer acknowledged that the demographic imbalance in West Germany necessitated utilising female labour. He thus promised to deliver job training to single women and promote equality, but only to an extent and only out of necessity. He furthermore promised to create a section of the federal government devoted to women's issues. He made it clear that his administration would only address these issues because of the post-war crisis. At the same time, while acknowledging the fundamental changes to German society, he proclaimed that the new West German government would idealise and promote the 'traditional' male breadwinner/female homemaker family model as a way to restore order to a society in upheaval.[33] Even if this model was the ideal, Adenauer and his administration faced an uphill battle. The rate of women, especially married women, in paid employment rose between 1950 and 1965, despite the efforts of the CDU/CSU.[34]

Despite Adenauer's pledges, it was the SPD and KPD who, seeking to carry out the promises contained in Articles 3 and 117, first proposed a series of measures to grant women more equality with men. Following up on Adenauer's own proposal, the SPD called for the creation of a department for women in the federal government. The Ministry of Interior then established a 'women's department' in the autumn of 1950; as a result, the Bundestag did not pursue any legislation or further discussion of this idea. The KPD also introduced a proposal to ensure equal wages for equal work.[35] The last pitch from the KPD gained little traction in the Bundestag, mainly because of strong anti-Communist sentiments developing in the West that limited available political opportunities.[36] Because the Socialist Unity Party in East Germany promised equal wages to men and women, the West German government was unwilling to consider any policy that resembled those of the Communists next door.

In addition to these proposals, the SPD/KPD suggested in November 1949 that the Bundestag incorporate *Gleichberechtigung von Männern und Frauen*, or 'equal rights of men and women', into all legislation.[37] This pitch became the most controversial of the three offered up by the two parties on the Left. In particular, they targeted the German Civil Code, a law that dated back to 1900 and had remained on the books. The Civil Code granted married men full authority over their wives, children and wives' property. The SPD and KPD sought to revise this law to align it with the principle of equality, but they faced resistance from the CDU/CSU and their coalition partners from the FDP, the German Party and the Centre Party. In the subsequent debates in the Bundestag on 1 and 2 December 1949, representatives from the CDU/CSU made their position clear: that 'equal rights' meant equal, but different, especially in marriage and the family. According to one CDU member, the Bundestag had an obligation to uphold the 'God-willed order of creation...especially in the fulfillment of marriage as a life union'.[38] Much as they had in the Parliamentary Council, Christian conservatives argued that the advantages of the family as the cornerstone of a stable society outweighed the risks of expanding equal rights to married women.

Unable to reach a compromise, the Bundestag elected to send the matter of family law to the Federal Ministry of Justice, where a lower-level official, lawyer and former judge, Maria Hagemeyer, drafted a memorandum with proposals for a new family law, publishing the document in three parts in 1951.[39] Hagemeyer drew upon her extensive legal experience, as well as predominant contemporary strains of argumentation within the legal profession, to create a set of proposals that honoured the sentiments of Articles 3 and 6. For instance, she supported keeping the paternal surname for the purposes of familial unity, but offered women the possibility of hyphenating their last names as a show of independence.[40] Hagemeyer and the Federal Ministry of Justice then circulated her memorandum among trade unionists, women's associations, legal professional organisations, the Protestant and Catholic Churches, and other interested parties. Over the next year, leaders and members of these organisations wrote to the Ministry of Justice with suggestions for the new legislation.

While the Ministry of Justice was in the midst of debating family law reforms, the Bundestag forged ahead with other gender policies and legislation. In January 1952, for instance, the Bundestag passed the Law for the Protection of Working Mothers, or the *Mutterschutzgesetz*. This law stemmed from a long tradition in Germany dating back to the German Empire, when Chancellor Otto von Bismarck had passed a series of protective measures for working mothers. The Nazis had introduced their own version in 1942. The Social Democrats revived the legislation in 1950, arguing that it provided vital protections for expecting and nursing working mothers, such as limiting their work hours, guaranteeing paid maternity leave and prohibiting employers from firing pregnant women.[41] While the SPD recognised the problematic parts of the Nazi-era legislation, they maintained that its provisions for working mothers could be useful in the post-war era. Furthermore, they argued that the Nazis had simply appropriated the Social Democratic programme of assisting working mothers, which meant it was not problematic to reclaim those goals.[42]

At the same time that the Bundestag debated the plight of pregnant workers and working mothers, it also addressed the outstanding issue of married female civil servants. In 1932, the Reichstag had passed a law that allowed the dismissal of married female civil servants from their posts in the federal government. The Nazis had subsequently passed more legislation in 1933 and 1937 that terminated all female civil servants at all levels. For the sake of reinstating the civil service as quickly as possible, the Bundestag resurrected old civil service laws. Under this legislation, women could only be appointed to a civil service job at the age of 35, in contrast to men, who could receive a post at 27. Furthermore, married women could be dismissed from their positions if their husbands held secure employment.[43] Both measures came under great scrutiny by Social Democrats, who argued that the provisions must be overturned for the sake of 'the social and economic quality of women'.[44] Meanwhile, their Christian Democratic opponents in the Bundestag asserted that dismissing married women was permissible because '*Beamtinnen* are more often absent from work than men'.[45] Furthermore, they argued that allowing female civil servants to retain their positions could threaten the status of male civil servants and 'destroy the natural order of the family'.[46] After a few years of debate, the Bundestag passed a new law in May 1953 that removed both of the controversial provisions.

While the Bundestag passed other gender-related laws, they made less progress on family law. Hagemeyer had solicited the insights of social organisations, which were happy to oblige. With these proposals in mind, the Ministry of Justice assembled a draft of family law in early 1952. The draft legislation retained some old measures, such as forcing women to take their husbands' surnames upon marriage, but it dismissed other provisions, such as the husband's right to make all decisions for his wife and family. The latter proposal, in particular, attracted the ire of more conservative Protestant and Catholic Church leaders, who argued that individual rights could not trump the family unit and paternal authority. Cornered, the Minister of Justice, left-liberal Free Democrat Thomas Dehler, settled on a compromise solution. This decision, however, did not satisfy the West German Chancellor, Konrad Adenauer, or the other Federal Cabinet members, who forced Dehler to reinstate the husband's unconditional right to decide.

In November 1952, the draft legislation finally went before the Bundestag. Once again, Bundestag members found themselves divided. Christian Democrats employed essentialist arguments against expanding married women's rights in family law. One CDU representative, for instance, asserted: 'Men and women can best develop their given characteristic to the best of their ability from their biological and functional differences in the service of the small community, with which they serve the welfare of the larger community.'[47] Meanwhile, Social Democrats pushed back against this interpretation, stressing that the Federal Republic had a responsibility to deliver equal rights to all citizens.[48]

In the end, the Bundestag reached no firm conclusions about the proposed legislation. It designated a special committee to pass the law by the constitutionally mandated deadline of 31 March 1953, but its members kept reaching impasses. The March deadline came and went with no law in sight. Thereafter, the Federal Republic was plunged into a period of 'legal chaos' until the Federal Constitutional Court ordered the Bundestag to pass new legislation in December 1953. During this period of legal chaos, the absence of a law clearly delineating the rights of married couples and their families forced judges to make decisions on their own. In some cases, such as those regarding unpaid alimony payments and the husband's right to decide, judges ruled in accordance with the principle of equality.[49] In many cases, however, judges ruled against women's equal rights. The absence of legislation proved problematic enough that the Federal Constitutional Court intervened.

By the end of December 1953, when the Federal Constitutional Court had handed down its ruling that the Bundestag must produce a new family law, politics in West Germany had changed dramatically. In 1949, voters had elected the Social Democrats and Christian Democrats in almost even numbers. By September 1953, the numbers tilted much more in favour of the Christian Democrats, who took 45.2 per cent of the vote in comparison to the SPD's 28.8 per cent.[50] The *Wirtschaftswunder* ('economic miracle') in West Germany had convinced many voters to support the Christian Democratic administration. Furthermore, the increasing anti-Communism in the West continued to narrow the political space for Social Democrats and Communists.[51] In fact, the Federal Constitutional Court ruled in 1956 that the Communist Party was prohibited.

Adenauer, chosen by the Bundestag for another term as Chancellor, took advantage of the CDU's rising popularity to begin implementing a series of social reforms. One of Adenauer's first moves was to create the Federal Ministry of Family Affairs in October 1953. He then appointed the conservative Catholic politician Franz-Josef Wuermeling as its leader. Wuermeling was outspoken in his beliefs that men and women were decidedly not equal, and that societies were 'naturally' patriarchal.[52] Wuermeling then went on to create several new policies aimed at supporting the male-breadwinner/female-homemaker family model as the basis of the Christian Democratic programme. For instance, he supported the creation of *Kindergeld* ('child allowances') in West Germany.

Despite having a clear majority in the Bundestag and the federal government, the Christian Democrats still struggled to pass the patriarchal family law they had envisioned for West Germany. Much like the earlier period, Social Democrats within the Bundestag opposed Christian Democratic proposals for the legislation. Meanwhile, outside the Bundestag, in society, independent women's associations and other social organisations mounted a campaign to petition the Bundestag and government to pursue more liberalising reforms of family law. In June 1957, the Bundestag finally passed the *Gleichberechtigungsgesetz* (Equal Rights Act). This law was ultimately a compromise between the Christian Democrats and Social Democrats. The new law preserved some aspects of the old Civil Code, such as female management of the household and the proviso that women could only work outside of the home if it was reconcilable with their obligations at home. At the same time, the new law removed old provisions such as the husband's right to decide and restructured marital property schemes, so it signified a major departure from the old Civil Code in certain aspects. The new law went into effect the next year, on 1 July 1958. Aspects of the legislation, such as the husband's right to make all decisions for the children, were challenged and overturned in court a year later in 1959.

A variety of legislation and policies passed in the 1950s demonstrated a clear agenda on the part of the ruling Christian Democratic government and its majority in the Bundestag to enforce a male-breadwinner/female-homemaker family model. They nevertheless faced opposition from the Social Democrats, Communists (until 1956), many women's associations and trade unions. While Bundestag politicians across the political spectrum preferred for women to stay at home if possible, they still had to grapple with the realities of changing family and marital structures after the Second World War. Furthermore, they had to take into account the context of the Cold War, which shaped these discussions as well.

'Outliers' in West Germany in the 1950s

While politicians, especially those in the CDU, constructed an ideal image of the male-breadwinner/female-homemaker family, they still had to confront the plethora of alternative family models that existed in (West) Germany after the end of the Second World War. In fact, the very existence of these different forms of families prompted politicians to frame discourses about the 'traditional' family in the 1950s in mostly implicit, but sometimes explicit, opposition to the prevalence of 'outliers', or non-traditional partnership and familial structures, in West Germany in the 1950s.

Above all, households headed by 'women standing alone', to use Heineman's phrase, stood out in West Germany. The deaths of approximately 5 million men – 40 per cent of whom were married – during the war had left a 'surplus' of 7 million women across Germany.[53] The 'surplus', broadly speaking, was comprised of unmarried women, married women and widows, though they often changed categories as they remarried or divorced. Some young women had married in haste, having never lived with their husbands, and stayed at home with parents during the war.[54] Some of these war brides suddenly found themselves widowed without having spent much time with their spouses.[55] Others pursued the option of a 'postmortem marriage', meaning that women could file for a marriage certificate with a dead male partner if they could prove serious intent to marry before the death.[56] Another large portion of the widowed population comprised older working mothers, married before the outbreak of the war, who had taken on the double burden of caring for the family – including all the necessary tasks like searching for food on the black market – and working full-time to aid the war effort.

Single women often found themselves creating new family structures after the war. Some of them remarried; presumably, many of them brought children into their new marriages, thus leading to a proliferation of stepfathers in the 1950s. Others set up female-headed households, either sharing a home with multiple generations of the family, or in some cases, other widowed families headed by single mothers. Yet others pursued 'uncle' or 'wild marriages', referring to non-marital cohabitation, in order to preserve the widow's pension, which she would lose upon remarriage.[57] These types of families came under intense scrutiny in West Germany. One women's organisation leader lamented to Wuermeling in 1955 that such women were offending the memories of their husbands by turning into concubines.[58] Wuermeling himself referred to such families as 'dwarf families' before the Bundestag in 1954, implying that their growth was stunted.[59]

Complete families, in the eyes of the Christian Democratic administration, consisted of a male breadwinner and a female homemaker.

Social Democrats, for their part, did not always disagree. They, too, idealised a family model in which women could remain at home, because they also subscribed to the notion that men and women were 'equal but different' and women were natural caretakers. The SPD, however, recognised that current circumstances did not fit their idealised vision, nor did they believe that the law should be used to implement a patriarchal model that would limit married women's rights. Rather, they argued that if single and married women and mothers had to work to support their families, then they needed support from child allowances and protective legislation.

In addition to their discourses about incomplete families, West German legislators attacked other models of partnership and romance that they believed undermined the 'traditional' family, such as homosexuality. After the Second World War, Paragraph 175 – the infamous provision of the Criminal Code that outlawed homosexuality – technically still remained in force. The Western and Soviet Allies repealed all Nazi legislation, but left this provision in place.[60] According to historian Clayton J. Whisnant, the law was rarely enforced for gay men in the dire crisis years of 1946 to 1947, partly for pragmatic reasons and partly because of legal uncertainty.[61] By the early 1950s, however, historian Robert G. Moeller recounts that West German cities had started enforcing the provision again, evinced by arrests of gay men in Frankfurt.[62] Lesbianism was never criminalised to begin with, and therefore harder to prosecute.[63] Meanwhile, Paragraph 175 came under the scrutiny of legal experts, politicians, doctors and religious organisations, especially after a controversial 1957 Federal Constitutional Court ruling. Advocates of repeal pointed to Article 3 of the Basic Law's promise of equality, arguing that criminalising sodomy between consenting male adults and ignoring lesbianism violated constitutional principles.[64] Contemporary discourses on the issue ranged from arguments about how decriminalisation would encourage 'sexual immorality' among young people to the blurred boundaries of public and private to raising questions about the 'naturalness' of homosexuality. In the 1950s, Adenauer, political Catholicism and the Christian Democratic Union still had a firm hold on the government and society. They aimed to keep (male) homosexuality illegal in order to discourage and marginalise homosexuality in society as a whole. Since homosexuality was seen as a corrupting or seductive force, in the eyes of the ruling Christian Democrats, it undermined the traditional family.[65]

The end of the Second World War forced Germans to reckon with the proliferation of 'non-traditional' family and partnership structures. In the West, the Christian Democratic government, strongly influenced by political Catholicism, asserted the prevalence of the 'traditional' male-breadwinner/female-homemaker family through various pieces of legislation, policies and propaganda. For them, 'incomplete' families and homosexuality presented divergences from the norm, not legitimate alternative familial and romantic models. At the same time, shifting societal norms in terms of demographics and openness to liberalisation provided a challenge to the West German government's efforts.

Conclusion

This chapter has examined the various discourses surrounding the state of the family during the long 1950s, in the wake of the destruction of the Second World War and in the context of the burgeoning Cold War. The immediate post-war years constituted a crisis of the family. While non-traditional family structures and high divorce rates were common – and many Germans had navigated a similar crisis following the First World War – contemporaries nevertheless emphasised throughout the late 1940s and the 1950s that the post-Second World War crisis was unique and demanded special attention. Throughout these debates – whether they concerned expanding married women's rights, working mothers, the civil service, or homosexuality – common trends in discourse were evident. First, there were frequent definitional debates: did equal mean without differentiation between the sexes, or did it refer to complementary gender roles? Under what circumstances was complete equality acceptable (such as allowing married women into the civil service), and when was it inappropriate (such as prosecution of homosexual acts)? Second, the historical legacies of the German Empire, the Weimar Republic and the Third Reich informed the post-war debates on the family and family policy. In particular, politicians constantly referred to the Nazi past, often as a smear against political opponents. Finally, the Cold War played a significant role in post-war political debates about the family. Christian conservatives asserted that any expansion of women's rights would lead the West to resemble the Communist East. Social Democrats and Communists (until 1956) rejected this notion. Still, they had to articulate their own vision very carefully in the context of the Cold War, where accusations of Communist sympathies had large political ramifications.

These discourses developed during a series of critical moments for West Germany. The changing political situation of West Germany, for instance, informed the positions its leading politicians took on the matters of marriage and the family. After 1945, Nazi family policies and beliefs about the racial hygiene of the family were rejected. At the same time, the emerging Cold War ensured that far-left positions, such as those promoted by the Communist Party of Germany in the West and the Socialist Unity Party in the East, were untenable in the West as well. The narrowing political space left the Social Democrats little room to manoeuvre, but they nevertheless presented some opposition to the ruling Christian Democrats, who controlled the Bundestag and federal government from 1949 to 1969. The CDU, for its part, attempted to implement a 'traditional' family model in response to the perceived crises precipitated by the Second World War.

Furthermore, the evolving economic growth of the fledgling West German state played into these debates as well. Initially, the Adenauer administration in the West reacted to labour shortages by pushing married women and mothers back into the home and favouring their husbands' breadwinning. Christian conservatives in particular used language about natural order and duties to support these discriminatory practices, while Social Democrats argued that changing sociological circumstances, such as the 'surplus' of women, many of whom had to earn money for their families, necessitated changing rights in the workplace and at home. By the mid-1950s, the 'economic miracle' had revived the West German economy. Legislators confronted a labour shortage that they dealt with by enlisting the paid, part-time labour of married women. This idea stood in stark contrast to the image the Adenauer administration hoped to continue with its family law reforms: that of a male-breadwinner/ female-homemaker family model, in which female labour was only employed under extenuating circumstances. By the early 1960s, female labour was seen as a way to help West German families support a burgeoning consumer culture, but not as a path to women's economic independence or liberation.

Finally, the gradual liberalisation of West German culture and society shaped the evolution of these debates as well. In the early 1950s, the West German government recognised the influence of the Protestant and Catholic churches on the general population and therefore sought out their guidance on all gender-related legislation and policies. In fact, the churches' dogmatic arguments resonated with the Christian conservative government, which forced the Minister of Justice to alter his legislative draft. Furthermore, many Germans were hesitant to abandon long-held ideas shaped by Christian teaching, about gender, women and the family. In the end, however, these religious arguments failed to sway other parties in the Bundestag. By the 1960s, the secularisation and liberalisation of West German society undermined the former strength of these arguments.

The history of the family in West Germany in the 1950s offers historians new insights into the longer history of gender and the family in German history. Historians have done an excellent job of outlining the different ways that, for instance, legacies of the pre-1945 era shaped the choices politicians made in the 1950s. In particular, historians have drawn out in detail the role of the rejection of National Socialism after the end of the Second World War. In many ways, politicians constructed their notions of the family in response to Nazi family policies that had centred on eugenic ideals. In addition, the entangled nature of the two Germanys in the context of the early Cold War also informed these debates significantly. At different points, politicians on both sides of the Iron Curtain cited the other Germany's gender and family policies as reasons to pursue different paths. This chapter paves the way for historians to pay more attention to the everyday lives of West Germans in the 1950s, especially those who did not neatly fit the 'traditional' male-breadwinner/female-homemaker family model. Did working mothers benefit from the new policies or the protective legislation under the Adenauer government? What was the everyday life of non-traditional families like? What about queer history in this period? All of these areas, and many more, deserve attention in a much deeper body of scholarly work on the history of the family in Germany.

Notes

1 'Walther von Hollander on the Breakdown of Marriages, Separation, Divorce (1946)', last accessed 12 November 2017, http://germanhistorydocs.ghi-dc.org/sub_document.cfm?document_id=4555.
2 Ibid.
3 C. Usborne, *The Politics of the Body in Weimar Germany: Women's Reproductive Rights and Duties* (Ann Arbor, 1992), p. 82; D. Blasius, *Ehescheidung in Deutschland 1794–1945* (Göttingen, 1987), pp. 157–8; M. Mouton, *From Nurturing the Nation to Purifying the Volk: Weimar and Nazi Family Policy, 1918–1945* (Cambridge, 2007), pp. 71–2; R. Bessel, *Germany after the First World War* (Oxford, 1993), p. 228; H. Boak, *Women in the Weimar Republic* (Oxford, 2015), p. 222.
4 See J. Chappel, 'Nuclear Families in a Nuclear Age: Theorising the Family in 1950s West Germany', *Contemporary European History* Vol. 26, No. 1 (2017), p. 1. Schelsky also published articles on the topic in English. See H. Schelsky, 'The Family in Germany', *Marriage and Family Living* Vol. 16, No. 4 (1954), p. 331. Supplemental Index, EBSCOhost (accessed 18 August 2017).
5 R. Moeller, *Protecting Motherhood: Women and the Family in the Politics of Postwar West Germany* (Berkeley, 1993); M. Niehuss, *Familie, Frau und Gesellschaft: Studien zur Strukturgeschichte der Familie in Westdeutschland 1945–1960* (Göttingen, 2001); E. Heineman, *What Difference Does a Husband Make? Women and Marital Status in Nazi and Postwar Germany* (Berkeley, 1999); C. Franzius, *Bonner Grundgesetz und Familienrecht: die Diskussion um die Gleichberechtigung von Mann und Frau in der westdeutschen Zivilrechtslehre der Nachkriegszeit (1945–1957)* (Frankfurt am Main, 2005); S. Buske, *Fräulein Mutter und ihr Bastard: eine Geschichte der Unehelichkeit in Deutschland, 1900–1970* (Göttingen, 2004).
6 D. Herzog, *Sex after Fascism: Memory and Morality in Twentieth-Century Germany* (Princeton, 2007).
7 D. Harsch, *Revenge of the Domestic: Women, the Family, and Communism in the German Democratic Republic* (Princeton, 2007).

8 Chappel, 'Nuclear Families in a Nuclear Age'.
9 C. Sachse, *Der Hausarbeitstag: Gerechtigkeit und Gleichberechtigung in Ost und West, 1939–1994* (Göttingen, 2002); L. Treber, *Mythos Trümmerfrauen: Von der Trümmerbeseitigung in der Kriegs- und Nachkriegszeit und der Entstehung eines deutschen Erinnerungsortes* (Essen, 2014); J. Freeland, 'Behind Closed Doors: Domestic Violence, Citizenship and State-Making in Divided Berlin, 1969–1990' (Ph.D. diss., Carleton University, 2015); A. Ruble, '"Equal but not the Same": The Struggle for '*Gleichberechtigung*' and the Reform of Marriage and Family Law in East and West Germany, 1945'68' (Ph.D. diss., University of North Carolina at Chapel Hill, 2017).
10 Usborne, *The Politics of the Body*, p. 82; Moeller, *Protecting Motherhood*, p. 32; Buske, *Fräulein Mutter und Ihr Bastard*, p. 196.
11 Statistisches Jahrbuch für die Bundesrepublik Deutschland, 1953, http://www.digizeitschriften.de/dms/img/?PID=PPN514402342_1952|log10&physid=phys63#navi.
12 Moeller, *Protecting Motherhood*, p. 32; Buske, *Fräulein Mutter und Ihr Bastard*, p. 196.
13 Heineman, *What Difference*, p. 251.
14 'Bevölkerung und Erwerbstätigkeit: Zusammenfassende Übersichten: Eheschließungen, Geborene und Gestorbene', last modified October 17, 2016, https://www.destatis.de/DE/Publikationen/Thematisch/Bevoelkerung/Bevoelkerungsbewegung/ZusammenEheschliessungenGeboreneGestorbene5126102157004.pdf?__blob=publicationFile.
15 Moeller, *Protecting Motherhood*, p. 29; Herzog, *Sex After Fascism*, p. 67.
16 Statistisches Bundesamt, last accessed 12 November 2017, https://www.destatis.de/DE/ZahlenFakten/GesellschaftStaat/Bevoelkerung/Ehescheidungen/Tabellen_/lrbev06.html.
17 Heineman, *What Difference*, p. 3.
18 C. Dollard, *The Surplus Woman: Unmarried in Imperial Germany, 1871–1918* (New York, 2009), p. 72.
19 Verhandlungen des Deutschen Bundestages, 5. Sitzung, 20. September 1949, 27.
20 Dollard, *The Surplus Woman*, p. 221.
21 Heineman, *What Difference*, p. 210.
22 Statistisches Jahrbuch für die Bundesrepublik Deutschland, 1953, http://www.digizeitschriften.de/dms/img/?PID=PPN514402342_1952|log10&physid=phys57#navi.

23 Ibid.
24 Ibid.
25 To be sure, opinion pollsters often asked leading questions and left little space for explanation of the choice of the answer.
26 E. Noelle and E. Neumann (eds), *The Germans: Public Opinion Polls 1947—1966* (Allensbach, 1967), p. 64.
27 Ibid.
28 Ibid., p. 73.
29 Ibid., p. 67.
30 H. Drummer and J. Zwilling, '1948/49 Als 'Anwältin der Frauen' im Parlamentarischen Rat', in *"Ein Glücksfall für die Demokratie": Elisabeth Selbert (1896-1986), die große Anwältin der Gleichberechtigung*, Hessische Landesregierung (Frankfurt am Main, 1999), p. 90; G. Notz, *Frauen in Der Mannschaft: Sozialdemokratinnen im Parlamentarischen Rat und im Deutschen Bundestag 1948-49 bis 1957. Mit 26 Biographien* (Bonn, 2003); P. Holz, *Zwischen Tradition und Emanzipation: Politikerinnen in der CDU in der Zeit von 1945 bis 1957* (Königstein, 2004), p. 118. Some male members of the Council, such as Ludwig Bergsträsser of the SPD, supported the 'four mothers' as well. See Moeller, *Protecting Motherhood*, p. 46. It is also necessary to note that while other parties like the KPD and FDP did not have female representation, prominent female party members did push from the outside, as will be shown later in this chapter.
31 Article 109 promised that men and women had 'fundamentally the same civic rights and duties', while Article 119 stated, 'Marriage, as the cornerstone of family life and the preservation and proliferation of the nation, stands under special constitutional protection. It is derived from the equality of both sexes.' Die Verfassung des Deutschen Reichs vom 11. August 1919, last accessed 12 November 2017, http://www.documentarchiv.de/wr/wrv.html#ZWEITER_ABSCHNITT02.
32 K. Jarausch, *After Hitler: Recivilizing Germans, 1945-1995* (Oxford, 2006), p. 146.
33 VDBT, 5. Sitzung, September 20, 1949, pp. 26-7.
34 C. von Oertzen, *The Pleasure of a Surplus Income: Part-Time Work, Gender Politics, and Social Change in West Germany, 1955-1969* (New York, 2007), p. 4.
35 Antrag der Fraktion der SPD, Drucksache 176, Verhandlungen des Deutschen Bundestages [1.] Deutscher Bundestag, 3. November 1949; Antrag der Fraktion der SPD, Drucksache 177, Verhandlungen des

Deutschen Bundestages [1.] Deutscher Bundestag, 8. November 1949; Antrag der Abgeordneten Renner und Genossen, Drucksache 206, Verhandlungen des Deutschen Bundestages [1.] Deutscher Bundestag, 15. November 1949.

36 Nathanius an die Herren Bundesminister, April 26, 1950, B141/2055/43, BArch Koblenz; Dehler an Ilk, August 3, 1950, B141/2055/48, BArch Koblenz; Ilk an Dehler, September 1, 1950, B141/2055/49, BArch Koblenz. In their correspondence regarding a committee on family law, neither side recommended or mentioned Communist Party members, although the party had more representatives in the Bundestag than the Centre Party and comparable numbers to other parties such as the DP and the Bayern Party. The Ministry's reluctance to engage with Communists on the issue reflected its leaders' ambivalence about the party.

37 Antrag der Fraktion der SPD, Drucksache 176, Verhandlungen des Deutschen Bundestages [1.] Deutscher Bundestag, 3. November 1949.

38 VDBT, 20./21. Sitzung, December 2, 1949, 626. Lehr was born in 1883, joined the Weimar-era DNVP, and studied law. He entered politics in the post-1945 period as the governor of the North Rhine region under the British occupation. See Kurt Düwell, 'Robert Lehr', last accessed 31 December 2016, http://www.kas.de/wf/de/37.8217.

39 Maria Hagemeyer, 'Denkschrift über die Anpassung des geltenden Familienrechts an den Grundsatz der Gleichberechtigung von Mann und Frau (Art. 3 Abs. 2 GG) erforderliche Gesetzesänderungen', Teil I, 5, B106/43313, BArch Koblenz.

40 Ibid., pp. 14–15.

41 Moeller, *Protecting Motherhood, pp.* 156–7.

42 Ibid., p. 157.

43 U. Wengst, *Beamtentum zwischen Reform und Tradition: Beamtengesetzgebung in der Gründungsphase der Bundesrepublik Deutschland 1948–1953* (Düsseldorf, 1988), p. 123.

44 'Für die Rechte der Frauen', *Gleichheit* 13 (1950), p. 2.

45 'Protokoll der Sitzung des Ausschusses fuer Frauenfragen am 5.2.50 in Bonn', February 5, 1950, 0133 Runschreiben, SPD-Parteivorstand-Frauenreferat, *Archiv der sozialen Demokratie der Friedrich-Ebert-Stiftung*, 4.

46 7. Februar 1950: Fraktionsvorstandssitzung, in H. Heidemeyer (ed.), *Die CDU/CSU-Fraktion im Deutschen Bundestag: Sitzungsprotokolle* (Düsseldorf, 1998), p. 204.

47 VDBT, 239. Sitzung, November 27, 1952, 11059.
48 VDBT, 239. Sitzung, November 27, 1952, 11060.
49 Moeller, *Protecting Motherhood*, p. 188.
50 D. Bark and D. Gress, *A History of West Germany*, 2nd ed. (Cambridge, 1993), p. 325.
51 C. Klessmann, *Zwei Staaten, Eine Nation: Deutsche Geschichte 1955–1970* (Göttingen, 1988), p. 59.
52 Moeller, *Protecting Motherhood*, pp. 101–2.
53 Heineman, *What Difference*, p. 48.
54 Ibid., p. 46.
55 Ibid., p. 47.
56 Ibid., p. 47.
57 Ibid., p. 168.
58 Ibid., p. 169.
59 VDBT, 15. Sitzung, February 12, 1954, p. 488.
60 R. Moeller, 'Private Acts, Public Anxieties, and the Fight to Decriminalize Male Homosexuality in West Germany', *Feminist Studies* Vol. 36, No. 3 (2010), pp. 528–52.
61 C. Whisnant, *Male Homosexuality in West Germany: Between Persecution and Freedom, 1945–69* (London, 2012), p. 23.
62 Moeller, 'Private Acts, Public Anxieties', p. 530.
63 Ibid., p. 531; Whisnant, *Male Homosexuality in West Germany*, p. 10.
64 Moeller, 'Private Acts, Public Anxieties', p. 531.
65 C. Whisnant, 'Styles of Masculinity in the West German Gay Scene, 1950–1965', *Central European History* Vol. 39, No. 3 (2006), pp. 359–93.

5

Continuities and ruptures: Women's agency and the West German family, 1960s–1980s

Sarah E. Summers

In August 1973, the Bielefeld resident Ingeborg Unterspann sent a letter to the Federal Minister of Youth, Family and Health Katharina Focke, of the Social Democratic Party of Germany (SPD), that highlighted the contradictions of motherhood in 1970s West Germany. She explained, 'I belong to the emancipated women who are attached to their occupation, but ... do not want to give up having a family'. Due to her lack of childcare options, Unterspann ended employment after the birth of her son. Her travels abroad exacerbated her frustrations with West German childcare infrastructure; she explained that for instance the Scandinavian nations eased the reconciliation of motherhood and work through full-day childcare and schools. She asked Minister Focke: 'Why is there not something similar in West Germany?'[1]

Unterspann's letter articulated the central influence on the discussion of and conflict over the family in politics, society and culture in Cold War West Germany from the 1960s until the 1980s. The desires and experiences of many West German women changed in these decades due to increased labour force participation and educational opportunities, pitting many against the male-breadwinner/female-homemaker model that formed the foundational gender roles of the Federal Republic.[2] The changing life course of women more than any other issue challenged the construction of the family in post-war West Germany beginning in the 1960s.

Studies such as Anselm Doering-Manteuffel and Lutz Raphael's *Nach dem Boom: Perspektiven auf die Zeitgeschichte seit 1970* argue that gender relations in Western Europe went through a permanent structural change in the 1970s, moving towards gender equality.[3] However, secondary literature on the family, family policy, and the welfare state in West Germany has long problematised this argument.[4] These studies find that the male-breadwinner/female-part-time earner and homemaker family model persisted in cultural and policy norms from the 1960s to the 1990s. Work by historians Wiebke Kolbe and Karen Hagemann outline the continued influence of the male-breadwinner family model on public policy from the 1960s onwards. Kolbe, in a comparison between Sweden and (West) Germany, demonstrates that while family policy gradually discursively acknowledged employed mothers, in practice, policy placed the burden of unpaid childcare unequally on mothers.[5] Hagemann's focus on the time politics of the half-day education system in the Federal Republic also demonstrates how this system reflected and reinforced, first, the Catholic ideology that the family was more powerful than state and society, and, second, Cold War discourse propagated by the Christian conservative Christian Democratic Union (CDU) and Christian Social Union (CSU) parties that socialisation in the family, as opposed to by the state, prevented the destruction of the family by authoritarian Communism such as that found in East Germany.[6]

This chapter does not contradict these assessments, but analyses how women's agency and activism contributed to stagnation and change in the family. Central to this analysis is the relationship between gender roles, employment and the family. This relationship became significant during the reconstruction of the Federal Republic following the Third Reich. As analysed by the historians Frank Biess and Robert G. Moeller, the male-breadwinner model replaced the militarised masculinity of the Third Reich. A man's ability to provide financially for his family formed the basis of masculinity, and thereby family and welfare policy.[7] Labour market participation thus became essential to the construction of the family in West Germany, as well as the relationship between the family, its members and the state.

The male-breadwinner family ideal influenced by Cold War discourses on the family and the Catholic Church, as well as long standing concerns over the socialisation of young children, also influenced the women's movement. While the autonomous women's movement offered a strong criticism of the family status quo both within the movement and in the mainstream press, policy outcomes reflected the moderate agenda of women active in the two largest political parties and the trade unions. Thus the women's movement also contributed to both the stagnation and the change of the West German family. The persistence of the male-breadwinner model also hinders investigating demographic trends on same-sex partners and families. Activist movements confirm their existence, but same-sex marriage was only legalised in the Federal Republic in 2017. Much of the statistical data for gay and lesbian parents is subsumed under the terms used by the federal government at this time.

To establish the 1960s to 1980s as a time of contestation over the family, the first part of this chapter examines demographic continuities and changes regarding the family via statistics. To what extent did the actions of West Germans confirm or deny the hegemony of the male-breadwinner family model? Second, it analyses family policy in these decades to establish the character of the family as defined by the state as well as the major influences on policy, and the influence of female politicians. This chapter concludes with a consideration of how the autonomous women's movement and feminist journalists in the mainstream press intervened in the debate over the family.

Demographic changes, 1960–89

In 1979, the West German press described a country on the verge of demographic collapse. Following the publication of the statistical decline of the West German birth rate, journalists and politicians alike claimed a crisis of the family that would result in the 'swift death of Germans'.[8] Several key demographic areas point to a change in values from the 1960s precipitated by the education of women, the increased employment of mothers and the social movements of the 1960s and 1970s. The same data also points to the continued importance of marriage after childbirth.

The raw number of women employed in West Germany rose steadily from the 1950s onwards, with slight drops during recessions in 1967 and 1968 and plateaus during the oil-shock recession of the 1970s (see Table 5.1). By comparison, the labour market participation of women

Table 5.1 Women's employment, 1950–89

Year	Total in 1,000	Percentage of total labour force	Percentage of women aged fifteen to sixty-five
1950	7,267	35.6	–
1954	8,050	35.9	–
1958	9,088	37.0	–
1964	9,785	36.6	49.6
1968	9,412	36.2	49.7
1972	9,760	36.5	47.6
1976	9,528	37.2	48.3
1980	9,829	37.3	50.2
1984	9,658	38.1	51.7
1989	10,794	38.9	55.5

Sources: *Statistisches Bundesamt*, 1950–89; Maier, p. 259.

aged fifteen to sixty-five in 1925 was upwards of 50 per cent, a percentage not repeated until 1980.[9] The most noticeable changes occurred, however, in the participation of women in full time education and the employment of mothers. In the 1970s alone, the number of women in post-secondary education tripled due to educational reforms in the 1960s.[10] And while women's employment participation stagnated overall, the labour participation of mothers increased 4–6 per cent across all categories (see Table 5.2). The proliferation of part-time employment drove this significant change. The East German government's erection of the Berlin Wall in 1961 cut off West Germany's migrant labour supply, creating a labour shortage for West Germany's booming economy. The subsequent 'modernisation' of the West German gendered division of labour was viewed as a compromise between the necessary role of mothers in the socialisation of children and the employment desires of mothers.[11] The migrant guest worker programme filled the remaining gaps in the labour market.[12]

Perhaps the most drastic change in the West German family from the 1960s onwards, however, was the birth rate and size of the family. The percentage of successful births per 1,000 persons decreased from 1900 until

Table 5.2 Employment rate of mothers in West Germany, 1950–85 (in % of cohort)

	All mothers			Married mothers		
	Children under eighteen	Children under fifteen	Children under six	One child under fifteen	Two children under fifteen	Three children under fifteen
1950	24	23	–	23	22	26
1961	35	33	30	37	32	32
1970	36	34	30	39	31	29
1980	42	41	34	46	37	32
1985	42	40	35	43	34	28

Sources: Statistisches Bundesamt Wiesbaden, 1950–85; Kolbe, 2002, p. 449.

Table 5.3 Birth rate developments in West Germany, 1950–90

Year	Total no. of births	Average no. of children per mother	% of births out of wedlock
1950	812,835	2.10	9.7
1960	968,629	2.37	6.3
1970	810,808	2.02	5.5
1980	620,657	1.44	7.6
1990	727,199	1.45	10.5

Source: Engstler et al., 2003, p. 71.

the 1980s. In 1900 in the German Empire, new-borns encompassed 36 per cent of the population for every 1,000 persons. By 1960, this percentage was 17.4. A slight 'baby boom' occurred in the 1960s when births per 1,000 persons reached 18.3 per cent in 1963.[13] However, the birth rate declined more sharply in the 1970s and 1980s (see Table 5.3).

Changing birth rate patterns in post-war West Germany correlated to changes in the life course of women. In 1972, the director of the German Institute of Demographic Research in Wiesbaden and the West German Ministry of Statistics Hermann Schubnell published his institute's findings with the Federal Ministry of Youth, Family and Health. He argued that one-fifth of the birth rate decline could be attributed to fewer women of child-bearing age due to a decline in the birth rate at the end of World War Two. He posited that a more significant cause, however, was women waiting longer to enter into marriage and motherhood, thus extending childbirth over the age of thirty in the case of a second, or even a first, child.[14] During the 'baby boom' of the 1960s, statistics from the Federal Ministry demonstrate women between the ages of twenty and thirty-two were choosing to have children at fairly equal rates (see Figure 5.1). The generation born in 1944 opted for its first child in its early twenties, and the 1930s generation was opting for a second or third child in its late twenties and early thirties. By 1975, the age of mothers giving birth narrowed to the early to mid-twenties, with few women from the 1944 generation choosing to have another child in their thirties. By 1988, the highest concentration of births shifted to mothers aged between twenty-five and thirty-three.

For Schubnell, this also indicated that mothers (and fathers) opted for fewer children overall, demonstrated by the dramatic decline in the number of children per mother.[15] The average children per mother increased from 2.1 in 1950 to 2.37 in 1960 with a subsequent decrease to 1.45 by 1990 (see Table 5.3). The decline in the birth rate was even more pronounced when compared to the average child per mother in 1900: 4.1 children.[16] Schubnell argued that this decline was made possible by more

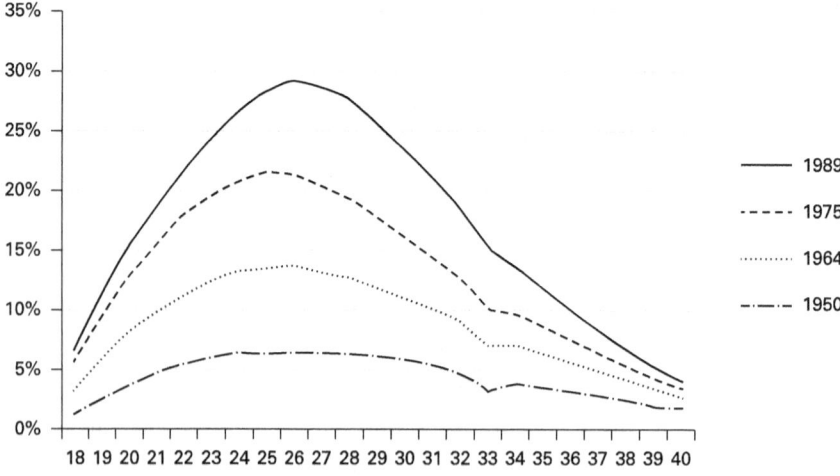

Figure 5.1 Number of births per year based on age of mother. Source: Statistisches Bundesamt Wiesbaden, 1991, p. 79.

reliable birth control in the form of the Pill. He estimated around 25 per cent of West German women took the Pill in 1972.[17]

The significance of the Pill in creating choices about how to balance family and employment for the generation of women born in the mid-late 1950s cannot be overlooked. Research by historian Eva-Maria Silies on the generational impact of the Pill on the life cycle and choices of West German women points to a staggering influence. By 1973, forty-eight per cent of young women between the ages of sixteen and twenty-two took the Pill, while fifty-nine per cent of women between the ages of twenty-three and twenty-nine used the Pill to control pregnancy and to help with the negative side effects of menstruation.[18] Silies's interview partners confirmed that the Pill offered them choices regarding career and family not afforded to their mothers.[19]

Finally, Schubnell identified the employment of mothers as a major indicator of the size of families. A qualitative and quantitative study conducted by the sociologist Rosemarie Nave-Herz in the 1970s and 1980s confirmed that the career ambitions of women exerted potentially the greatest influence on the decision of couples to conceive.[20] Nave-Herz theorised that rather than forging a new form of partnership and motherhood, women in West Germany still conceived of motherhood as prioritising the family and household. This perception conflicted with career ambitions and thus women chose either career or family.[21] Nave-Herz concluded that changes in schooling and employment for women did not produce a significant change in the conception of the gendered division of labour in the home.[22] Scholars also identified family policies that encouraged the home care of children rather than promoting employment resulting in some women choosing either career or motherhood.[23]

From the 1960s onwards, marriage remained the dominant form of cohabitation between heterosexual couples in West Germany, even as the meaning of the institution changed. In the 1950s and 1960s, heterosexual marriage was the only socially, culturally, and legally acceptable means of engaging in an emotional sexual relationship and legitimating children resulting from that relationship. The necessity of marriage to engage in legal sexuality was reinforced by Paragraph 175 of the Civil Code and paragraphs of the *Lex Heinze* adopted during the German Empire and still on the books in West Germany. Paragraph 175 criminalised sexual acts between men and bestiality. The *Lex Heinze* outlawed pornography, prostitution, same-sex relationships, and other forms of 'procurement', which was often interpreted as including pre-marital sexual relationships. Authorities occasionally enforced paragraphs via such actions as 'procurement' convictions for parents allowing their daughter's fiancé to spend the night in their home.[24] The importance of marriage was also protected by its material benefits for women who still had fewer opportunities for economic self-sufficiency and the ability to acquire accommodation in a country with a severely depressed infrastructure following the Second World War.[25] Divorce was also tightly regulated through the so-called 'guilt clause' necessary for a legal divorce. In cases where a judge declared the wife the guilty party, which occurred often, she was denied financial support from her ex-husband.[26]

Nonetheless, we can observe important changes in marriage patterns from the 1960s onwards. After an increase in marriage rates in the 1950s, the marriage rate as a percentage of the population began to steadily decline in the 1960s, reaching almost half the 1950 rate in 1980 (see Table 5.4). This decline can be attributed to a younger generation that put into practice new philosophies towards partnership and sexuality influenced by the student protest and women's movements.[27] The SPD/FDP coalition also stripped the last vestiges of the *Lex Heinze* from West German law in 1973, which allowed for the open practice and acceptance of pre-marital sexual relationships with fewer material repercussions. As

Table 5.4 Marriage and divorce rates in West Germany, 1950–88

Year	Marriages	Per 1,000 residents	Divorces	Per 1,000 residents
1950	535,708	10.7	84,740	1.77
1960	521,445	9.4	48,780	0.915
1970	444,510	7.3	76,520	1.24
1980	362,408	5.9	96,222	1.6
1988	397,738	6.47	128,897	2.1

Source: Statistisches Bundesamt Wiesbaden, 1950–88.

part of the same wave of reform, the West German Bundestag lowered the age of consent in Paragraph 175 first to twenty-one in 1969, and then eighteen in 1973, and eliminated the bestiality clause.[28]

A 1985 publication from the Ministry of Youth, Family and Health on non-marriage partnerships estimated that between 1972 and 1982 this form of relationship increased by 277 per cent, with between 1 million and 2.5 million West Germans deciding to enter into an unmarried partnership.[29] The ministry also made clear that non-marriage partnerships did not coincide with a particular educational milieu or social class, making it ubiquitous.[30] These changes reflected shifting perceptions of the function of marriage in West German society. The student protest movement and the women's movement called into question the prevailing sexual morality, the gendered division of labour, and the institution of marriage among the post-war generation of West Germans who came of age in the late 1960s and 1970s.

Despite these challenges to the institution of marriage, it by no means died out. The same ministry survey found that while many West Germans no longer considered marriage necessary for emotional and sexual relationships, West Germans did continue to have a traditional conception of marriage and the family, as it was still considered an important step once a couple decided to have children. This contributed to the steady increase in the average age of marriage for West German women. We can see the average age of marriage for women increasing from twenty-five in 1960 to just over twenty-eight in 1989.[31] These statistics also take into account remarriage as a result of divorce, a growing trend in West Germany beginning in the 1960s. However, the sociologist Rosemarie Nave-Herz contended that by the 1970s, 64 per cent of divorcees remarried.[32]

Divorce also challenged the male-breadwinner family. An immediate post-war surge in divorces as returning soldiers and their spouses faced difficulties after long separations stabilised in the 1950s. Unlike divorce trends in later decades, divorces in the late 1940s tended to occur between young spouses with few if any children. The increase in divorce rates beginning in 1970 predated the First Law for the Reform of Marriage and Family Law passed in 1976. Instead, divorces increased as judges began declaring more and more men guilty in divorce proceedings. As the threat of a guilty verdict decreased, women initiated divorce proceedings on a larger scale.[33]

The demographics of the family between 1960 and 1989 reinforce the change and stagnation thesis. Marriage was still by far the most popular choice of heterosexual partnership and was still considered to be a necessary condition in the case where a couple decided to have children. However, increased educational and employment opportunities affected the age of marriage and the size of the West German family. Furthermore, the activism of a younger generation of West Germans who came of age in the late 1960s and 1970s popularised non-marriage partnership before childbirth.

Legislating the West German family

A similar change and stagnation can be found in West German family policy. Between 1960 and 1990, family policy gradually recognised working mothers and the equal role of both parents in the upbringing of children, even while in practice promoting the care of children by mothers. Policy reinforced the male-breadwinner/female-part-time-earner-and-caregiver gendered division of labour due to the continued importance of Cold War discourses on the family and cultural norms regarding the role of mothers in the socialisation of children. Yet change occurred because of economic and social realities and the increased importance of women and women's issues in politics.

Since the founding of the Federal Republic, family policy focused primarily on the interests of the child. Since the nineteenth century, with the exception of the social democratic milieu and some education and social reformers, the bourgeois ideal 'male-breadwinner/female homemaker' was considered to be the best practice in childrearing. The family played a central role in childrearing and mothers were seen as the best possible educators.[34] The Catholic Church further reinforced the significance of the family as above state and society. This doctrine became institutionalised with the election of the conservative CDU/CSU coalition under Chancellor Konrad Adenauer as the FRG's first government. According to Catholic teachings, the state should support the family, but not interfere with the private sphere.[35] The advent of the Cold War cemented these long-standing ideals in West German politics, culture, and society. The female homemaker became the bulwark against the invasion of Communist ideology from the East, represented by the employed mother who relied on state education and childcare (i.e. Communist indoctrination) to raise her children.[36]

Beginning in the 1960s, the increased desire and demand for employment among women and mothers, as well as the needs of the West German labour market, resulted in family and education policy that supported the part-time employment of women. The turn towards part-time work for mothers achieved a broad consensus among influential institutions in West Germany: the two main political parties (SPD and CDU), trade union organisations and confessional groups.

The SPD saw a political opportunity to break the CDU's domination of the women's vote and responded to changing social patterns with the 'Guidelines for Social Democratic Family Policy' in April 1961. Here, the party acknowledged the new significance of paid employment in the lives of West German women and the role it played in altering their position in the family and in society. Historian Christine von Oertzen argues that, in acknowledging other reasons beyond economic necessity for married women to take up employment, the SPD returned to its socialist roots by defining emancipation through productive labour.[37] In any case, the party was clearly supporting part-time employment. In her 1961 essay, the SPD's women's affairs director, Hety Schmitt-Maass, declared that women had a right to paid employment and to choose whether or not they wanted to enter the workforce. Part-time labour, in her opinion, provided the opportunity for women to do just that, while also not neglecting their duties in the home.[38]

Such a clear and supportive stance on women's employment resulted in electoral benefits. In the 1961 election, married and employed women began shifting their support to the SPD, not least because of the CDU's limited response. The CDU's Women's Union spearheaded a response to shifting patterns of women's employment. However, it did not receive the support of the party executive. CDU executives would not accept a new direction until after their devastating defeat in the 1972 federal elections.[39]

Christine von Oertzen argues that the political and societal recognition that married women might work out of desire rather than economic necessity was a definitive turning point in gender relations and the family in West Germany.[40] However, family, education and economic policy did not entirely follow suit and continued to reinforce the importance of mothers as caregivers, particularly for children under the age of three. Karen Hagemann outlines in her research on the time politics of childcare and education in West Germany that the expansion of part-time employment among West German mothers did not include an expansion of state-funded child care, part-time or otherwise, which stagnated until the 1970s.[41] Politicians and West Germans considered crèches for children under three a last resort, for instance in the case of single mothers, and coverage remained less than 1 per cent.[42] The creation of the Guest Worker programme in the late 1950s must also be understood in the context of maintaining the 'male-breadwinner/female-part-time-earner-and-homemaker' division of labour in the family. The migrant labour contracted to fill the labour shortage helped to preserve the gender order of West German citizens.[43] Thus while the political rhetoric around the relationship between employment and family for women changed in the 1960s, policies did not catch up to social and economic realities, and in fact supported the continued perception of mothers as the best caregivers.

This discrepancy between rhetoric and policy evolved in the 1970s, when the SPD formed a new Bundestag majority with its liberal coalition partner the Free Democratic Party of Germany (FDP). The SPD policy reforms in the 1960s contributed to the SPD's electoral success and the dramatic drop in the CDU/CSU's so-called 'Women's Bonus', the higher ratio of female to male voters that had ensured the CDU/CSU's majority in the 1950s and 1960s.[44] Women also joined the SPD in record numbers. Between 1970 and 1980, women as a percentage of total membership increased from 18.7 to 23 per cent.[45]

The importance of women to the SPD's electoral success and their growing presence in the party lent credence to a supportive environment for policies affecting working mothers. However, cultural norms and

Cold War discourses intensified internal family policy debates. The SPD revisited its family policy in 1970 as part of a larger reform of the Godesberger Programme platform of 1959, called the *Orientierungsrahmen '85* (Orientation Framework).[46] The party nearly unanimously passed the document at the 1975 Mannheim party congress except for those relating to family policy.[47]

The tabling of family policy in 1975 resulted from generational conflicts among members of the women's faction in the SPD, the *Arbeitsgemeinschaft sozialdemokratischer Frauen* (AsF or Working Group of Social Democratic Women). The party placed the responsibility for writing suggestions for family policy in the hands of the AsF; however, the feminist positions of the old generation that comprised the leadership often clashed with those of the younger generation. The ideology and actions of the New Left and autonomous women's movement strongly influenced the younger generation. Many also participated in the *Junge Sozialdemokraten* (Young Social Democrats, or Jusos), the youth wing of the party that tended to promote more radical positions.[48] Unhindered by fears of communism, the younger women promoted dual-earning households out of desire rather than necessity.[49] A group of female Jusos in 1975 eventually formed a separate working group to draft more radical suggestions, such as the expansion of full-day childcare. Anni Jensen best expressed the worries of the older, more conservative leaders of the AsF in a letter to party manager Holger Borner, in which she showed concern that such suggestions would 'bring Marxist approaches to our family policies'.[50]

Despite the SPD's struggles, the 1970s was a decade of considerable legislation affecting the family that took into account the same changes that had caused so much internal strife. Under SPD minister Katharina Focke, the Federal Ministry of Youth, Family and Health initiated a *Tagesmütter Modellprojekt* (Nanny Model Project) in 1974. Modelled on a similar programme in Sweden, the study hoped to popularise a new form of childcare for the infants and toddlers of employed mothers who could not cease employment after the birth of their children. The ministry and cooperating state and local governments paid stay-at-home mothers with their own children a meagre, untaxed wage to care for an additional two to three children in their home. Moderate feminists, represented by the women's lifestyle magazine *Brigitte*, offered public support for the initiative by meeting with local legislators.[51]

The reactions to the project demonstrate the limits of the federal government's ability to provide full time child-care infrastructure for West German children under the age of three. Child psychologists and paediatricians who were proponents of the 'motherly deprivation' thesis publicly criticised the project in the media and at an information conference with Minister Focke, arguing that absences of the mother due to employment 'can lead to profound damage in the entire process of child development'.[52] Furthermore, they connected the employment of mothers to the 'crisis of the family', contending that the experience of childrearing should be the parents' primary focus, not finding self-worth through employment.[53]

Perhaps the most progressive legislation was the First Law for the Reform of Marriage and Family Law, passed in 1976, which aimed to achieve the equality of women in marriage and divorce law. The law finally codified changes in divorce proceedings by eliminating the guilt clauses that had worked against women. Furthermore, the law also revised Paragraph 1356 of the West German civil code that codified the gendered division of labour in the family. The language of the statute, which had received little revision since 1900, enforced the patriarchal rights of husbands over their wives and families, and obligated women to their families first before seeking wage labour outside the home. The new law both promoted the freedom of couples to determine the most effective gendered division of labour for their family and bound both spouses to the interests of their home.[54]

The other major advancement in family policy in the 1970s spearheaded by the SPD/FDP coalition was the implementation of a paid maternal leave policy in May 1979. Paid maternity leave recognised the importance of employment in the life course of West German mothers, and aided in their reconciliation of family and employment. Furthermore, it was the realisation of policy advocated by female members of the SPD, and their female colleagues in the West German Trade Union Federation (DGB) since the 1950s, considered important for maintaining women's equality in the home and the workforce. The bill extended an already existing *Mutterschutz* (mother's protection) law that provided paid leave one month before and two months after the birth of the child. The new law provided six months of paid leave of up to 750 DM, depending on the salary of the mother before childbirth, with employment guaranteed should the mother want to return to her position following the birth of her child. In addition, she maintained her insurance and retirement benefits.[55]

While the bill received a positive reaction, women in the DGB, the SPD, and the autonomous women's movement expressed mixed feelings about the structure of the bill. First, many felt the bill contradicted the SPD's commitment to an equal gendered division of labour in the home because it excluded fathers from taking leave. SPD parliamentarian Renate Lepsius voiced this concern in a Bundestag debate in March 1979, arguing that the inclusion of fathers 'would have made clear the responsibilities of the father in their children's upbringing and would have conformed to the partnership practiced more seriously in young marriages'.[56] Women in the DGB worried that the meagre subsidy of *up to* 750 DM would make the leave economically unviable for the more vulnerable families in West Germany. Instead, they proposed a subsidy of 68 per cent of income, the equivalent to unemployment benefits.[57] The average monthly income for women in 1979 was 1,700 DM for industrial work and 2,170 DM for white-collar jobs.

Despite the SPD's reforms, the re-election of the CDU/CSU to a political majority with its coalition partner the FDP in 1983 marked yet another decade of change in federal family policy. However, rather than signal a return to the CDU/CSU's traditional male-breadwinner family policy of the 1950s and 1960s, the CDU/CSU built on the policy developments of the SPD/FDP in the 1970s. Understanding family policy under the new government requires contextualisation within the modernisation process that occurred in the party in the 1970s in response to their devastating loss of both the women's vote and the election in 1972. The CDU 'modernised' both their party structure and their platforms to appeal to a broader stratum of voters. As a result, a powerful coalition emerged between three organisations within the party representing the new target constituencies: the Christian Democratic Employees Association (CDA), representing workers' interests, the CDU Women's Union, and the CDU Youth Union.[58] A noticeable growth in female membership also contributed to the Women's Union's power in the party. Between 1970 and 1980, women's membership grew from 13 to 21 per cent.[59]

The need to attract women voters back to the party and the visible increase in women's membership resulted in a more 'modernised' image of women meant to appeal to the new emancipated housewife rather than the traditional 'children, church and kitchen', while maintaining its core conservative, confessional base. The emergence of the autonomous women's movement in the late 1960s and increased discussion of the women's question in West German media and society inspired the president of the Women's Union Helga Wex and her colleagues to incorporate some aspects of emancipatory rhetoric. However, they presented themselves as a unified, conservative counter-image to autonomous and social democratic women's activists. Their ideology emphasised equal treatment of employed mothers and housewives, a significant rhetorical shift for the CDU since the 1960s.[60]

Wex signalled this new direction in CDU women's policy in a 1973 article in the Catholic political magazine *Die neue Ordnung*. Wex argued that 'modern women' faced a dilemma between their families, their obligation to raise their children, and their right to seek individual fulfilment through employment.[61] The article also announced the Women's Union's solution to a mother's dilemma between employment and remaining in the home: *Erziehungsgeld* (Upbringing Money). This family policy would provide a subsidy to either parent (but mostly the mother) who took up childrearing as his or her main occupation in the first year of the child's life, regardless of the parent's previous employment status. The CDU confirmed the Women's Union position in the 1975 *Mannheimer Declaration*, the new party platform for the reformed CDU. The party now officially acknowledged mothers as homemakers and members of the labour force, as long as this did not affect their childrearing duties.[62] However, the CDU/CSU's status as minority Bundestag faction limited its ability to act.

This changed when West Germans voted the CDU/CSU as the parliamentary majority with the FDP and Helmut Kohl was sworn in as chancellor. By 1986, *Erziehungsgeld* replaced the SPD/FDP's 1979 maternal leave law. The law provided a stipend of 600 DM per month for the first six months of a child's life. The subsidy would be adjusted for income for the remaining six months, and was paid to the primary parent responsible for childcare, regardless of employment status. Unlike the *Mutterschaftsurlaub* passed by the SPD, either parent was eligible. The law also included a clause guaranteeing job protection for the parent taking employment leave and the opportunity to work part-time for the duration of the leave (after the mandatory twelve-week health-protection leave for mothers). The CDU/CSU also offered flexibility for the parents to split the parental leave and the *Erziehungsgeld*. The final law also included a provision that allowed the stay-at-home caregiver to maintain eligibility for social insurance during the period of leave.[63]

The rhetorical acceptance of mothers' employment and the subsequent changes in family policy resulted from the confluence of electoral necessity and the greater visibility of women in the political parties who wanted more discussion of the changing life course of West German women. However, change was limited by both male and female politicians' acceptance of established cultural norms regarding the socialisation of children and the power of the CDU/CSU's discourse on the family in the Cold War context.

The West German women's movement and the family

The women's movement outside of West German institutions presented the strongest critique of the male-breadwinner family model. Rather than reject family and marriage outright, the New Women's Movement that began in the late 1960s widely debated the role of the family, parenthood, and the gendered division of labour in women's lives. However, while these feminists exhibited changes in marriage and family values, strategic and ideological concerns limited the movement's ability to induce change in the structures that reinforced the male-breadwinner model in West Germany.

Questioning the male-breadwinner/female-part-time-earner-and-homemaker gendered division of labour in the home and advocating for the individuality of mothers played a central role in the early New Women's Movement. The *Aktionsrat der Befreiung der Frau* (Action Council for the Liberation of Women) in West Berlin and the *Frauenforum* (Women's Forum) E.V. in Munich, led by single mothers Helke Sander and Hannelore Mabry, respectively, placed motherhood and the reconciliation of family, work, and politics at the centre of their activism. In the late 1960s, before legalised abortions and the Pill's widespread accessibility, motherhood was much more common among feminists. Their feminist theories centred on the 'mother question', i.e. how best to combine motherhood with public activism and employment. Sander, in West Berlin, criticised the economic and emotional dependencies of women on family and husband and believed the solution to be a recasting of the social and cultural image of mothers to independent women who happened to be mothers, free to follow their own pursuits.[64] Mabry, in Munich, defined the goals of the *Frauenforum* as eliminating the double burden of employed mothers, improving the situation and role of women in politics, and ending overall discrimination against women in the family, job market and the law.[65]

To explain the root of female inequality in society, autonomous feminists turned to class analysis.[66] For example, the *Aktionsrat* argued that capitalism created a double role for women as unpaid reproducers in the home and as cheap labour in the workforce. The result was an unequal gendered division of labour in the home and in the workforce, as well as the double burden of mothers, both of which took an emotional toll on women.[67] Many West German autonomous feminists argued that socialist theory should recognise the benefits of women's unpaid labour in child-bearing and housework instead of focusing on paid employment.[68]

While the autonomous women's movement offered a clear rhetorical critique of West German gender roles in family and society, its autonomous theory of praxis limited its ability to change government policy and institutions that underpinned the male breadwinner family model. Autonomy, as defined by the sociologist and movement member Ute Gerhard, was 'individual self-determination and the institutional independence from heretofore-existing political forms and organisations'.[69]

This mistrust of institutions was a legacy of the student protest movement of the 1960s. West German student activists argued that the continued participation of former National Socialists in public life contributed to the authoritarianism of West German political and university institutions. This mistrust of institutions also evolved to include a criticism of the patriarchal culture of these institutions.[70]

Thus, rather than seek change to state institutions, the early autonomous movement focused on self-help projects. For example, the need to find a practical solution to the short supply of childcare instigated the largest project undertaken by the *Aktionsrat*, the *Kinderladenbewegung* (Store Front Daycare Movement) in West Berlin. Members converted cheap storefronts into childcare facilities. In most cases, the funding did not exist to hire a full time early childhood educator, so the mothers took turns. *Kinderläden* removed many ideological and practical objections to state-run childcare for activist mothers. On the ideological level, the *Aktionsrat* expressed extreme mistrust of state-run *Kindergärten*, arguing that they propagated a 'hierarchical structure' and 'authoritarian relationships', which they connected to their parent's generation and their relationship with the Third Reich.[71] Furthermore, they viewed the *Kinderläden* as an emancipatory space that provided mothers with the time and opportunity to reflect on their own situation as women away from the isolation of the home.[72] On the practical level, the *Kinderläden* provided (part-time) childcare while mothers attended classes or went to work. Creating their own childcare options was particularly important because of the small number of available state-financed kindergarten places.[73] The project goals eventually shifted towards anti-authoritarian pedagogy as more fathers became active and realised the potential of the *Kinderläden* to change 'authoritarian' childcare practices in West Germany.[74] Within a few years, several daycares opened in other cities in West Germany, such as in Munich.[75]

While the *Kinderladenbewegung* demonstrated an ideological reluctance to engage with West German educational institutions, the Wages for Housework campaign of the late 1970s offers an example of the attempt to politicise the homemaker role of many West German women. This intense debate over the definition of work, the gendered division of labour in the home, the best means to reconcile family and work, and their consequences for women's emancipation began in Italy and was adopted by West German autonomous feminists in several cities in 1976. The movement demanded a government wage for housewives in order to empower women's reproductive roles and housework.[76] Activists questioned whether paid labour outside the home ensured women's emancipation and instead argued that providing a monetary value for housework would equalise the status of housewives with those who earned an income in the job market. The writings of the political scientist and Wages for Housework activist Hannelore Schröder directly attacked Karl Marx's gendered separation of production and reproduction that diminished women's work in society.[77]

Rather than glorify the male-breadwinner family model, the Wages for Housework movement believed that the wage provided an easy solution for the unequal career opportunities for women, the social realities of mothers, and the government's lack of response to these issues. Gisela Bock, a historian of German history and then a research assistant at the Free University of West Berlin, argued that such a subsidy would change the basic inequalities of the West German welfare system that guaranteed a 'vicious cycle of dependency … poverty for single mothers, poverty and discrimination for lesbians, overworking of the double burdened'.[78]

While the Wages for Housework debate was more an isolated debate within the movement, an important avenue of transmission for criticisms against the male-breadwinner family model articulated by the West German women's movement to the West German public was the mainstream illustrated magazine *Stern* and the popular women's lifestyle magazine *Brigitte*. An analysis of these two magazines helps to bring into focus what informed the wider public's understanding of feminism, since the media was in many cases the only exposure to feminism of most West Germans. The magazines portrayed women and men not only as the embodiment of the ideals of feminism as interpreted by journalists, but also as the victims of long-term structural and cultural inequalities in West German society.

Parallel to the Wages for Housework movement and CDU policy, *Brigitte* and *Stern* advocated for the importance of the West German housewife. *Brigitte* featured a series of articles authored by the sociologist Helga Pross, famous for her study *The Realities of Women* (partially funded by *Brigitte*), which investigated the world of the housewife.[79] In a 1975 article, Pross contended that the attractiveness of employment outside the home diminished the popularity of the housewife role. In order to maintain housewives' worth, Pross suggested (similar to Christian Democratic politicians in the 1970s) that housewives should receive pensions and other 'material recognition'. Furthermore, society should recognise the role of raising children as being more important than aspirations beyond the home.[80]

The psychological burdens of housewives and housework, popularised by Betty Friedan's 1963 study *The Feminine Mystique*, which was translated into German in 1966, also framed the discussion of housewives.[81] In 1974, *Stern* ran a series of articles under the heading of 'The Psychological Suffering of the Woman'. The Problem that Has No Name identified by Friedan became the basis for an examination of the psychological burdens of housewives, especially older housewives beyond child-bearing age. A gynaecologist in Hamburg confirmed, based on recent findings, that: 'Women with employment and intellectual interests fair better with aging than those who have oriented their lives towards their husband and children.'[82]

Out of the desire to renegotiate the relationship between men and women emerged the 'new family man'. This figure stood in sharp contrast to the male breadwinner, emphasising a new masculinity based on the contributions men could make in the home. He supported his wife's career and shared responsibilities in the home, or raised his children alone as a single father. Equally important, men desired and embraced this new construction of masculinity. This 'new family man' related to the increased popularity of the *Partnerehe* (partnership marriage) in West German political and cultural discourse, supported by the First Law for the Reform of Marriage and Family Law and the alteration of Paragraph 1356 of the Civil Code.

Stern and *Brigitte* demonstrated that the values promoted in the proposed new law already existed and exposed the structural inequalities that prevented the full exercising of the *Partnerehe*. A 1975 *Brigitte* article profiled two *Partnerehen*. Both parents worked and shared the household and childcare duties. In the Friebe-Baron family, both parents were trained pastors who worked with patients in mental health clinics. Their partnership benefited from flexible work schedules, so much so that Jochen was able to spend ample time at home after the birth of their daughter. The career decisions he made in order to support his wife and child did not come without some doubt. Jochen recalls: 'It is hard to break free from the work ethic instilled in me. I often have to remind myself to work through it in peace and act instead on values.'[83]

While the magazines portrayed fathers as equal partners, *Stern* and *Brigitte* also analysed the impact of divorce on fatherhood. In a 1975 article titled, 'Fathers Become Good Mothers' the journalist Maren Delcke at *Stern* profiled the lives of divorced fathers who took on the role of primary caregivers to their children. These fathers learned how to cook and clean and stepped back from their career ambitions. Peter Dewor became the confidant of his three teenaged daughters in all matters concerning puberty and sexuality. Delcke also made a point of explaining how Dewor even took his oldest daughter to the gynaecologist to get the Pill after her sixteenth birthday. The article attributes the capabilities of single fathers to cultural changes. The article quotes a psychologist arguing: 'The fathers have discovered their children.'[84]

While both magazines applauded men for defying the male-breadwinner role, they also discussed the difficulties preventing widespread changes in gender roles. Christine Heide described these problems in *Stern* in an article titled 'Farewell to Superman'.[85] In its premise, Heide uses the difficulties of forging a partnership in marriage to criticise the West German political parties for not doing more to allow the practice of the equitable gender roles they in fact supported. Heide profiled Peter and Lottemi Doormann, parents to two children. Peter was an editor and Lottemi a journalist and activist in the women's and citizen initiative movements. Lottemi's career ambitions and the financial necessity of Peter's employment strained their relationship. However, the parents avoided state institutions as a solution. Between school and the children attending a parent-run *Kinderladen* after school (where Lottemi had to volunteer once a week), Lottemi was able to work four days a week.

But Peter's work hindered his participation. He volunteered at the *Kinderladen* once a month, and he had to take a holiday to do it.

The difficulties of the Doormann family in putting an equitable gendered division of labour in the home into practice, despite Peter and Lottemi's values, summarises the contradictions of the enduring critique of the West German women's movement on the family. The women's movement initiated a considerable change in values, one that was reflected in the partnership decisions of a younger generation of West Germans. However, the women's movement was also limited in its ability to exact changes in those institutions such as family policy and childcare that continued to propagate a male-breadwinner family model.

Conclusion

The proliferation of part-time employment for mothers in the 1960s began a new chapter in the contestation over gender roles, changing values, childrearing and policy in West Germany from 1960 until 1989. The impact of these changes in values and the life course of women on the family were palpable during these decades. Demographic changes denote that the employment of mothers, and later the student protest and feminist movements, affected non-marriage partnership and birth rate patterns, facilitated by the introduction of the birth control Pill. Couples began putting off marriage until they had children, and the size of families decreased over time. Divorce became more prevalent.

Concurrent to these developments, the CDU/CSU's hyper-politicisation of family policy, reinforced by Cold War politics, remained influential in the political realm, even after its electoral defeat in 1972. The issue of reconciliation of family and employment split the SPD generationally, even while it championed progressive legislation on marriage and paid leave for mothers. An older generation of female politicians who supported the male-breadwinner model out of political necessity and personal beliefs clashed with a younger generation less stigmatised by communism. Across the aisle, the CDU/CSU 'modernised' its family policy stance in the 1970s after facing electoral defeat. But its rhetoric was not entirely matched by legislation that supported the desire of many mothers to work after the birth of their children.

The West German autonomous women's movement offered a grass roots cultural challenge to the male-breadwinner model, but was limited in its ability to challenge state policy due to autonomous political beliefs. Journalists at mainstream publications challenged the male-breadwinner by offering images of homemakers and fathers who prioritised their families. West Germany began questioning the male-breadwinner model by the 1970s, but it remained powerful in politics, culture and society.

Notes

1   BArch K 189/6128/150 'Letter from Ingeborg Unterspann 3.8.1973'.
2   R. Moeller, *Protecting Motherhood: Women and the Family in the Politics of Postwar West Germany* (Berkeley, 1993); U. Frevert, 'Umbruch der Geschlechterverhaltnisse? Die 60er Jahre als geschlechterpolitischer Experimentierraum', in A. Schildt, D. Siegfried and K. Christian Lammers (eds), *Dynamische Zeiten: Die 60er Jahre in den beiden deutschen Gesellschaften* (Hamburg, 2000), pp. 642–60; F. Biess, *Homecomings: Returning POWs and the Legacies of Defeat in Postwar Germany* (Princeton, 2006).
3   A. Doering-Manteuffel and L. Raphael, *Nach dem Boom: Perspektiven auf die Zeitgeschichte seit 1970* (Göttingen, 2008), p. 110. For a gendered critique of their argument, see J. Paulus, E. Silies and K. Wolff (eds), *Zeitgeschichte als Geschlechtergeschichte: Neue Perspektiven auf die Bundesrepublik* (Frankfurt am Main, 2012).
4   J. Lewis, 'Gender and the Development of Welfare Regimes', *Journal of European Social Policy* Vol. 2, No. 3 (1992), pp. 159–73; M. Daly, *The Gender Division of Welfare: The Impact of the British and German Welfare States* (Cambridge, 2000); C. Kuller, *Familienpolitik im föderativen Sozialstaat: die Formierung eines Politikfeldes in der Bundesrepublik 1949–1975* (Munich, 2004); I. Naumann, 'Child Care and Feminism in West Germany and Sweden in the 1960s and 1970s', *Journal of European Social Policy* Vol. 15, No. 1 (2005), pp. 47–63; K. Hagemann, K. Jarausch and C. Allemann-Ghionda, 'Children, Families, and States: Time Policies of Childcare and Schooling in a Comparative Historical Perspective', in K. Hagemann,

K. Jarausch and C. Allemann-Ghionda (eds), *Children, Families, and States: Time Policies of Childcare, Preschool, and Primary Education in Europe* (New York, 2011), pp. 3–50.

5. W. Kolbe, *Elternschaft im Wohlfahrtsstaat: Schweden und die Bundesrepublik im Vergleich 1945–2000* (Frankfurt am Main, 2002), pp. 45–50.

6. K. Hagemann, 'Between Ideology and Economy: The "Time Politics" of Child Care and Public Education in the Two Germanys', *Social Politics* Vol. 13, No. 2 (2006), pp. 217–60; K. Hagemann, 'Die Ganztagsschule als Politikum', *Zeitschrift für Pädagogik*, No. 54 (2009), pp. 209–29; K. Hagemann, 'A West German "Sonderweg"? Family, Work, and the Half-Day Time Policy of Childcare and Schooling', in Hagemann, Jarausch and Allemann-Ghionda (eds), *Children, Families, and States*, pp. 275–300.

7. Moeller, *Protecting Motherhood*; Biess, *Homecomings*.

8. J. Neander, 'Frei, aufgeklärt und emanzipiert eilen die Deutschen dem Aussterben entgegen', *Die Welt*, 30 March 1979.

9. K. Hausen, 'Frauenerwerbstätigkeit und erwerbstätige Frauen. Anmerkung zur historischen Forschung', in G. Budde (ed.), *Frauen arbeiten: weibliche Erwerbstätigkeit in Ost- und Westdeutschland nach 1945* (Göttingen, 1997), p. 31.

10. B. Hille, 'Geschlechtstypische Präferenzen und Benachteiligungen – Weibliche Jugendliche in Bildung, Ausbildung und Studium', in G. Helwig and H. Nickel (eds), *Frauen in Deutschland, 1945–1992* (Bonn, 1993), pp. 215–21; E. Kolinsky, *Women in Contemporary Germany: Life, Work, and Politics*, 2nd ed. (Providence, 1993), pp. 120–1.

11. C. von Oertzen, *Teilzeitarbeit und die Lust am Zuverdienen: Geschlechterpolitik und gesellschaftlicher Wandel in Westdeutschland 1948–1969* (Göttingen, 1999).

12. M. Mattes, *'Gastarbeiterinnen' in der Bundesrepublik: Anwerbepolitik, Migration und Geschlecht in den 50er bis 70er Jahren* (Frankfurt am Main, 2005).

13. W. Hubbard, *Familiengeschichte: Materialien zur deutschen Familie seit dem Ende des 18. Jahrhunderts* (Munich, 1983), p. 93.

14. H. Schubnell, *Der Geburtenrückgang in der Bundesrepublik Deutschland: die Entwicklung der Erwerbstätigkeit von Frauen und Müttern* (Troisdorf, 1973), p. 63.

15. Ibid., p. 101.

16. Hubbard, *Familiengeschichte*, p. 93.

17. Schubnell, *Der Geburtenrückgang in der Bundesrepublik Deutschland*, p. 11.

18 E. Silies, 'Erfahrungen des Bruchs? Die generationelle Nutzung der Pille in den sechziger und siebziger Jahren', in Paulus, Silies and Wolff (eds), *Zeitgeschichte*, p. 210.
19 Ibid., p. 216. See also Silies, *Liebe, Lust, und Last. Die Pille als weibliche Generationserfahrung in der Bundesrepublik 1960–1980* (Göttingen, 2010).
20 R. Nave-Herz, *Kinderlose Ehen: Eine empirische Studie über die Lebenssituation kinderloser Ehepaare und die Gründe für ihre Kinderlosigkeit* (Weinheim, 1988), p. 45.
21 Ibid., p. 47.
22 Ibid., p. 56.
23 L. Oláh, 'Family Policies and Birth Rates: Childbearing, Female Work, and the Time Policy of Early Childhood Education in Postwar Europe', in Hagemann, Jarausch and Allemann-Ghionda (eds), *Children, Families, and States*, pp. 113–31.
24 E. Heineman, 'Sexuality in West Germany: Post-Fascist, Post-War, Post-Weimar, or Post-Wilhelmine?', in F. Kiessling and B. Rieger (eds), *Mit dem Wandel leben: Neuorientierung und Tradition in der Bundesrepublik der 1950er und 60er Jahre* (Cologne, 2011), p. 244.
25 Kuller, *Familienpolitik im föderativen Sozialstaat*, p. 40; E. Heineman, *What Difference Does a Husband Make?: Women and Marital Status in Nazi and Postwar Germany* (Berkeley, 1999), pp. 137–75.
26 U. Frevert, *Women in German History: From Bourgeois Emancipation to Sexual Liberation* (Oxford, 1997), pp. 285–6.
27 W. Kraushaar, *1968 als Mythos, Chiffre und Zäsur* (Hamburg, 2000); M. Marx Ferree, *Varieties of Feminism: German Gender Politics in a Global Perspective* (Stanford, 2012).
28 Paragraph 175 was not fully eliminated from the civil code until 1994. It is estimated that over 50,000 men were convicted under this statute in West Germany alone. See R. Moeller, 'Private Acts, Public Anxieties, and the Fight to Decriminalize Male Homosexuality in West Germany', *Feminist Studies* Vol. 36, No. 3 (2010), pp. 528–52; C. Whisnant, *Male Homosexuality in West Germany: Between Persecution and Freedom, 1945–69* (New York, 2012).
29 Bundesministerium für Jugend Familie und Gesundheit, *Nichteheliche Lebensgemeinschaften in der Bundesrepublik Deutschland* (Stuttgart, 1985), p. 21 and p. 169.
30 Ibid., p. 8 and p. 171.
31 Statistisches Bundesamt Wiesbaden, *Statistisches Jahrbuch für die Bundesrepublik Deutschland* (Stuttgart, 1991), p. 76.

32 R. Nave-Herz, 'Kontinuität und Wandel in der Bedeutung, in der Struktur und Stabilität von Ehe und Familie in der Bundesrepublik Deutschland', in R. Nave-Herz (ed.), *Kontinuität und Wandel der Familie in Deutschland. Eine zeitgeschichtliche Analyse* (Stuttgart, 2002), p. 64.
33 Kuller, *Familienpolitik im föderativen Sozialstaat*, p. 52.
34 Frevert, *Women in German History*, pp. 15–18.
35 L. Rölli-Alkemper, *Familie im Wiederaufbau: Katholizismus und bürgerliches Familienideal in der Bundesrepublik Deutschland 1945–1965* (Paderborn, 2000).
36 Moeller, *Protecting Motherhood*.
37 C. von Oertzen, *The Pleasure of a Surplus Income: Part-Time Work, Gender Politics, and Social Change in West Germany, 1955–1969* (New York, 2007).
38 Ibid., p. 52.
39 Oertzen, *Teilzeitarbeit*, p. 56.
40 Oertzen, *The Pleasure of a Surplus Income*, p. 31.
41 Hagemann, 'Between Ideology and Economy', p. 236.
42 J. Reyer and H. Kleine, *Die Kinderkrippe in Deutschland: Sozialgeschichte einer umstrittenen Einrichtung* (Freiburg im Breisgau, 1997).
43 Mattes, *'Gastarbeiterinnen' in der Bundesrepublik*.
44 F. Bösch, *Macht und Machtverlust: die Geschichte der CDU* (Stuttgart, 2002).
45 W. Pausch, *Die Entwicklung der sozialdemokratischen Frauenorganisationen: Anspruch und Wirklichkeit innerparteilicher Gleichberechtigungsstrategien in der Sozialdemokratischen Partei Deutschlands, aufgezeigt am Beispiel der Arbeitsgemeinschaft sozialdemokratischer Frauen* (Frankfurt am Main, 1985), p. 118, p. 142 and p. 166.
46 H. Schmidt, 'Komissionsbericht Orienteriungsrahmen '85', in *Protokoll Parteitag der Sozialdemokratischen Partei Deutschland Hannover 1973*, Vorstand der SPD (Bonn, 1973), pp. 268–71.
47 Vorstand der SPD, *Protokoll Parteitag der Sozialdemokratischen Partei Deutschlands von 11. bis 15. November 1975 Mannheim* (Bonn, 1975), p. 1191.
48 D. Süss, 'Die Enkel auf den Barrikaden: Jungsozialisten in der SPD in den Siebzigerjahren', *Archiv für Sozialgeschichte* Vol. 44 (2004), p. 68. Sixty-five per cent of the 156,000 new SPD party members in 1972 were under the age of thirty-five.
49 R. Lepsius, *Frauenpolitik als Beruf: Gespräche mit SPD-Parlamentarierinnen* (Hamburg, 1987), p. 96; Pausch, *Die Entwicklung der sozialdemokratischen Frauenorganisationen*, p. 172.

50 AdsD/SPD-PV/Referat Frauen/10322/'Brief von Anni Jensen an Holger Borner', 1.
51 S. Pape, 'Wir brauchen Tagesmütter sofort!', *Brigitte*, 8 August 1973; S. Pape, 'Wir fordern eine neuen Beruf: Tagesmütter', *Brigitte*, February 1973; S. Pape, 'Sie wollen schnell handeln', *Brigitte*, 1973.
52 Quote in J. Pechstein, 'Das Projekt Tagesmütter: Stellungnahme und Widerspruch aus kinderärztlicher Sicht', *Süddeutsche Zeitung*, March 23, 1974. See also BArch K 189/6149, Fold. 13 'Modellprojekt "Tagesmütter" – Expertentagung des BMJFG am 13. – 14. Juli 1974 im Schloss Lehbach (Bergish-Gladbach)'.
53 J. Bowlby, *Maternal Care and Mental Health: A Report Prepared on Behalf of the World Health Organization as a Contribution to the United Nations Programme for the Welfare of Homeless Children.*, 2nd ed. (Geneva, 1952); W. Kolbe, 'Kindeswohl und Müttererwerbstätigkeit: Expertenwissen in der schwedischen und bundesdeutschen Kinderbetreuungspolitik der 1960er- und 1970er- Jahre', *Traverse: Zeitschrift für Geschichte* No. 2 (2001), pp. 124–35.
54 BT-Drs. 7/650 'Erstes Gesetz zur Reform des Ehe- und Familienrechts (1.EheRG)', 4.
55 BT-Drs. 8/2613 'Entwurf eines Gesetzes zur Einführung eines Mutterschaftsurlaubs'.
56 Deutscher Bundestag – 8. Wahlperiode – 144. Sitzung. Bonn, 15 March 1979, 11391.
57 AdsD/DGB Parteivorstand/Referat Frauen/4021 'Niederschrift über die Sitzung des Bundesfrauenausschusses des DGB am 14.11.1978'.
58 G. Pridham, *Christian Democracy in Western Germany: The CDU/CSU in Government and Opposition 1945–1976* (London, 1977), pp. 223–5; S. Wiliarty, *The CDU and the Politics of Gender in Germany: Bringing Women to the Party* (New York, 2010), p. 89.
59 Kolinsky, *Women in Contemporary Germany*, p. 210; Wiliarty, *The CDU and the Politics of Gender*, p. 85.
60 ACDP IV-003-067/1 – CDU Bundesfrauenvereinigung Vorstandssitzungen 18 Januar 1974 bis 5 März 1974/ 'Ergebnisprotokoll der Sitzung der Kommission "Frauen" am 18.1.1974', 2.
61 H. Wex, 'Politik für die Frau: Politische Aspekte zur Situation der Frau heute', *Die Neue Ordnung* No. 4 (1973), pp. 270–1.
62 CDU, 'Mannheimer Erklärung. Unsere Politik für Deutschland', 1975, p. 115.

63　CDU, 'Mannheimer Erklärung'.
64　H. Sander, 'Versuch, Die Richtige Fragen Zu Finden', 1968, 1, Berlin/A/Rep. 400/20. Aktionsrat (2)/Berlin/Folder Handapp. Träger I-7, FFBIZ.
65　'Bericht über die erste Grossveranstaltung des Frauenforums München', *Information des Frauenforums* 1 (1972), pp. 3–17.
66　Ferree, *Varities of Feminism*, p. 59; F. Haug, 'The Women's Movement in West Germany', *New Left Review* No. 155 (February 1986), pp. 50–74.
67　Aktionsrat der Befreiung der Frauen, 'Selbstverständnis Der Aktionsrats Zur Befreiung Der Frauen', 1968, Berlin/A/Rep. 400/20. Aktionsrat(1)/Berlin/Folder 1, FFBIZ.
68　L. Doormann (ed.), *Keiner schiebt uns weg: Zwischenbilanz der Frauenbewegung in der Bundesrepublik* (Weinheim, 1979), pp. 43–9; Sommeruniversität für Frauen. Dokumentations-gruppe., *Frauen als bezahlte und unbezahlte Arbeitskräfte: Beiträge zur Berliner Sommeruniversität für Frauen, Oktober 1977*, vol. 1. Aufl. (Berlin: Frauenbuchvertrieb, 1978).
69　U. Gerhard, 'Westdeutsche Frauenbewegung: Zwischen Autonomie und dem Recht auf Gleichheit', *Feministische Studien* Vol. 10, No. 2 (1992), p. 42; K. Schulz, *Der lange Atem der Provokation: Die Frauenbewegung in der Bundesrepublik und in Frankreich, 1968–1976* (Frankfurt am Main, 2002); G. Notz, 'Die autonomen Frauenbewegungen der Siebzigerjahre', *Archiv für Sozialgeschichte* Vol. 44 (2004), pp. 123–48.
70　K. Schulz, 'Macht und Mythos von 1968: Zur Bedeutung der 68er Protestbewegung für die Formierung der neue Frauenbewegung in Frankreich und Deutschland', in *1968 – Von Ereignis zum Gegenstand der Geschichtswissenschaft* (Göttingen, 1998), pp. 256–72; G. Notz, *Frauen in der Mannschaft: Sozialdemokratinnen im parlamentarischen Rat und im deutschen Bundestag 1948/49 Bis 1957: Mit 26 Biographien* (Bonn, 2003).
71　Aktionsrat der Befreiung der Frauen, 'Modell einer demokratischen Kindergartensstätte', 1968, Berlin/A/Rep. 400/20. Aktionsrat(2)/Berlin/Folder Handapp. Träger I/30, FFBIZ.
72　Aktionsrat der Befreiung der Frauen, 'Analyse und Strategie der Frauenemanzipationsbewegung', 1968, 56–7, Berlin/A/Rep. 400/20. Aktionsrat(2)/Berlin/Folder Handapp. Träger I/55-58, FFBIZ.
73　Hagemann, 'Between Ideology and Economy', p. 236.
74　H. Berndt, 'Zu den politischen Motiven bei der Grundung erster anti-authoritarer Kinderladen', *Auschwitz und die Pädagogik*, 1995, p. 243; Z.d.s. Kinderläden, *Kinder im Kollektiv* (Berlin, 1969).

75 E. Zellmer, *Töchter der Revolte?: Frauenbewegung und Feminismus in den 1970er Jahren in München* (Munich, 2011).
76 G. Bock and M. Glöckler, 'Lohn Für Hausarbeit – Frauenkämpfe Und Feministische Strategie', in *Frauen Als Bezahlte Und Unbezahlte Arbeitskräfte. Beiträge Yur 2. Berliner Sommeruniversität Für Frauen – Oktober 1977*, Dokumentationsgruppe der Sommeruniversität e.V. (ed.) (Berlin, 1978), pp. 206–9.
77 H. Schröder, 'Unbezahlte Hausarbeit, Leichtlohnarbeit, Doppelarbeit. Zusammenhänge und Folgen.', in *Frauen als bezahlte und unbezahlte Arbeitskräfte: Beiträge zur Berliner Sommeruniversität für Frauen. Oktober 1977*, Dokumentationsgruppe der Sommeruniversität für Frauen e.V. Berlin (ed.) (Berlin, 1978), pp. 108–18.
78 G. Bock, 'Lohn Für Hausarbeit-Perspective Der Frauenbefreiung', in Doormann (ed.), *Keiner schiebt uns weg*.
79 H. Pross, *Die Wirklichkeit der Hausfrau: Die 1. Repräsentatitive Untersuchung über Nichterwerbstätige Ehefrauen: Wie leben Sie? Wie denken Sie? Wie sehen Sie sich selbst?*, 1.–10. Tsd. (Reinbek bei Hamburg, 1975).
80 H. Pross, 'Wer hat die Hausfrau abgewertet?', *Brigitte*, 1975.
81 B. Friedan, *The Feminine Mystique* (New York, 1963).
82 I. Randschau, 'Schmerz Der Aus Der Seele Kommt', *Stern*, 1974.
83 S. Pape, 'Wir führen eine Partnerehe', *Brigitte*, 1975.
84 M. Delcke, 'Aus Vätern wurden gute Mütter', *Stern*, 1975.
85 C. Heide, 'Abschied Vom Supermann', *Stern*, 1975, pp. 74–5.

6

Vanguard of the working mother: The East German family between change and continuity

Donna Harsch

The single most significant development in the East German family between 1949 and 1990 was the accelerating probability that its mother and/or wife would work for wages. From the early 1960s, a rapidly rising percentage of women worked through every phase of childrearing. In an era when the 'working mother' remained relatively uncommon in the West, she was typical in the German Democratic Republic (GDR). In 1966, women there worked outside the home at the highest rate in the industrialised world, comprising 49.1 per cent of the total workforce. The high proportion of employed mothers and wives was the intended result of policies implemented by the ruling Socialist Unity Party (SED), the East German Communist party. Although the SED set in motion this historic development, it did not foresee its complex, often unwanted, outcomes, including a rising divorce rate driven by wife complainants, teachers worried about unprepared pupils, demands for privately owned labour-saving appliances, and, in an economy starved for labour, wives/mothers leaving full-time work for part-time employment. Most alarming to the SED was a downturn in the birth rate. In 1964, the very year the GDR achieved its goal of drawing a majority of young married mothers into wage labour; it also recorded the first decline in the fertility rate of East German women since 1946. Clearly, the family's internal dynamics were not adapting to the working-mother model as predicted. In response to the entangled economic, demographic and cultural consequences of the working-mother family, the SED adjusted its social and economic policies as well as its discourse about the family. The SED changed the East German family, this chapter argues, but the East German family also bent the arc of socialist state policy.

The chapter briefly surveys the situation of the East German family after the defeat of Nazism. It then summarises the SED's understanding of the family and lays out the main phases and social consequences of the party's family-related policies. Turning to the experiences of East Germans inside the family, it discusses relationships between spouses and between parents and children. Finally, it addresses the evolution of sexuality in the GDR.

In the wake of total war: Post-war crisis and stabilisation of the family

From 1945 through 1949, a multi-sided crisis afflicted the German family – above all, the urban family.[1] Whether killed in the war or held as prisoners of war, millions of soldiers did not return home at the war's end. As late as 1950, women headed one-third of households in East Germany. Women had to care for their children and elderly parents under dire conditions that placed extraordinary burdens on the family, the central social institution in the face of the collapse of public services and private enterprises. Allied bombing had destroyed or damaged a substantial percentage of housing in cities. Severe food shortages spread through every zone of occupation. The worth of German currency plummeted; rationing systems did not function well; the black market surged.[2]

The Soviet zone of occupation (SBZ) was even more crisis-ridden than the Western zones. In the spring of 1945, as the Red Army entered German-populated territory, its soldiers raped untold numbers of women. The wave of mass rape peaked during the Battle of Berlin that raged for more than a week before surrender on 8 May. It is estimated that the number of women raped in Berlin exceeded 100,000.[3] Many thousands of women became pregnant; many searched frantically for someone to abort the pregnancy, while many others buried infants who did not survive the time of scarcity. Memory of mass rape – and the refusal of the Soviet military administration to punish offending soldiers – deeply alienated many women from the Red Army, its occupying administration and Russians in general.[4] Meanwhile, masses of destitute people were streaming into Eastern Germany. Between 1945 and 1948, around 11 million German refugees fled Poland, Czechoslovakia and elsewhere in Eastern Europe. The ratio of women to men was even higher among refugees than among the native population. The majority of these refugees moved on to the (consolidated) Western zone but 3–4 million remained in the much smaller SBZ. When the GDR was founded in 1949, 'settlers' (as the SED called them) made up around 20 per cent of the population.[5]

Married couples also suffered from psychological and sexual crises. Returning from captivity, husbands were often depressed and immobilised by defeat and dearth. Wives were exhausted by scrounging for food, water and fuel.[6] Therapists at hastily organised 'marriage and sexual counselling centres' tried to help husbands who were impotent and wives who recoiled in disgust from dispirited, wasted partners.[7] The divorce rate shot up; husbands (who had much higher chance of remarriage) filed most of the suits. Fleeting affairs occurred more frequently than earlier. In 1946, three times as many babies were born out of wedlock as in 1939.[8]

The family recovered from this acute crisis as food supplies improved, inflation and the black market were brought under control, and peacetime economic activity ramped up. By 1950, the family's typical pre-war demographic profile seemed to be re-emerging in East Germany: a husband/wife pair in which the husband worked for wages and the wife worked in the household or on the family farm. The return to 'normalcy' reflected a very strong urge to marry. Around 95 per cent of women who came of age in the 1950s became wives. The divorce rate fell after its post-war spike.[9] The ratio of women to men in the population began to shrink, as did the percentage of female-headed households. The birth rate headed back up after 1946.[10]

The party's vision of the family

The SED published no official ideological treatise on the family. From its ideas and policies on the 'woman question' and its family-related laws, one can, however, reconstruct leading Communists' post-war understanding of the ideal family. The SED supported women's public and private equality as citizens, workers, and spouses. The East German constitution guaranteed women's equal rights. Communists recognised that the Constitution would not lead to actual equality for women. The private oppression of women in the family was, they believed, a major reason that women were unable to gain the education or take the jobs that would have helped them attain equal standing with men. The Ministry of Justice contemplated reforms of family law that would dismantle patriarchal privileges and liberalise divorce. Even these specific reforms of family law would not, they knew, change social customs and prejudices about gendered abilities and natures. To achieve actual equality, women had to work for wages. The working woman would, like the working man, become a class-conscious citizen of a socialist society. An independent livelihood would give her autonomy within the family. Thus, paid employment, state propaganda explained, would emancipate women from both public discrimination and private tyranny. The nuclear family would become a companionate and egalitarian partnership between spouses. Communists were also strongly pronatalist. Children, they believed, not only made a family, but also represented the future of socialism. Books about marriage and housekeeping, fiction, pamphlets and press articles portrayed large families as the happiest families. They also presented maternity as fulfilling female nature.[11]

In the early 1920s, the Bolsheviks had gone through a phase of anti-family rhetoric and policy, but all that was long gone in the Soviet Union by the time Communists came to power in East Germany. The SED's approach to modernising the family was pragmatic and reformist, rather than transformative or revolutionary. Neither in principle nor in practice did the SED entertain utopian ideas about the abolition of marriage, communalisation of the family, or even, free love. Nor did the SED adopt an egalitarian, gender-neutral approach to unpaid labour inside the family. While party officials did not reify women's household labour and did hope that men would do a bit more, they did not question the de facto status of housework as female labour, much less actively propagate housework or childcare by men/husbands/fathers. Believing that domestic labour had stultifying effects on the social consciousness of anyone who performed it, they were not eager to burden men with housework. Rather, they envisioned gradually moving much labour out of the home and into the hands of paid workers. School and factory kitchens, laundry services, and crèches and kindergartens would provide the midday meal to family members, wash their dirty clothes and care for young children while their parents worked.

This plan was laudable but expensive to realise. The focus of the SED was on the revival and expansion of heavy industrial production, not services or consumer goods. The GDR's early Five Year Plans invested few resources in socialised or commercial services, residential housing, household goods, textiles, or public transportation. The SED, then, left the wife/mother to perform the unpaid labour of social reproduction, while it squeezed consumption and services in favour of production. A woman's work was cut out for her: the typical wife/mother had to care for her family in crumbling, cramped, damp apartments, most without hot water or a toilet, not to speak of a washing machine. At the shops, she had to queue for hours to buy low-quality goods.

The SED did not transform the family but did politicise it, especially in the early years of social upheaval and Stalinist repression. Communists wanted all family members to become active socialists and tried to engage them in the appropriate mass organisation (women's league, youth leagues, cultural organisations, trade unions, the party itself). Education policies discriminated against the children of bourgeois parents. The children of active Christian or dissident parents had absolutely no chance of attending university. Party stalwarts gathered information on suspected 'saboteurs' and 'layabouts' in the 1950s; in the 1970s and 1980s, thousands of 'unofficial collaborators' provided State Security with potentially damning personal information about even their own family members. It was rare, however, for the party to intervene directly in the family and extremely rare for the state to take children from their parents for political reasons.[12] The family enjoyed considerable privacy within its internal world, and family bonds took on great significance. The family essentially was the private sphere. Civil society did not exist, due to the suppression of non-state organisations, press and institutions, except the churches. By the 1960s, the family was the centrepiece of what Günter Gaus dubbed a 'niche society' made up of thousands of private corners to which people withdrew after work and official activities to spend time with family and friends. In the words of Paul Betts, 'Private life – generally associated with liberal society – assumed its most political power and personal value under authoritarian regimes.'[13]

Policies and social consequences, 1950–70

The SED did not have an explicit family policy but implemented disparate policies and laws that affected the family: women's employment and qualification; reproductive health; childcare and other socialised services; consumer production; and family law. Family-related policies intersected with *Frauenpolitik* ('women's policy'). *Frauenpolitik* was continually guided by two priorities: female employment and a high birth rate. In the mid-1960s, however, these commitments began to shift position as the first priority of *Frauenpolitik*. Before then, female employment ranked higher. Fertility was seen as on the right track, women's workforce participation left much to be desired. By the late 1960s, women of every family situation were committed to working outside the home but were reducing their fertility rate. Thus, pronatalism began to overtake employment as the primary goal of *Frauenpolitik*.

The 1960s was a decade of flux in economic and social policy. Three intertwined transitions influenced family-related policies. In the 1950s, economic planners focused intensely on the quantity of production, number of workers, and size of the population (even as SED policies drove 3 million East Germans to flee to West Germany between 1949 and 1961). In the 1960s, managers, planners and SED officials came to believe that the quality of labour was as critical as its quantity to the building of Socialism. Policy-makers started to think seriously about how to raise the qualification level of women workers and, to a lesser degree, about how to enhance child development. The shift in emphasis from quantity to quality was related to a swing away from heavy reliance on social and economic disincentives towards greater use of positive incentives to influence, for example, women's readiness to train for skilled work or have more babies. The SED rehabilitated social-scientific approaches to social issues, rather than denounce academic expertise as 'bourgeois'. After reluctantly acknowledging that Socialism had not overcome family conflict or dysfunction, the SED encouraged sociologists, psychologists, and sexologists to study child development, delinquent youth, the causes of divorce, or techniques to enhance sexual satisfaction.

Employment

The SED's mobilisation of women's labour was not only ideologically, but also instrumentally motivated, for the GDR was plagued by labour shortages from the early 1950s onwards. The daily press, illustrated weeklies, and women's magazines highlighted the benefits of employment for women and emphasised the state's commitment to equal pay, socialised services, and women's committees on the shop floor. To encourage mothers and especially wives to work, the GDR retained a National Socialist perk: a monthly paid 'housework day' for all married women and for single mothers with children under fourteen years old. Initially, however, most policies did not incentivise employment but penalised non-employment and were directed not at wives but at women 'standing alone' – widows, divorced women, and never married women. Officials reduced and, in some cases, took away war widows' pensions; they lessened or eliminated welfare payments to single mothers; and they gradually abolished the payment of alimony. By the mid-1950s, virtually all women 'standing alone' worked for wages, even if they had small children. Wives entered the workforce slowly, unless their husband was a low-wage worker. In 1960, 56.7 per cent of wives of employed husbands worked for wages.[14] The proportion of married mothers' employment increased unevenly. In 1956, Minister of Justice Hilde Benjamin lamented that only 18.6 per cent of wives with young children worked for wages. Most married mothers dropped out of the workforce after the birth of their first child. They typically returned to employment after their children had reached kindergarten age (three years old).

By 1958, the vast majority of the remaining labour reserves left in the GDR were women: 2,207,700 women of working age, but fewer than 400,000 men were not employed.[15] Not coincidentally, the GDR ended rationing for basic foods in 1958, thus, raising the cost of living. Planners also moderately expanded consumer goods production. Walter Ulbricht, First Secretary of the Politburo, touted 'the 1,000 little things' that women could now buy. These measures aimed to push and pull wives into the workforce. They had some effect, but no breakthrough occurred. Many families with a stay-at-home wife could afford higher prices for food and even buy 'little things', for throughout the 1950s a steadily increasing percentage of husbands moved into the socialist 'middle class' as skilled workers, managers, engineers, and the like.

As men were climbing the social scale, women workers languished in unskilled and semi-skilled jobs. They faced discrimination from managers, trade union officials, and even SED factory committees in male-dominated (and higher paying) industries. Given the reluctance of young married mothers to enter employment and of all women to get qualified, the SED leadership realised that it could no longer treat women as the instruments of a labour policy that mainly benefited men. In December 1961, a much-publicised 'Women's Communique' introduced a campaign that acknowledged that women's emancipation had not occurred and promised major improvements in their work situation. Travelling committees of SED women met with women workers and with housewives, informing them that mother-friendly qualification programmes would allow them to train for skilled diplomas while on the time clock and assuring them that men would no longer be allowed to assign women to the worst-paid positions on the shop floor. The SED also expanded crèche places.[16]

The dam broke. By 1965, 79.5 per cent of women twenty-five to thirty-nine years old (the prime child-bearing and childrearing years) were employed, as were 70 per cent of wives. By 1967, 55 per cent of women with three or more children at home were employed (almost all women with three or more children were married). Even more gratifying to state planners, the female workers' qualification rate rose impressively. By 1970, 41 per cent of women workers had a professional degree or skilled diploma; their level of qualification outpaced men's in rural occupations, commerce, health and administration. Most pleasing of all to the SED was that the higher the educational level of the woman, the higher the likelihood that she worked outside the home.[17]

Even as it celebrated the achievement of forging the first generation of skilled women workers in German history, the SED faced the consequences of its disinterest in domestic labour. Women began to retreat from full-time employment. To draw wives into the workforce, in 1959 the party allowed a few state enterprises to offer part-time jobs to members of 'housewife brigades'. News of this experiment spread quickly. Soon, women in enterprises of every type were asking for a reduction in their hours. They threatened to take a job in another factory or office if denied this request. Given the shortage of labour, plant directors usually relented. In 1960, 14.9 per cent of all women workers and employees worked part-time; by 1964, 24.2 per cent did; by 1969, 31 per cent had reduced their hours. Surveys showed that more than half of women workers wanted to work part-time.[18] Investigations by the SED Women's Commission revealed that nearly all part-timers were married.[19] More surprisingly, the majority of part-timers were unskilled or semi-skilled workers – a sign that the working-class family, in particular, was not adapting to the working-mother model.[20]

Reproduction

The Department of Mother and Child (in the Ministry of Health) implemented the GDR's reproductive and natalism policies, guided by the Law for the Protection of Mother and Child and the Rights of Women (1950). This law instituted programmes intended to encourage maternity and decrease infant and maternal mortality. Pregnant workers and employees received a paid five-week leave before delivery and six weeks afterwards (increased to eleven weeks after birth in 1956). A woman received a 100 Deutschmark (DM) lump sum for her third, 250 DM for her fourth and 500 DM for her fifth child. Families received modest monthly allowances for the fourth and subsequent children. Single mothers got the same benefits, although few of them had three or more children. The law created the framework for reproductive healthcare:

registration of pregnant women; pregnancy counselling including medical examinations; explication of social and legal rights, and hygiene education; medical care for nursing mothers; medical observation of children.[21] The Department set up pregnancy counselling centres, worked to identify all pregnant women, and used small monetary rewards to entice women to attend prenatal examinations.[22] By 1958, medical personnel examined 100 per cent of pregnant women at least once.[23] After overcoming resistance to clinic birth in rural areas and from midwives, the GDR managed to hospitalise child delivery fully by the early 1960s.[24] Paediatric care for young children (including vaccinations against tuberculosis, small pox, etc.) was ever better developed. These programmes (combined with antibiotics and an improved standard of living) dramatically reduced rates of maternal, infant and child mortality.

The Mother and Child Law included a major penalty for women who tried to reduce their fertility by ending a pregnancy: a very strict abortion law that allowed abortion only for 'eugenic' reasons or if the pregnancy resulted from rape. The rate of authorised abortion was extremely low: per 10,000 births, 2.7 in 1952 and 0.7 in 1962.[25] Contraceptive means such as condoms and pessaries were scarce, though not illegal. The most common method was 'probably' *coitus interruptus*.[26] In 1961, the GDR's pharmaceutical industry was the fifth in the world to develop a hormonal ovulation blocker. Only 3 per cent of 'pill' production was, however, prescribed to East German women (who had a medical indication against pregnancy); the rest was sold for hard currency on the world market.[27] Although access to birth control was poor, couples managed to hold fertility in limits (abetted by recourse to illegal abortion). The rise in fertility was solid but there was no 'baby boom'. Births per 1,000 women of child-bearing age increased between 1947 and 1963: 1947: 55.7/1,000; 1950: 75.0/1,000; 1963: 90.0/1,000.[28] After that, fertility tumbled. In 1970, there were only 69.7 births per 1,000 women. In that year, deaths per 1,000 outnumbered births.[29]

The SED's response to the falling birth rate was neither a crackdown on illegal abortion nor the criminalisation of contraceptives. Rather, a commission comprised of physicians and representatives from the Democratic Women's League gathered data on who petitioned for abortions, and why. They found that rapid succession of births, the difficulty of caring for several young children while pursuing qualification, and women's double burden drove them (with support from their husbands) to apply for a termination or to risk an illegal procedure. The commission recommended a de facto relaxation of abortion regulation in cases, which met certain criteria including age, number of children, frequency of pregnancies, etc. Introduced in 1965, this complicated half-measure created administrative difficulties for the Department of Mother and Child as the number of applications shot up and every case had to be evaluated by a committee of physicians.

Institutional childcare

In the 1950s, the number of places in crèches and kindergartens expanded but lagged woefully behind mothers' increasing employment rate. By 1958, 36.2 per cent of children (aged three to six) attended kindergarten, while 8.3 per cent of infants and toddlers had a place in a crèche. The majority of working mothers had to find private providers, often their own mothers.[30] Women workers and their spokeswomen in the SED and Department of Mother and Child complained often and loudly about the toll of lacking childcare on women's ability to work. In the 1960s, coverage expanded considerably but still did not meet need. In 1970, 64.5 per cent of three- to six-year-olds attended kindergarten, while crèches could accept 29.1 per cent of infants and toddlers.

Initially, concern about the quality of daycare focused on basic issues such as safety, space, sun and nutrition. In the late 1950s, however, the Department of Mother and Child talked to women who had stopped work so they could care for their children at home because of their slow cognitive and motor development in the crèche. These complaints prompted comparative studies by psychologists of 'home' and 'crèche' children. The evidence suggested that crèche children, especially those who stayed in weekly homes from Monday through Saturday, entered kindergarten 'verbally and emotionally behind' those raised solely in the family and suffered from having less physical contact with their parents.[31] In the early 1960s, experts and ordinary women participated in a lively debate in the daily press and women's periodicals about whether babies should stay home with their mothers or, instead, crèche care could and should be improved. The debate did not cause any diminution of the state's commitment to women's employment, but it did highlight the maternal role in childrearing.[32]

Mechanising the household

In the 1950s, socialised services, especially the factory laundry, were introduced with much fanfare in enterprises with majority female workforces. Practice did not fulfil propagandistic promises. The laundries were often laughably inefficient. In the huge chemical concerns around the town of Dessau, 17,000 women workers could have their linens washed in the factory laundry only twice a year. Lucky was the worker who could, instead, get her washing back in eight to nine weeks.[33] In the 1960s, most public laundries were located along city streets, not in the factory. Waiting times declined but remained high. Complaints about service and quality actually rose as standards of cleanliness increased.[34]

Rather than perfect the public laundry, planners touted a 'rationalisation model' – that is, the electrification of housework done at home. This dream fired the imagination of East German women. They yearned for devices that would make their homes easier to maintain – and with good reason: wives spent an average of six hours more a day on housework than did husbands.[35] The East German woman's magazine, *Die Frau von heute*, stoked the desire for the modernised home by running articles on consumer appliances produced by East German industry. Women flocked to demonstrations of these wares, only to become frustrated when they had to wait for months or even years to receive the washing machine, vacuum cleaner, or mixer they had seen on display.[36] In the 1960s, consumer production leapt upwards. By the end of the decade, more than half of households owned a refrigerator and a washing machine.[37] Rather than save time, these devices raised standards of cleanliness and cookery. In 1970, housework claimed 47.5 hours per week in a four-person household. Women performed 90 per cent of this work, thus working a full second shift at home.[38]

Family law

In 1954, the Ministry of Justice presented a draft family law for public discussion. At hundreds of information sessions, citizens seemed to accept its proposed elimination of the patriarchal division of property, income and family decision-making. Urged on by Protestant and Catholic clerics, however, many people criticised its guarantee of the wife's right to work as evidence that the state was pushing wives into paid labour. Above all, they objected to the plan to liberalise divorce by introducing a no-fault 'irretrievable breakdown' rule and eliminating alimony. Older wives, many of whom had never worked for wages and had no skills, led the popular outcry. Many East Germans, including Communist women, sympathised with their opposition. The Ministry of Justice withdrew the draft law – and for a decade, there was no public discussion of family law.[39] Meanwhile, using the equal rights provision of the Constitution, the courts implemented shared division of property and decision-making. Divorce reform occurred in a piecemeal fashion. Family court judges often denied a husband's petition for divorce, but the higher courts overturned such rulings and also denied petitions for alimony.[40]

Over time, popular anxiety about divorce dissipated as women's financial independence rose. By the mid-1960s, it was the SED that worried about divorce – and a declining rate of marriage and rising rate of single motherhood.[41] For every 1,000 inhabitants, there were 1.3 divorces in 1958; in 1969, 1.7.[42] In 1965, 9.8 per cent of babies were born out of wedlock, rising to 13.3 per cent five years later. The data showed that single mothers and young divorced mothers had, on average, fewer children than married women.[43] Worries about the quantity of fertility were accompanied by experts' concerns that children's psychological development might be harmed by the trauma of divorce or, as we have seen, overexposure to institutional childcare (on which single and divorced women relied more than did married mothers).

Rather than tighten divorce regulation or discriminate against single motherhood, the state responded with a vigorous pro-marriage and pro-family message. In 1965, the Ministry of Justice introduced a new draft family law for public discussion. This draft (which became law) proclaimed the family 'the basic cell of society' and credited it with 'determining the personality in socialist society'. At thousands of sessions about the law, attended mostly by women, spokespeople from the Ministry of Justice touted its support for both the two-earner couple and *Familienerziehung* (family nurture/upbringing). They emphasised that the new law encouraged husbands to do more work in the household. Popular support for the law ran high. The press joined the discussion with articles on the importance of the family to socialist society, on the one hand, and the difficulty of women's double burden, on the other.[44]

To reduce the rate of divorce, state agencies introduced an odd mix of collective and individual remedies, a combination that was symptomatic of the transitional nature of policy in the 1960s. On the one hand, the Ministry of Justice encouraged family court judges to prescribe 'collective intervention'. In collective intervention, the work collective of the defendant (typically the husband) met with the couple and tried to convince the wife to stay with her husband, while admonishing him to straighten up and fly right. Collective intervention was very unpopular, did not work and soon disappeared. The Ministry of Health, on the other hand, revived the post-war (and Weimar) practice of sexual and marriage counselling. Sessions included information on contraception, advice about sexual techniques, and a truncated version of psychotherapy. Initially, almost no one took advantage of this modern approach to marital troubles, but by 1970 counselling centres were attracting ever more clients, especially in Berlin. Clients were 60–80 per cent women and were disproportionately well-educated.[45]

The emphasis on 'family upbringing' signalled the increasing focus on child development, arguably, a modern perspective. Yet concern about children was paired with a conventional understanding of the mother as the parent most responsible for 'upbringing'. Asked why they switched to part-time work, some women referred to teachers who insisted that they as mothers must answer for a child's poor academic performance.[46] In justifying decisions to terminate parental rights, judges held employed and single mothers to standards of care associated with the full-time housewife/mother, but did not make gendered comments when chiding neglectful fathers.[47]

Muttipolitik, 1971–89

In 1971, Erich Honecker replaced Walter Ulbricht as First Secretary of the Politburo of the SED. At the Eighth Party Congress, he proclaimed the 'main task' was to raise 'the material and cultural standard of living of the people'. Called the 'Unity of Economic and Social Policy', the new programme channelled investment towards private income, private consumption and social consumption. By 1980, every household in the GDR owned a refrigerator, washing machine and television. Every third household owned a car. The state subsidised the cost of children's clothing and other basic goods. A residential construction programme built 500,000 housing units in the 1970s (the population was c. 17 million). The provision of socialised childcare leapt forwards. By 1980, 92.2 per cent of three- to six-year-olds were in kindergarten, increasing to 95.1 per cent in 1989; in 1980, 61.2 per cent of birth to two-year-olds had a place in a crèche, rising to 80.2 per cent in 1989. The state raised the minimum wage, pension and holiday. Without cutting pay, it reduced the working week to forty hours (from forty-five) for women with three or more children younger than seventeen. It extended maternity leave to eighteen weeks. Upon first marriage, a couple whose members were twenty-five or younger could receive a 5,000 DM credit that worked similarly to the National Socialist marriage loan: the birth of each child reduced the principle until, with three children, the couple owed nothing. Families with three or more children received tax credits.[48] These measures were clearly aimed at bolstering fertility, while also helping employed mothers and low-wage workers (most of whom were women).

In 1972, however, an about-turn in reproductive policy seemed destined to doom the effort to increase fertility: the GDR legalised first trimester abortion. Simultaneously, the Ministry of Health made the 'Pill' available at no cost to any adult woman (after a medical examination). The reform of abortion regulation was multi-determined. Looking to the East, the SED wanted to end 'abortion tourism' to Poland (where abortion was legal). Looking to the West, the SED aimed to impress the women's movement in West Germany (where abortion was illegal). Looking inwards, it hoped to impress female Communists and ordinary women who had taken to charging the SED with hypocrisy on the 'woman question'. Not surprisingly, the rate of abortion shot up and fertility continued to fall. Rather than re-enact restrictions, the SED introduced massive positive incentives to raise fertility. In 1976, paid maternity leave for a first child was extended to twenty-six weeks; a second child brought a mother a paid 'baby year' and the guarantee of her job upon return to work. The maternalist and family bias of Honecker's programme, popularly dubbed *Muttipolitik*, became even more pronounced over time. In 1979, women received the 'baby year' for the first child; in 1986, they received eighteen months' leave for the third child. Monthly child allowances were raised repeatedly. Residential construction boomed throughout the 1980s (as the GDR fell into serious debt).[49] Socialised daycare was massively expanded, underlining the state's belief in its benefits for children and mothers. Yet, simultaneously, the 'baby year' allowed mothers to care for infants at home, thus, recognising the value of maternal care for very young children.

These generous policies boosted fertility but also soon lost their charge – and, thus, the state had to provide ever more incentives. Efforts to encourage marriage also had a temporary effect. Divorce rose substantially in the 1980s (3.0 per 1,000 population). In 1989, one-third of babies were born to a single mother, although the statistic is misleading since many couples lived in stable cohabitation. *Muttipolitik* did keep women in the workforce and on the education track. In 1989, 92 per cent of East German women were employed, in training, or at a university or technical college. More than 80 per cent of all women employees had completed a qualification programme. Yet women workers' rate of part-time employment remained relatively high (27.6 per cent in 1983).[50]

Husbands and wives

In the 1950s, East German marriages basically fitted one of two models: companionate marriage with a gendered division of labour or patriarchal marriage. Urban-dwelling couples typically consulted about major family decisions, but husbands rarely performed any significant housework or childcare. Furthermore, a husband's employment, education and political activities took precedence over the wife's.[51] In the countryside, farmer-husbands often ruled the roost, refusing, for example, to let their wives join rural production cooperatives. The Protestant Women's League, with its active rural base, propagated a message about morality in marriage that supported the authoritarian behaviour of husbands.[52] As criticism of the draft family law of 1954 revealed, most East Germans did not believe a wife should work full time or even at all.

As it turned out, couples jettisoned that belief fairly easily. Within a decade, women's employment was utterly normalised. Yet domestic relations between spouses changed minimally. In 1967, the SED Women's Bureau concluded: 'The egalitarian socialist marriage has not materialised.'[53] Especially in rural districts, working mothers filed for divorce because household tasks and childrearing were 'almost completely loaded' on them. When the Women's Commission questioned women about why they did not train for qualified positions, women often described a modified patriarchal relationship: a husband allowed his wife to work for wages but controlled the money she earned and would not let her go out with friends, much less take a training course. Commissioners heard story after story about functionaries in the party, unions, government bureaucracy and economy who feared that their wives would 'develop beyond them'. These men avoided any workplace discussion of women's domestic burdens 'because the obvious consequences would reach into their own families'.[54] Asked why they wanted to work part-time, young married mothers cited 'concern about my children' and the necessity to 'balance familial, household, and occupational responsibilities'. Their husbands, many reported, had decided their part-time work was better for the family.[55]

Some evidence suggests that women's understanding of marriage was becoming more modern, even if men's was not. Now that women filed most of the cases, 'incompatibility' became one of the top five grounds for divorce. A new legal ground leaped to sixth place in the 1960s: 'Disagreements about children's upbringing and/or how to run the household.' Most divorces, however, were provoked by age-old male behaviours. Three of the top five grounds were the same in 1968 as ten years earlier: infidelity, 'abuse of alcohol' and the catchall 'ill-considered' marriage (commonly claimed as a ground in young marriages).[56] Male infidelity remained the number-one reason for divorce, while male alcohol abuse became relatively *more* important between 1958 and 1968. As of 1968, complainants could cite more than one ground for divorce. The 'especially common combinations' all included 'male violence' as a cause.[57] In rural areas, in particular, marital conflict arose most often from 'an understanding of male/female relations that is still far from socialist. Violence, abuse of alcohol, and the nearly complete burdening of women with housework are characteristic of marriage [in the countryside].'[58]

Over time, increased rhetoric about the need for husbands to help in the household and with childcare did influence the domestic division of labour. Women reported in the 1970s and 1980s that husbands helped with food shopping, household chores and childcare.[59] Husbands or male live-in partners became more interested in domestic life. A survey conducted in 1988 found that more than 60 per cent of both women and men wanted more time for home and family-related activities.[60] A quite vibrant private life emerged in East Germany as couples had more money to spend, enjoyed a two-day weekend and longer summer holiday, and bought a car (after a long, long wait) with the freedom of movement it allowed. Together, families watched television in the evenings, spent weekends at small dachas built with friends' help from hard-to-find construction materials, and in the summer went camping along the Baltic or even Black Sea.

Even as the family became more central to men's lives, women became more vocal about their deep dissatisfaction with gender relations in the GDR. Women writers were allowed to publish books critical of gender relations in the GDR, most notably *Guten Morgen Du Schöne* by Maxie Wander, that in nineteen monologues by women, conveyed deep anger about sexist attitudes and behaviour in private relationships. Directors produced popular films such as *The Legend of Paul and Paula* (1973) and *Solo Sunny* (1980) that depicted with honesty and sensitivity the resilience of single mothers/women and the joys and sorrows of their lives.

Parents and children

Families may have spent more leisure time together as a result of Honecker's social reforms, but during the week mothers, fathers, and even very young children spent many hours a day away from each other and out of the home. Given everyone's busy schedules, daily life ran smoothly only if parents and children followed well-planned routines. Studies of family life in East Berlin showed that it was conventionally gendered, but had unconventional generational relationships at least by Western standards of family relations. The mother prepared what the children needed for the day, made dinner, supervised homework, and tucked them in after they watched East German television's popular sign-off programme, 'The Sandman'. After both parents left for work (with infants, toddlers or kindergartners in tow), school-age children got up, made breakfast, and headed off for school on their own. Both mothers and fathers believed that this routine taught their children necessary responsibility and independence. With long hours spent outside the home and well-established routines inside the home, children's lives were highly regulated. Yet, they also enjoyed free space and time, as long as they got to school and came home on time.[61] Moreover, if their mornings ran unconventionally, parent/child relations in the evenings corresponded to patterns in the West. And generational cooperation in running the household also contributed to strong family bonds.

East German families did not all function, of course, like well-run, happy teams. Parent-child relations could be fraught due to paternal abuse, disorganised households, controlling parents, uninvolved parents or rigid parents. Former East Germans have recently published family memoirs and autobiographical novels that tell moving stories about distant, difficult or deeply fissured relationships between parents and children in the GDR. The authors of these books were very often the children or grandchildren of dedicated Communists. These parents, especially fathers, rejected children, especially sons, who privately criticised the GDR or, worse, spoke out publicly or, worst of all, refused to serve in the military or applied to leave the GDR. The books portray a private world of denial and secrets in which parents repressed both their political disappointment with socialism and their emotional tensions with family members and seemed to care less about their children as individuals than as models of socialist convention. They also suggest that these comfortably well-off families of Communist functionaries, living in suburban homes, functioned more like isolated atoms than cells within a social web. The authors' need to come to terms with life inside these monads confirms the emotional power of family bonds in the GDR.[62]

Heterosexuality

Many East (and West) Germans experienced (or at least remember) the immediate post-war years as a time of scarcity, loss, and existential anxiety, but also as years of freedom and experimentation, including in their sexual lives. Many men and women had to find or wanted to find a new partner or they simply desired a fling for pleasure and affection in the midst of so much misery. The loosening of sexual mores began, Dagmar Herzog argues, during the Third Reich, a consequence of war conditions and a rejection of National Socialist discourse about the body. In East Germany, the post-war relaxation no doubt left traces of change in sexual behaviour in the 1950s, but did not cause a radical shift. The SED did not stoke post-war anxieties about sexual disorder as did West German conservative Christian politicians, but it did discourage sexual experimentation.[63] In the 1950s, the press and Ministry of Justice used accusations of homosexuality, promiscuity and prostitution to tar even mildly defiant youths who donned Western jeans and T-shirts and danced to rock music.[64] And the police tried, without great success, to repress a revived nudist culture that had deep roots in pre-war Germany.[65]

Divorce court proceedings provide some information on ordinary people's sex lives. Judges took the date of 'last marital intercourse' as the main marker of irreconcilable difference between spouses. Husbands who wanted a divorce often claimed their wife had refused sex for years. They may have exaggerated, but their wives did not specifically deny such claims, suggesting that many middle-aged women led unsatisfying sex lives.[66] Among younger women, fear of pregnancy thwarted desire. According to physicians, some women expressed resentment of male partners who were 'only out to satisfy themselves'.[67] East German adults were often ill informed about the physiology of sex and contraception.

Sex education became part of the secondary school curriculum only in 1959. Parents did not routinely explain the 'facts of life' to their children. Sex was a taboo subject in many proletarian households, although educated mothers often enlightened a daughter if they found out she was sexually active.[68] In the 1950s, a small number of 'marriage and sexual counselling centres' operated in a few cities. Their few clients were mainly women who rarely asked 'questions about difficulties in marital intercourse and about conjugal life or [made] requests for sexual advice'.

Extramarital sex was not infrequent. Male infidelity had long been and remained the primary ground for divorce. In the early 1950s, people believed that male adultery was more widespread than before the war due to the 'surplus of women'.[69] Although less common than male infidelity, adultery by the wife was one of the top five grounds for divorce. Prenuptial sex was even more widespread. Statistics were not gathered until the 1960s, but interviews with women who married in the 1950s suggest that many brides were pregnant. Judging by the matter-of-fact way interviewees mention this fact, women did not feel great moral misgivings about sleeping with a 'serious' companion. An eighteen-year-old worker from a village, for example, met her first boyfriend shortly after she left home to work for the railway. They had sex soon after meeting and got married when she found out she was pregnant.[70]

In 1956, the GDR published its first sexual advice book for older adolescents/young adults: *The Question of Sex. A Book for Young People*. A year later East Germans could purchase an advice book for married couples, *The New Marriage Book*. Dr Rudolf Neubert, the author of both books, explained that couples could learn to have sex that would not result in pregnancy and which both partners could enjoy. The marriage book emphasised that sex was for pleasure, not just procreation. A couple in a loving and long-term (heterosexual) relationship, he assured readers, could and should indulge sexual desires in any way wanted by both partners. Women, he explained, were as capable of arousal as men, but might require more time and varied techniques to reach 'satisfaction'. Sexual skill was learned, not inborn, he insisted, although he did not provide instructions.[71] Neubert propagated sexual enlightenment more explicitly than any other public voice in the 1950s. His message reached a wide audience, for the marriage book was instantly popular; its twenty-first edition appeared in 1976.

Whether encouraged by Neubert's books or by a rising sense of entitlement, employed and educated women adopted a higher standard of sexual gratification and knowledge in the 1960s. In petitions that requested permission for an abortion, educated letter-writers assumed that they deserved a sexually satisfying life.[72] Data on the causes of marital discontent tell a similar story. From information collected by the Ministry of Justice, one sees that 'sexual grounds' doubled as a cause of divorce between 1958 and 1968. Female adultery as a ground also increased relative to male infidelity. In 1971, the Ministry of Health collected information on who visited the marriage and sexual counselling centres, and why. Sixty to eighty per cent of clients were women, most between twenty-five and forty years old. From 1964 to 1969, four main motivations sent people to the counselling centres in East Berlin: 23 per cent asked for contraception or an abortion; 23 per cent came about marital violence or alcoholism; 22 per cent wanted to talk about their own or their spouse's adultery; and 19 per cent raised sexual matters such as 'frigidity, impotence, and sexual disorder'.

Women's rising belief that they both wanted and deserved good sex was certainly related to the universal availability of the Pill after 1972. They did not experience the Pill as purely liberating, not only because of its physical side effects, but also because of men's assumption that every woman would now instantly jump into bed with them. Still, the decline in fear about pregnancy transformed the experience of sexual intercourse for many women.[73] Women's interest in sex was also fostered by the appearance of books on sexual enlightenment written by sexologists who were much more explicit about how to reach sexual fulfilment than Neubert's marriage book. In the Honecker era, East Germany became known for such books and for a thorough and ubiquitous programme of sexual education at the secondary school level. Physicians and psychologists offered sex therapies which aimed to enhance, especially, women's enjoyment of sex. Overall, women seemed to get what they wanted. In surveys from the 1980s, women reported high rates of orgasm and overall satisfaction with their sex lives.[74] In the same decade, the

GDR became famous for a nudist beach culture that presented itself as family-friendly and matter-of-fact, not titillating or erotic. Having given up the effort to repress *Freikörperkultur*, the state now celebrated nudism as a sign of socialism's healthy version of sexual liberation.[75] Not surprisingly, older East German heterosexuals look back nostalgically on the 1980s as a sort of sexual paradise.

Homosexuality

The East German criminal code retained the German law that in 1871 criminalised male homosexual activity (female homosexuality was never criminalised). The police enforced Paragraph 175. Meanwhile, the state directed anti-gay discourse at young East German men who adopted Western youth fashions and musical tastes. Outside the public eye, however, there were a few psychiatrists, including members of the SED, who argued for the decriminalisation of sodomy. In both 1952 and 1958, the Ministry of Justice seriously considered arguments to decriminalise sex between consenting adult men. Paragraph 175 was kept on the books, however, out of fear that, if decriminalised, homosexual activity would spread and endanger youth. In addition, some Communists believed that homosexuality was a 'vice of Western capitalism' and a 'typical manifestation of degeneration among the ruling classes'. They expected it to wither away in socialist society.[76] It did not, of course. After 1957, consenting adults were not prosecuted under Paragraph 175. As in the case of anti-abortion law, a commission was created in the 1960s to study legal reform. Its members accepted the medical opinion that homosexuality was not an illness, but a biologically based orientation. In 1968, the GDR decriminalised homosexual acts between consenting adult men. It set the age of consent, though, at eighteen years of age, while it was fourteen for heterosexual encounters.[77]

Legalisation did not mean that gay men (or lesbians) came out of the closet. Homophobia was widespread in the populace. The anti-gay atmosphere made it hard to find a partner. In the 1970s and 1980s, attitudes liberalised to some extent, but homosexuals still felt compelled to hide their sexuality or face discrimination from co-workers and managers. They worried about exposure by a Stasi informant. The Stasi was known to blackmail gay men in politically sensitive positions. A gay rights movement began to be organised clandestinely in the 1970s, but, unable to meet legally, soon dissipated. In the 1980s, the situation improved because the Protestant churches now enjoyed considerable freedom from state interference. An environmental movement cohered, for example, under the protection of the churches. Gay-rights working groups also took advantage of the sanctuary offered by the churches. Activists worked to have the state recognise and commemorate the pink triangle victims of National Socialism at the concentration camps Buchenwald, Ravensbrück and Sachsenhausen (located in East Germany). Their most dramatic act was to lay wreaths in commemoration of gay and lesbian victims at Buchenwald (1983) and Ravensbrück (1984). The police cracked down on these actions. In the 1980s, some gay advertisements were allowed in the press, a gay organisation was recognised and produced a newsletter, and several educational televisions shows addressed popular homophobia.[78]

Conclusion

In the 1950s, the SED neglected the family, its division of labour, and its needs, even as it also promoted measures that would modernise the family by equalising women's standing under family law, recognising the rights of single mothers and their children, and liberalising the terms of divorce. Rather than a family policy, the state followed a *Frauenpolitik* that promoted women's employment and pursued measures to raise fertility. It did so without seriously considering, much less addressing, the consequences of these combined policies on the family and, indeed, on each other. In the 1960s, confronted with these unexpected consequences, the SED became ever more aware of the family's significance as a social institution and introduced various piecemeal measures to ease women's double burden and make it easier for women to qualify for skilled occupations. The decision to carry out major social reforms to address the contradictions of women's policy came in the 1970s. Honecker's 'unity of economic and social policy' suggested that the SED now understood that the family mattered. It placed the family at the centre of its new social programmes and even used a domesticated legitimising rhetoric that portrayed the GDR as a 'home' and, thus, like a family. Yet the family that the SED now celebrated and even reified was the same one it had earlier neglected: a nuclear family based on imbalanced gender relations. It was certainly of great social significance that the GDR forged a family model in which an employed and trained wife/mother was the norm. Yet that family defied the Communist assumption that public change would force a transformation in private relationships. Instead, after having been changed by state policy, the nuclear family bent state policy towards the needs of the real-existing private relationships.

Notes

1. E. Heineman, 'The Hour of the Woman: Memories of Germany's "Crisis Years" and West German National Identity', *The American Historical Review* Vol. 101 (1996), pp. 354–95.
2. D. Harsch, *Revenge of the Domestic: Women, the Family, and Communism in the German Democratic Republic* (Princeton, 2007), pp. 22–7; *Statistisches Jahrbuch der Deutschen Demokratischen Republik* (1955), p. 22.
3. N. Naimark, *The Russians in Germany: A History of the Soviet Zone of Occupation, 1945–1949* (Cambridge, 1995), pp. 68–85, 75, 109, 91–3, 117 and 104–5; I. Schmidt-Harzbach, 'Eine Woche im April, Berlin 1945: Vergewaltigung als Massenschicksal', *Feministische Studien* Vol. 2 (1984).
4. Naimark, *The Russians in Germany*, pp. 123, 129 and 135. See also Harsch, *Revenge of the Domestic*, pp. 37–8; E. Heineman, *What Difference Does a Husband Make? Women and Marital Status in Nazi and Postwar Germany* (Berkeley, 1999), p. 127; Bundesarchiv Berlin (hereafter BArch), DQ1, 323, Bl. 128–37 Deutsche Zentralverwaltung für Volksbildung, Abt. Frauenausschüsse, Protokoll 3.9.46.
5. Statistisches Jahrbuch der Deutschen Demokratischen Republik (1955), p. 19; P. Seraphim, *Die Heimatvertriebenen in der Sowjetzone* (Berlin, 1954) pp. 15, 55 and 64.
6. K. Poutrus, 'Von den Massenvergewaltigungen zum Mutterschutzgesetz: Abtreibungspolitik und Abtreibungspraxis in Ostdeutschland, 1945–1950',

in R. Bessel and R. Jessen (eds), *Die Grenzen der Diktatur. Staat und Gesellschaft in der DDR* (Göttingen, 1996), pp. 174–5.
7 SAPMO-BArch, IV2\\17\\51, Bl.162, 1.2.47. Richtlinien für Eheberatungsstellen; Bl. 216, 19.5.47.
8 Naimark, *The Russians in Germany*, pp. 126–8; Poutrus, 'Von den Massenvergewaltigungen zum Mutterschutzgesetz', p. 175.
9 H. Trappe, *Emanzipation oder Zwang? Frauen in der DDR zwischen Beruf, Familie und Sozialpolitik* (Berlin, 1995), p. 103.
10 Heineman, *What Difference Does a Husband Make?*, p. 211.
11 Harsch, *Revenge of the Domestic*, pp. 33–40 and pp. 143–6.
12 I. Markovits, *Justice in Lüritz: Experiencing Socialist Law in East Germany* (Princeton, 2010).
13 P. Betts, *Within Walls: Private Life in the German Democratic Republic* (Oxford, 2010), p. 3. See also Harsch, *Revenge of the Domestic*, pp. 315–17.
14 *Statistisches Jahrbuch der DDR* (1966), p. 452.
15 H. Benjamin, 'Wer bestimmt in der Familie', *Neues Deutschland*, 1 February 1958.
16 Harsch, *Revenge of the Domestic*, pp. 184–7 and pp. 242–4.
17 Ibid., pp. 247–9.
18 Ibid., pp. 250–4.
19 SAPMO-BArch, DY34/5471, Entwurf, Thesen ... 7.1.67. S.7; DY30/IV B-2/17/731 Analyse ... Frauen in Industriebetrieben ... 30.7.70, S.6.
20 SAPMO-BArch, DY34/4298. Arbeitsgruppe Frauen, 14.1.66. Einschätzung ... S.2.
21 Harsch, *Revenge of the Domestic*, pp. 62 and 133; S. Major, 'Zur Geschichte der außerklinischen Geburtshilfe in der DDR'. Medical Dissertation: Humboldt University, Berlin (2014), pp. 21–5.
22 BArch, DQ1 2512, Richtlinien für die Tätigkeit der Schwangerenberatungsstellen 7.9.1953.
23 DQ1/5331, Bericht zum Ministerialratsbeschluss von 8.7.54, Gesundheitschutz für Mütter, 29 May 1957.
24 Harsch, *Revenge of the Domestic*, pp. 136 and 139–43; L. Falwell, *Modern German Midwifery, 1885–1960* (London, 2013), pp. 124–36; Major, 'Zur Geschichte der außerklinischen Geburtshilfe in der DDR', pp. 35–54.
25 Harsch, *Revenge of the Domestic*, pp. 143–51. Before 1945 (and after in West Germany), Paragraph 218 of the German criminal code criminalised abortion. During the years of the SBZ, there was both a de facto and de jure liberalisation of abortion regulation.

26 R. Neubert, *Das neue Ehebuch. Die Ehe als Aufgabe der Gegenwart und Zukunft* (Rudolstadt, 1957), pp. 98–9.
27 A. Leo and C. König, *Die 'Wunschkindpille'. Weibliche Erfahrung und Staatliche Geburtenpolitik in der DDR* (Göttingen, 2015); D. Harsch, 'Society, the State, and Abortion in East Germany, 1950–1972', *The American Historical Review* Vol. 102 (1997), pp. 54–84; Harsch, *Revenge of the Domestic*, pp. 264–73.
28 *Statistisches Jahrbuch der Deutschen Demokratischen Republik* (1973), p. 35.
29 Harsch, *Revenge of the Domestic*, pp. 135–7.
30 Trappe, *Emanzipation oder Zwang?*, p. 127.
31 DQ1/2963, DFD (Frau & Staat), Einschätzung des Standes der Realisierung der vom Bundesvorstand getroffenen Vereinbarungen mit dem Ministerium für Gesundheitswesen, 31 Oct. 1960, p. 4.
32 DY 34/9820, Arbeitsökonomie und industriesoziologische Aspekte der Teilzeitarbeit, 1970; DY 34/11873, Analyse über die Teilbeschäftigung in VEB Schuhkombinat Banner des Friedens, [1970]; G. Obertreis, *Familienpolitik in der DDR 1945–1980* (Opladen, 1985), pp. 157 and 205.
33 DY 34, 39/94/5571, Protokoll über die Lage der werktätigen Frauen im Bezirk Halle der IG Chemie, 18 Oct. 1956; A 1544, RdB Halle (Arbeit), Arbeitskreis der Arbeitskraftsreserven (Chemieprogramm), 20 Apr. 1959, pp. 28–9.
34 Harsch, *Revenge of the Domestic*, p. 275.
35 H. Ulbricht et al., *Probleme der Frauenarbeit* (East Berlin, 1963), p. 28.
36 SAPMO-BArch, DY 31/Folder 338, DFD (Frau & Staat), Auswertung der Handelskonferenz der Zentralkomitee der SED, [1960?], pp. 5–6; K. Pence, 'Schaufenster des sozialistischen Konsums: Texte der ostdeutschen "consumer culture"', in A. Lüdtke and P. Becker (eds), *Akten, Eingaben, Schaufenster: Die DDR und ihre Texte* (Berlin, 1997), p. 114.
37 Harsch, *Revenge of the Domestic*, p. 183.
38 DY 34/9137, Studie zur Begründung des langfristigen Planes der Frauenarbeit im Kombinat, 25 June 1970, p. 17.
39 A. Ruble, '"Equal but not the same": The Struggle for "Gleichberechtigung" and the Reform of Marriage and Family Law in East and West Germany, 1945–1968'. Dissertation University of North Carolina (2017).
40 Markovits, *Justice in Lüritz*, pp. 77–8.
41 D. Harsch, 'Sex, Divorce, and Women's Waged Work: Private Lives and State Policy in the Early German Democratic Republic', in J. Massino and S. Penn

(eds), *Gender and Everyday Life under State Socialism in East and Central Europe* (London, 2010), pp. 97–114.

42 Brandenburgisches Landeshauptarchiv (BLHA), Rep. 601, Bezirkstag und Rat des Bezirks Frankfurt/Oder. Akte: 8294. Ehescheidung; Oberstes Gericht der DDR. Präsidium. 9.9.70. Ursachen und Tendenzen der Ehescheidungen ... S. 4.

43 Harsch, *Revenge of the Domestic*, pp. 232–4 and pp. 297–9.

44 Ibid., pp. 284–6 and p. 293; A. Port, 'Love, Lust, and Lies under Communism: Family Values and Adulterous Liaisons in the German Democratic Republic,' *Central European History* Vol. 44 (2011), pp. 478–505.

45 Harsch, *Revenge of the Domestic*, pp. 286–91 and pp. 295–6.

46 Ibid., p. 240.

47 Markovits, *Justice in Lüritz*, pp. 79–80.

48 B. Bouvier, *Die DDR – ein Sozialstaat? Sozialpolitik in der Ära Honecker* (Bonn, 2002), pp. 71 and 180; G. Helwig, 'Frauen im SED-Staat', in Deutscher Bundestag (ed.), *Materielen der Enquete-Kommission 'Aufarbeitung von Geschichte und Folgen der SED-Diktatur in Deutschland'. Bd. III/2. Rolle und Bedeutung der Ideologie, integrativer Faktoren und disziplinierender Praktiken in Staat und Gesellschaft der DDR* (Frankfurt am Main, 1995), pp. 1265 and 1238; Harsch, *Revenge of the Domestic*, pp. 304–5.

49 Harsch, 'Society, the State, and Abortion'; Harsch, *Revenge of the Domestic*, pp. 306–7.

50 M. Dennis, 'The East Germany Family: Change and Continuity,' in C. Flockton and E. Kolinsky (eds.), *Recasting East Germany: Social Transformation After the GDR* (New York, 1999), pp. 83–100; Harsch, *Revenge of the Domestic*, p. 313.

51 See descriptions of marriages in: BArch, DQ1/5145 (Herr) H. Heduschka, Cottbus an das MfG, 23.4.54; Dr. Neumann an Heduschka, 4.5.54; Dr. Wenzke an das MfG, 6.7.54; 'Wir wollen darüber offen sprechen,' *Die Frau von heute*, 2 January, 13 February, 6 March 1953; interview by author with Frau CT, Bernau, 27 July 1998.

52 Leipziger Stadtsarchiv, IV A-2/17/474. Abteilung Landwirtschaft. Anmerkungen ... Landwirtschaft, 10.1.63; BArch-Berlin, DO4/360, Bl. 241 Stunde der Frau Marktkirche.

53 SAPMO-BArch, DY34/4290. Bl. 134, Zusammenarbeit mit dem Ministerium der Justiz, 1966/67.

54 SAPMO-BArch, DY34/4298. Arbeitsgruppe Frauen, 14.1.66. Einschätzung ...; DY 30/IV 2/17/71, Bericht über den Einsatz Karl-Marx-Stadt vom

28.8.-7.9.62, fo. 117; BArch, DP1/VA 1445, vol. 2, Information über den Verlauf der öffentlichen Diskussionen zum Entwurf des FGB, 25 July 1965, fo. 23; Bericht über die Diskussion zum Entwurf FGB, 6 Oct. 1965, fo. 56.
55 DY 34/11873, Einschätzung einiger Ursachen für den zunehmenden Übergang der Frauen von der Voll- zur Teilbeschäftigung ... (Zeitraum 1968 bis 1969), pp. 1–2; DY 30/IV 2/2.042/20, Entwicklung der Beschäftigung der Frauen in der Produktion, 24 Nov. 1971, fos. 245, 247.
56 Erfahrungen aus einem Gerichtspraktikum in Familiensachen, *Neue Justiz* 1961, pp. 779–80.
57 BLHA, Rep. 601, Akte: 8294. Ehescheidung ... 9.9.70. Also see J. Freeland, 'Behind Closed Doors: Domestic Violence, Citizenship and State-Making in Divided Berlin, 1969–1990'. Dissertation, Carleton University (2016).
58 DY34/4290. Bl. 134, Zusammenarbeit mit dem Ministerium der Justiz, 1966/67. Buro Margot Müller, Untersuchung..., 9, 16, 23–5; Heinrich, Goeldner, and Schilde, Rechtsprechung, *Neue Justiz* 1961, 778.
59 Interview by author with Frau CT, Bernau, 27 July 1998.
60 W. Thaa et al., *Gesellschaftliche Differenzierung und Legitimitätsverfall des DDR-Sozialismus* (Tübingen, 1992), pp. 166–8 and pp. 172–7.
61 D. Kirchhöfer, 'Alltägliche Lebensführungen von Kindern in der DDR – Arrangements zwischen Traditionalität und Modernisierung', in E. Badstübner (ed.), *Befremdlich anders. Leben in der DDR* (Berlin, 2000), pp. 271–93.
62 See, e.g., M. Brasch, *Ab jetzt ist Ruhe. Roman meiner fabelhaften Familie* (Frankfurt am Main, 2012); E. Ruge, *In Zeiten des abnehmenden Lichts. Roman einer Familie* (Reinbek, 2011); B. Honigmann, *Eine Liebe aus nichts* (Reinbek, 1991); B. Honigmann, *Ein Kapitel aus meinem Leben* (Munich, 2004); M. Maron, *Pawels Briefe* (Frankfurt am Main, 1999).
63 D. Herzog, *Sex after Fascism: Memory and Morality in Twentieth-Century Germany* (Princeton, 2005).
64 M. Fenemore, *Sex, Thugs, and Rock 'N' Roll: Teenage Rebels in Cold-War East Germany* (New York, 2007), pp. 138–48.
65 J. McLellan, *Love in the Time of Communism: Intimacy and Sexuality in the GDR* (Cambridge, 2011), pp. 4–15 and pp. 33–6.
66 See cases in *Neue Justiz* (NJ), 1954: 247; 1956: 284, 514, 543, 736–7; 1958, 139; 1959: 714, 716; BArch, DP1/VA, Akte 1362, Bl.3, 15.12.55, R.W. an MfJ; Bl.5, Abschrift of Urteil; Bl.39, SR an JM der DDR, 17.12.55.
67 Neubert, *Das neue Ehebuch*.
68 Leo and König, *Die 'Wunschkindpille'*, pp. 63, 103 and 135.

69 Neubert, *Das neue Ehebuch*, pp. 184–6.
70 Interview with Frau RB, June 28, 1996 (conducted by author and Martina Dietrich). Also see interviews in Leo and König, *Die 'Wunschkindpille'*, pp. 103 and 135.
71 Neubert, *Das neue Ehebuch*, pp. 142–56; R. Neubert, *Die Geschlechterfrage. Ein Buch für junge Menschen* (Rudolstadt, 1956), pp. 93–9.
72 Harsch, *Revenge of the Domestic*, p. 297.
73 Leo and König, *Die 'Wunschkindpille'*, pp. 153 and 224–7.
74 Herzog, *Sex after Fascism*, pp. 204 and 214.
75 McLellan, *Love in the Time of Communism*, pp. 4–15, 205–13 and 33–6. Herzog, *Sex after Fascism*, pp. 206–14.
76 McLellan, *Love in the Time of Communism*, p. 115; E. Huneke, 'Morality, Law, and the Socialist Sexual Self in the German Democratic Republic, 1945–1972'. Dissertation University of Michigan (2013), pp. 144, 145 and 148; J. Evans, 'Homosexuality and the Politics of Masculinity in East Germany,' in K. Hagemann and S. Michel (eds), *Gender and the Long Postwar: The United States and the Two Germanys, 1945–1989* (Baltimore, 2014), pp. 344 and 346.
77 Evans, 'Homosexuality and the Politics of Masculinity in East Germany', p. 342; McLellan, *Love in the Time of Communism*, p. 117.
78 Evans, 'Homosexuality and the Politics of Masculinity in East Germany', pp. 349 and 351; McLellan, *Love in the Time of Communism*, pp. 122–3, and 132–5.

7

German family policy since reunification

Sigrid Leitner

Introduction

Post-reunification Germany has seen a fundamental change in family policy, which has left the post-war male breadwinner model of West Germany behind and has developed a new understanding of shared parenthood and continuous labour market participation of both parents. This development arose first with the expansion of public childcare for children aged three to six years from the mid-1990s, and later on also for children under three years of age. Since 2013, a legal right has existed for every child over one year old to claim a childcare place. As a result, the take-up of childcare has largely increased in West Germany and is still widespread in East Germany. Improved childcare has enabled parents (particularly mothers) to take up work quickly after the birth of a child and to work longer hours. Thus, the political goal of enhancing mothers' employment rate, especially in West Germany has been complemented with the intention of increasing mothers' weekly working hours. In 2007, the introduction of an earnings-related parental leave benefit set further incentives for an early re-entry into the labour market after the first birthday of the child. Moreover, the parental leave reform reserved two months of paid leave exclusively for fathers and thus has promoted gender equality in parenting – or at least has enhanced the participation of fathers in childcare.

This *Leitbildwandel* (change of normative framework) reflects not only changed attitudes within the younger generations, but also different traditions between East and West Germany regarding the roles and responsibilities of mothers and fathers. The traditional male breadwinner model has been substituted increasingly by a one-and-a-half-earner model as well as by a two-full-time-earner model. However, the picture remains mixed and there are still policies in place, which support a traditional division of labour within the family, for example, the *Ehegattensplitting* (a tax benefit for married couples with only one earner or a low-earning second earner). The new family policy is also linked to the European Union employment strategy, which aims at mobilising human resources in order to increase economic growth. As a result, German labour market policy has become very rigid in terms of enforcing labour market participation. Everybody who is able to work should be in work or at least plausibly prove that he/she is actively trying to find work. This applies also to parents, at the latest when their youngest child is older than three years and to caring relatives of dependent adults. Thus, the political aim to increase (especially female) employment is framed primarily by economic reasoning. This also holds true for the new reconciliation policies for caring relatives, which aim at prolonging homecare settings for as long as possible in order to save costs. Long standing feminist demands for gender equality in the labour market and within the family have only been secondary drivers of the policy changes. Nevertheless, gender equality arguments have been prominent at least in the political discourse around childcare.

In addition to the description of policy change and the discussion of its main drivers, this chapter also analyses empirical data on the development of parental employment, the expansion of childcare, the take-up of parental leave by fathers and the provision of professional care services in order to give the full picture of contemporary family life in Germany. Moreover, the shortfalls of the new family policy are pointed out. On the one hand, parental and care leave regulations reproduce social inequalities and the rigid demand for labour market participation is coerced most strongly on low income parents. Thus, the choices of parents and carers about their labour market participation and the sharing of (child) care depend highly on their socio-economic status. High income and medium income families do have choices, while low-income families do not. On the other hand, the current feminist debate on care criticises the new adult worker framework of family policy for neglecting care responsibilities. While the focus is on general labour market participation, the question of how care for children and dependent adults should be best organised is not answered properly by the current family policy, especially when it comes to old age care. A more balanced policy is required, and recent proposals from the federal Ministry of Family Affairs demand 'more time for families' addressing also the responsibility of enterprises. The implications of these latest developments for the situation of families are outlined in this chapter.

The expansion of public childcare

Already before reunification, the employment rates of West German mothers had been rising. In 1991, 48 per cent of West German and 83 per cent of East German mothers with a child aged three to six years were employed.[1] Thus, the demands for public childcare became more prominent, especially in West Germany, where public childcare was less well developed. Interestingly, reunification brought with it a new policy driver: GDR and FRG laws on abortion had to be harmonised. While the GDR had a more liberal regulation, which allowed abortions until the twelfth week of pregnancy, abortion law in the FRG was more restrictive by requiring counselling and special indications for an abortion. During the reunification process, FRG abortion law was extended to Eastern Germany. Due to political protests from feminists who rather wanted the more liberal GDR regulation to become the reunification standard, compensation was found in the introduction of the right to a childcare place for children aged three to six years. Thus, while the autonomy of women was (kept) reduced by restricting their right to abortion, (West German) women's possibilities for labour market participation in spite of motherhood were increased by a right to childcare.[2] The political deal did not hold any benefits for East German women since they got the restrictive abortion law while the coverage of childcare was already at high levels.

Due to financial reasons, the right to a kindergarten place was delayed until 1996 and then only gradually introduced until 1999.[3] Nevertheless, the percentage of children aged three to six years attending a kindergarten increased from 77 per cent in 1994 to 90 per cent in 1998.[4] In 2016, the quota was 95 per cent with only half of all places providing full-time care (more than 35 hours per week).[5] Thirty-eight per cent of the places provided care for twenty-five to thirty-five hours per week and 13 per cent provided care for up to twenty-five hours per week. The present coverage meets the expectations of parents quite well, which also reflects a high percentage of (voluntary) part-time employment of mothers.[6] A modernised male breadwinner model has been enabled by the expansion of kindergarten places with an employment rate of 68 per cent for women in West Germany and 73 per cent in East Germany. However, 52 per cent of parents wish for more flexible opening hours of kindergartens, i.e. earlier than 8 am or later than 5 pm.[7]

Despite the right to a kindergarten place, German family policy still referred to a strong male breadwinner model for families with children less than three years of age. Up to the turn of the century, a long and low paid parental leave, as well as a lack of childcare for young children in West Germany, characterised the institutional framing. In 2002, a new public discourse on how to raise the birth rate entered family policy. Due to the racist, pronatalist nature of family policy during the Nazi regime, pronatalist policies were a long-standing taboo after the Second World War. But now, the Ministry of Family Affairs established a positive connection between a high fertility rate, female employment and reconciliation policies. The expansion of early education and care was seen as fundamental for an increase of the employment rate of mothers as well as for an increase of the fertility rate. An early return of mothers to the labour market resembled a short-term strategy to avoid labour shortage. A high fertility rate was needed in the long run to guarantee the quantitative reproduction of the future labour force, hence to secure future economic growth.[8]

This new economic paradigm first resulted in a law that obliged the municipalities to expand childcare for children less than three years old. The aim was a national coverage rate of 20 per cent until 2010, which implied 230,000 new places in West Germany. Due to the historical legacy of the GDR, the situation in East and West Germany was completely different. In 1989, 56 per cent of children under the age of three were in

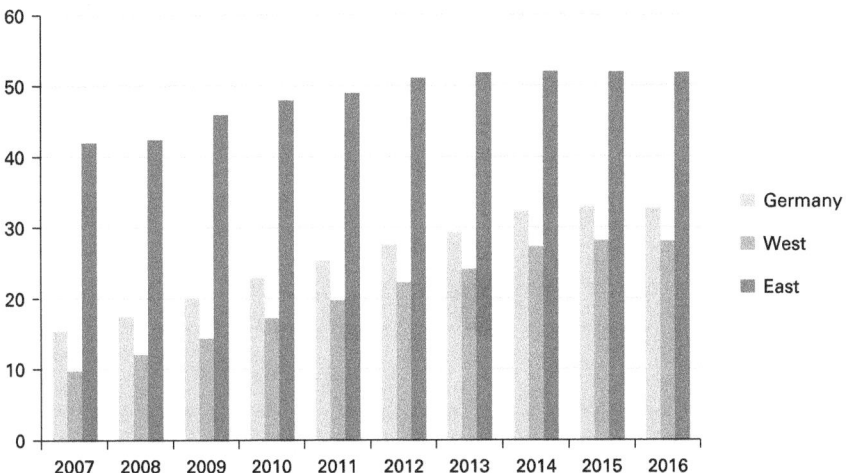

Figure 7.1 The expansion of childcare for children under three (coverage rate). Source: http://www.sozialpolitik-aktuell.de/tl_files/sozialpolitik-aktuell/_Politikfelder/Familienpolitik/Datensammlung/PDF-Dateien/abbVII28.pdf, 14 November 2017.

institutional childcare in East Germany. The coverage decreased after reunification, but was still at 36 per cent in 1998 (West Germany: 3 per cent).[9] Since the municipalities did not comply sufficiently, a legal right to a childcare place starting from the first birthday of the child was introduced and has been implemented since 2013. This measure finally boosted the coverage rate (see Figure 7.1). In 2016, one-third of all children less than three years had a childcare place (West: 28 per cent, East: 52 per cent). However, the supply still did not meet the demand: 43 per cent of parents in the West and 59 per cent of parents in the East need childcare for young children.[10]

The reform of childcare leave regulations

Already in 1979, a paid maternal leave of six months with a capped earnings-related benefit was introduced by the coalition government of the Social Democrats and the Liberals (FDP) in order to protect working women's health and well-being.[11] Thus, fathers and non-employed mothers were consequently excluded from the regulation. Paid parental leave was only introduced in 1986. Since the employment rate of women was increasing and the problem of reconciling work and family life affected not only single mothers, but also a rising number of married women, the then incumbent and dominant Christian Democrats acknowledged the necessity of childcare leave.[12] At the same time, Christian Democratic ideals of 'good' childcare shaped the design of the new parental leave and benefit. In order to support the stability of families and the well-being of young children, one of the parents – preferably the mother – should be entitled to opt out of employment fairly long-term.[13]

The so-called *Erziehungsgeld* (parental benefit) was available up to the second birthday of the child for all parents: mothers or fathers, employed or unemployed. The payment was a low flat-rate benefit of 300€ per month which did not attract average fathers to take parental leave anyway. It rather called for a male breadwinner in order to support the mother on leave financially. The more so, because the *Erziehungsurlaub* (parental leave period) could last until the third birthday of the child, thus only the first two years of the leave were paid for. These regulations supported a traditional family model with a non-employed wife and stay-at-home mother, as well as a modernised breadwinner model involving a three-phase model of (1) female employment before giving birth, (2) parental leave and (3) (part-time) return to the labour market when the child started to attend the kindergarten. As pointed out above, this was complemented by a very low level of childcare places for children aged less than three years and the introduction of the right to a (half-day) childcare place for children aged three to six years in the second half of the 1990s.[14]

In line with the economic arguments that led to the right to a childcare place from the first birthday of the child, the parental benefit was reformed fundamentally by the grand coalition in 2007. The Social Democrats went through a process of 'political learning' and were definitely saying farewell to the sequential model of female life course. The negative labour market effects of the rather long spells of parental leave induced the Social Democrats to change their position towards the promotion of continuous working careers and the simultaneity of work and childcare.[15] The motives of the Christian Democrats to shift away from the (modified) traditional breadwinner model need further explanation. Most importantly, the Christian Democratic Party no longer holds a concerted normative position with regard to gender roles and family models. Two competing groups can be distinguished, struggling for power along an intra-party cleavage: on the one hand, the right-wing 'Fundamentalists', who stick to the traditional breadwinner norm and the sequential model of the female life course, and on the other hand, the moderate 'Realos', who promote a modernised family model in which men and women continuously participate in the labour market and children are taken care of outside the family early on.[16] The latter describe a paradigmatic middle-ground position and can be linked to the new discourse on the economics of childcare policy initiated by the Social Democrats. The Ministry of Family Affairs strategically used this economic reasoning to push forward the above-described reforms.[17] This discursive strategy also worked in lessening the ideological differences within the Christian Democrats about women's gender role.[18] Thus, the economic re-framing of childcare policy makes the reforms appear reasonable and forward-looking, the more so since the discursive hegemony was also brought forward by international organisations (see below).[19]

The new benefit called *Elterngeld* replaces 67 per cent of the parent's previous income (with an upper limit of 1,800€ and a minimum amount of 300€). The benefit is still universally available to all parents, including also formerly non-employed parents who are entitled to the minimum benefit. The benefit span has been shortened from two years to one year and can be prolonged for another two months if these are taken by the other parent (generally the father). Furthermore, part-time employment up to thirty hours per week can be combined with part-time *Elterngeld*, and both parents are allowed to take part-time leave simultaneously. It can be expected that the incentive of a reasonable replacement rate and the non-transferable entitlement will increase fathers' take-up of parental leave. At the same time, mothers might react to the shortened paid leave period with an early re-entry into the labour market, although a long unpaid leave period until the third birthday of the child is still possible – especially for mothers with a high earning breadwinner. Together with the expansion of childcare for children under three, the new parental benefit might initiate the farewell from the male breadwinner model.

Goodbye male breadwinner?

The employment rate of mothers has risen considerably since the introduction of the *Elterngeld*, especially among mothers with children between one and three years old. Whereas in 2006, only 33 per cent of mothers with a child between one and two years were employed, the percentage rose to 41 per cent in 2012. And while 42 per cent of mothers with a child between two and three years were employed in 2006, the percentage climbed to 54 per cent in 2012. Thus, the new reconciliation policy seems to support the early re-entry into the labour market for mothers. The increase is most of all an increase of mothers' part-time work (fifteen to thirty-two hours per week), whereas a stable 10 per cent work less than fifteen hours per week and only 11–15 per cent work full-time. However, it is also interesting to note that the employment rate of mothers with a child under one year has decreased from 17 per cent in 2006 to 10 per cent in 2012.[20] This shows that the new earnings-related benefit enables more mothers to stay at home during the first year of the child than the old flat-rate benefit. When we consider fathers' employment, it seems to be steadily above 80 per cent, regardless of the age of the child, and only 6 per cent of fathers work part-time.[21] Data show that with regard to all families with a child less than three years, only one parent (mostly the father) is employed in 59 per cent of all cases. In 33 per cent of these families, both parents work, but only in 14 per cent of all cases do parents share work and care equally. Thus, the male-breadwinner model is still dominant in families with young children although we also see change.

The leave take-up rate of fathers has increased steadily since the introduction of the new parental leave regulation in 2007. Before the reform, less than 5 per cent of parents on paid parental leave were fathers. Shortly afterwards, 20 per cent of fathers with a child born in 2008 were on paid parental leave, and even 32 per cent of fathers with a child born in 2013 were on paid parental leave. Of these fathers on leave, 79 per cent took up to two months of leave; the average duration of fathers' paid leave is 2.8 months. In comparison, 96 per cent of all mothers with a child born in 2013 were on paid parental leave. Most mothers on leave (92 per cent) took ten to twelve months; on average mothers were on paid leave for 11.6 months. Thus, the non-transferable right of two months paid leave for 'the other partner' was mostly used by fathers. The average benefit for fathers amounted to 1,143€ per month; the average benefit for mothers was 601€ per month.[22] This mirrors the wage differences between the sexes before the birth of the child, as well as higher rates of female non-employment before parenthood. It also indicates that most mothers on leave cannot live independently from other sources of financial support, mostly the income of a breadwinner, but for lone mothers, welfare benefits play an important role. Fathers with higher education and fathers with a female partner who has been employed before giving birth are more likely to take parental leave. Fathers who do not take parental leave mostly do so because of financial reasons (48 per cent) or due to employment-related restrictions (35 per cent). Only 20 per cent argue that childcare is a mother's task.[23] Thus, the financial needs of young families are not met by the 67 per cent replacement rate, which is an important factor for fathers' decision not to take parental leave, but the situation at the workplace, that is the lack of a family-friendly working culture, also influences the (low) take-up rate of fathers. Thirty-eight per cent of fathers on leave take their leave simultaneously with the mother of the child.[24] Thus, these fathers act as secondary caregivers only. Fathers with longer spans of parental leave share care work more equally with their female partners even after the leave ends and they rate their relationship to the child as more intense in the long run.[25]

The latest development in German reconciliation policy was the introduction of the *Elterngeld Plus* in 2015. The new regulation gives additional options to parents who combine part-time employment (up to a maximum of thirty hours per week) and part-time paid parental leave. Each month in part-time prolongs the duration of part-time paid parental leave. The benefit of part-time parental leave is reduced according to the income from part-time work (for example, half of the benefit if working half-time), but for each month on part-time leave another month of part-time leave is granted. Thus, the span of the paid parental leave period can be extended up to a maximum of twenty-four months (plus four months for the other parent). If both parents are on part-time leave simultaneously for a minimum of four months, another four months of paid part-time leave are granted to the couple. The *Elterngeld Plus* clearly fosters shared parenthood and the employment of both parents in the frame of a part-time earner/part-time carer model. First empirical data show that about 17 per cent of parents opted for the *Elterngeld Plus* in 2016.[26]

The persistence of the male breadwinner model

Although the recent reform policies set incentives for alternatives to the traditional breadwinner model, other policies are still in place that support the old model. First of all, non-employed wives are covered in health insurance and long-term care insurance without paying contributions if their husband is gainfully employed and contributing to the social security system. This way, the costs for medical treatment and long-term care of non-employed wives are carried by the social security system instead of the family. The male earner is unburdened from financial responsibility and the breadwinner model gets subsidised. Secondly, married couples can receive tax benefits if they follow a traditional division of labour. The incomes of the couple are added together and then the sum is divided by two as if each of the partners earned the same income, for example, if the husband has a high income, this income is taxed as if it was two small incomes. Within the frame of a progressive tax system the so-called *Ehegattensplitting* (tax benefit for married couples) leads to tax savings for couples with very unequal partner incomes. Married couples with two earners benefit less than couples with only one earner. Couples who are not married do not benefit at all.[27] Last but not least, widow pensions also support the idea of the male breadwinner model. They substitute the breadwinner's income after his death. Since 1986, a widower pension has existed also, which at least allows for the idea of female breadwinners, but in most cases the widower pension is substituted by the own income of the widower, whereas the widow pension is crucial for women's self-sufficiency in old age.[28]

These instruments of family policy are legitimised by article 6 of the German constitution that states: 'Marriage and family are especially protected by the state.'[29] During the post-war period, marriage and family constituted two sides of the same coin. Thus, non-married couples with children are not supported by the social policy instruments described above, whereas married couples without children are supported by the system. In addition, married couples with an equal division of labour are not supported, which stands in contrast to the new ideals of shared parenthood. With rising divorce rates, lone parent families and patchwork families challenge the norm of the married couple family. But up to now, all attempts (from the political left) to reduce the benefits of the *Ehegattensplitting* have failed. The 'sacred cow' of support for married couples seems to be too popular.

In 2001, the introduction of registered partnerships for homosexual couples at least expanded the support for married heterosexual couples step by step to registered same-sex couples. First, only the coverage of non-employed partners in health and long-term care insurance was granted; later on, same-sex couples were also entitled to widow and widower pensions and were allowed to benefit from the *Ehegattensplitting*.[30] This equal treatment of registered same-sex couples with married couples was initiated by the Social Democrats and the Green Party, who built a coalition government from 1998 to 2005. The Christian Union only gradually gave up resistance to this reform. However, since October 2017, same-sex couples have been allowed to marry. The bill was passed with the votes of the Social Democrats, the left-wing party (Die Linken), the Green Party and seventy-five votes from the CDU/CSU. A total of 226 Members of Parliament from the CDU/CSU rejected the bill.[31] The benefits of the married couple breadwinner model were thus extended to registered same-sex couples with a division of employment and care between the partners. All in all, the breadwinner model is still popular. A population survey of men and women aged twenty-four to forty-three years asked for the ideal working time for parents of young children. It appeared that West German women prefer mostly part-time work between

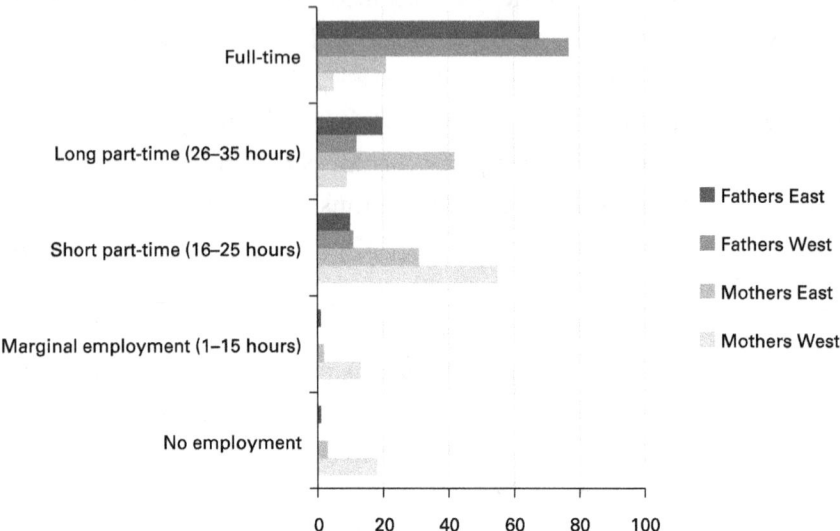

Figure 7.2 Attitudes towards the ideal weekly working times of parents with a child aged two years. Source: Bujard, Martin (2017): Wie passt das zusammen? Familienbilder junger Menschen und Parteipositionen zur Familienpolitik, in: *Aus Politik und Zeitgeschichte* 67 (30–1), 12.

sixteen and twenty-five hours per week. Only 5 per cent opt for a full-time job and 18 per cent agree to non-employment (see Figure 7.2). In contrast, East German women focus on part-time work between twenty-six and thirty-five hours per week. Twenty-one per cent prefer full-time work and only 3 per cent opt for non-employment. With regard to fathers, 77 per cent of West German and 68 per cent of East German men preferred full-time employment. Only 23 per cent in the West and 30 per cent in the East opted for part-time work.

The population survey shows on the one hand that only a minority of the younger generation in Germany opts for the male breadwinner model. On the other hand, a minority also prefers the equal sharing of work and childcare between the sexes. The vast majority favours a flexible dual earner model with the mother working part-time when the child is very young and expanding working time to long part-time or full-time when the child becomes older. Although most fathers avoid part-time work due to lower earnings and restricted career prospects, they want to be more active fathers, as is also intended by the new *Elterngeld*. However, instead of cutting their working time, they reduce their time for leisure and sport to enable activities as fathers.[32]

In 2012, the coalition government of the Christian Union and the Liberal Party introduced the *Betreuungsgeld* (cash transfer for childcare), which constituted a small flat-rate cash benefit (150€ per month) between the first and the third birthday of a child. This benefit was a reaction to the introduction of the right to a childcare place from the first birthday of the child and represented the ambivalence of contemporary German family policy with instruments against and for the breadwinner family model. The *Betreuungsgeld* was only granted if a child did not take advantage of a publicly subsidised childcare place. It enabled parents with a male-breadwinner income to prolong the care of young children at home until the third birthday and was promoted by the government to increase the choice of parents with regard to childcare. The opposition parties from the left were highly critical and labelled the benefit as *Herdprämie* (award for stay-at-home mothers) that set an incentive for the non-employment of mothers within financially privileged married couples. In 2015, the Federal Constitutional Court abolished the *Betreuungsgeld* due to the fact that the federal state has no legislative competencies in the realm of childcare. The law was thus not consistent with the German constitution. Currently four of the sixteen *Länder* provide a decentralised kind of *Betreuungsgeld* in order to give parents more 'choice'.

The impact of international organisations

Since the turn of the century, the Organisation for Economic Cooperation and Development (OECD) and the European Union (EU) have been active policy drivers in childcare policy. The OECD focused on Early Childhood Education and Care (ECEC) and documented the development of this policy in different countries in order to promote the importance of ECEC for educational success in the long run.[33] Furthermore, the OECD broached the issue of reconciliation of work and care. The 'Babies and Bosses' serial analysed reconciliation policies in thirteen countries and marked the importance of childcare for the employment of parents.[34] The resulting recommendations for national policy development were very clear. The expansion of childcare is a necessity in order to guarantee a high level of education for future generations and to enable the employment of parents. Recent publications deal with the question of convergence in national family policies and show that the expansion of childcare together with tax incentives for part-time work lead to higher female employment rates.[35] In addition, paid childcare leaves are seen to have positive effects on the increase of female employment, even though the balance seems to be mixed with regard to effects on wage levels after returning to work. Leaves that last longer than one or two years rather seem to result in negative effects on employment rates and wage levels.[36] Paid leaves that are shared between parents are noted to affect the employment of mothers positively. The OECD recommends the introduction of daddy-months in connection with high benefits and flexible conditions of leave taking.[37] Thus, it is not astonishing that the OECD's evaluation of the German reforms in reconciliation policy is highly affirmative.[38] The OECD frames reconciliation policy twofold: with regard to children their education prospects are in focus, while with regard to parents, labour market aspects, especially the increase of mothers' employment rate, dominate.

The EU connects reconciliation policy strongly with labour market policy. The European employment strategy is based on what was phrased by Lewis as the 'adult worker model'.[39] This model implies that every adult person who is able to work should be in employment regardless of existing responsibilities for caregiving. In 2000, the European Council recommended in its Lisboa-Strategy to increase the average female employment rate across the EU from then 51 per cent to more than 60 per cent by 2010. Two years later, the European Council promoted common aims (the so-called 'Barcelona targets') for the expansion of childcare in order to minimise parents' obstacles to employment. Until 2010, at least 90 per cent of children aged three to six years and 33 per cent of children less than three years should have a childcare place to enable the employment of both parents. In the subsequent strategic programme 'Europe 2020', which dates from June 2010, the European Council set the target at an employment rate of 75 per cent for men and women aged twenty to sixty-four years. This, of course, will require a further expansion of childcare, but new targets have not been formulated in this regard. Moreover, to include fathers in the task of childcare, the European Institute for Gender Equality recommends a well-paid, time-flexible and non-transferable childcare leave for fathers as well as more flexibility at the workplace with regard to daily and weekly working hours.[40] Gender equality could not be achieved with long and highly paid parental leave. In general, reconciliation of work and childcare has become an important topic within the European employment strategy. Nevertheless, the EU has not yet formulated targets with regard to the reconciliation of work and old age care.

In contrast, the OECD has dealt with long-term care for the aged and infirm and warned of the growing disparity between increasing care needs and decreasing care provision within the family.[41] The OECD also carried out country comparisons of long-term care policies, which showed a common international trend. People dependent on care should be enabled to live at home for as long as possible and caring relatives should be enabled to reconcile work and care.[42] Supporting caring relatives creates a 'win-win-win' situation for the cared for, the carer and the public finances. However, cash transfers for care are assessed as ambivalent because they are mostly low level, whereas care leave and support through short-time care, care counselling and care courses are benchmarked as adequate.[43] Reconciliation of work and old age care has also become a topic of German family policy in recent years.

Reconciliation of work and old age care

For quite a long time, the care of elderly people at home was not dealt with at all in family policy. Caring for a frail elderly relative was more or less automatically defined as the responsibility of the family, which was in line with the male breadwinner model of the conservative German welfare state. The increase of female employment together with the ageing of the population and people living longer made care for elderly relatives by family members (mostly women) more and more difficult. In addition,

Table 7.1 Benefits from long-term care insurance in euros per month

Degree of dependency	Care at home		Residential care
	By caring relatives	By mobile care services	
Degree 1	–	–	125
Degree 2	316	689	770
Degree 3	545	1,298	1,262
Degree 4	728	1,612	1,775
Degree 5	901	1,995	2,005

Source: http://www.pflegeversicherung-tarif.de/pflegeversicherung/leistungen-gesetzliche-pflegeversicherung, 14 November 2017.

the costs of residential long-term care were growing rapidly although the increasing care needs were met with only moderate increases of professional care until the introduction of long-term care insurance in 1995. Long-term care insurance is financed by contributions from employers and employees and grants flat-rate benefits for people with care needs. The flat-rate varies depending on the quantity of care needed and can be used to co-finance residential care or homecare with two alternative possibilities for homecare: the *Pflegegeld* for care by relatives and benefits in kind for mobile care services (see Table 7.1). This has resulted in an expansion of professional care. Between 1999 and 2015, the number of residential care homes increased from 8,859 to 13,596 and the number of places in residential care grew from 645,456 to 928,939. At the same time, the number of mobile care services increased from 10,820 to 13,323 and the number of people receiving mobile care expanded from 415,289 to 692,273.[44] This development also demonstrates a trend from non-professional care by relatives to professional care by mobile and residential care.[45]

However, most frail elderly people in Germany are still cared for by family members at home. In 2015, 2.08 million out of 2.9 million people in need of care were looked after at their homes. 1.38 million were cared for exclusively by relatives without the support of professional mobile care services.[46] Most caring relatives are women, although the percentage of caring men has risen from 17 per cent in 1991 to 28 per cent in 2010. About half of all men who care for relatives are in their pension age, in general one-third of all caring relatives are pensioners. However, of those caring relatives who are younger than sixty-five years, an increasing share is employed (59 per cent in 2010). Half of all employed (mostly male) carers worked more than thirty hours per week, 34 per cent reduced their working time when they took over care and 15 per cent stopped working while on care duty.[47]

Long-term care insurance not only improved professional care provision, but also the situation of caring relatives. If they provide care for more than fourteen hours per week (since 2017: more than ten hours per week) caring relatives are covered by accident insurance and pension insurance. The cash benefit for homecare (*Pflegegeld*) constitutes a kind of low wage for caring relatives (especially with lower degrees of care intensity), although it is paid to the person in need of care and not to the caring relative. Thus, caring relatives depend on the transfer of the *Pflegegeld* from the person they care for. Feminist critique has pointed out that routed wages like the *Pflegegeld* usually manifest the sex division of labour as well as the male breadwinner model.[48]

With the introduction of care leave regulations (*Pflegezeit* and *Familienpflegezeit*) the reconciliation of work and care became prominent on the political agenda. Under the *Pflegezeit* regulation it is possible to take a short leave of up to ten days, which is paid at 90 per cent of the former wage (*Pflegeunterstützungsgeld*). The short time span allows for the organisation of a reliable homecare situation after a sudden emergency of care needs. The *Pflegezeit* also allows for a longer but unpaid leave up to six months in order to care for a dependent relative. The *Familienpflegezeit* on the other hand offers a reduction of the weekly working time by (up to) 50 per cent for a maximum time span of two years. During the leave period, caring relatives can opt for an interest-free grant, which has to be paid back after return to (full-time) work.

The care leave regulations have been strongly criticised.[49] Firstly, the simultaneity of employment and care is difficult to maintain, especially with increasing degrees of dependency, and supportive mobile and short-term inpatient care services are rarely used because they are too expensive for many families. The OECD classifies Germany among the countries with the highest percentage of out-of-pocket payments for care services.[50] Only Switzerland and Portugal shift an even higher percentage of the costs at those depending on care and their relatives. Secondly, the leave regulations are not flexible enough. Although the typical time span for homecare is up to two years, there are nevertheless many cases with considerably longer spans of homecare.[51] These situations are not covered by the leave periods. Last but not least, the lack of wage replacements results in social and gender inequalities. The income reduction due to full-time or part-time leave has to be financed by the caring relatives themselves. Low-income earners can hardly afford to take care leave, especially if they cannot rely on an (adequate) partner income. The right to care thus requires not only time rights like care leaves, but also 'enabling financial circumstances'. The interest-free grant is not an attractive option. Lacking cash transfers for caring relatives and routed wages foster the gendered take-up of care leave with the resulting financial dependencies within the family and difficulties of re-entering the labour market after longer spans of homecare. There are no incentives to include men in care.

Shortfalls of the adult worker family model

Contemporary German family policy focuses on the reconciliation of employment and care for children and/or dependent family members. While the traditional male breadwinner model provided resources for family care due to the non-employment of wives and the attached support policies for married couples, the new *Leitbild* of family policy builds on the employment of both men and women. This general orientation towards the adult worker model for both sexes ties in with gender equality arguments that also contain shared responsibilities for childcare (although not for old age care). Non-employment due to childcare duties is supported for mothers and fathers, but only for limited time spans. Longer parental leave periods are only possible in combination with part-time work or if the income of the employed partner is high enough to support the non-employment of the other partner. With regard to the care of elderly and frail family members, support for part-time employment or non-employment is even more restricted. The message is very clear: continuous employment should be the source of income for both sexes notwithstanding their care obligations.

This new paradigm is mirrored in labour market policy. In 2005, new regulations for long-term unemployment benefits were introduced that match a workfare policy of activation and control instruments. Long-term unemployed persons have to take up any job they are offered by the employment agency regardless of their qualifications. Furthermore, beneficiaries have to prove that they are constantly applying for jobs. If they do not comply, their benefit is reduced. This workfare ideology is also applied to long-term unemployed parents starting from the third birthday of their youngest child.[52] Moreover, the *Elterngeld* is deducted from long-term unemployment benefits. Thus, childcare by parents who are long-term unemployed is not 'paid for' at all. Caring relatives who are long-term unemployed are also obliged to work. The employment agency assesses if the care responsibilities allow for (part-time) work and if care could be organised differently in order to allow for (part-time) work of the family carer. In contrast to the *Elterngeld*, the *Pflegegeld* does not reduce benefits for long-term unemployment. In general, these regulations of labour market policy show the primary importance of employment obligations and the secondary importance of care responsibilities towards children and dependent family members. Nevertheless, professional care provision is not able to unburden families from their care responsibilities to a meaningful degree. The vast majority of care is still carried out within the family, now mostly by increasingly employed women who have to deal with this double burden. The situation has already been coined as a 'reproduction crisis' and affects family life.[53]

About two-thirds of all parents and caring relatives (younger than sixty-five years) are employed. The existing supply of care services is not sufficient in terms of quantity and not adequate in terms of flexible hours and adaptability. Reconciliation of work and care therefore remains a difficult task. In addition, more and new conflicts arise for employed carers of children and the elderly. Changes in the organisation of work, the multiplication of tasks and worsening working conditions have resulted in precarious situations such as job insecurity, low wage despite full-time work, increased work intensity or increased demands for flexible working times and places.[54] These developments put more and more pressure on employees who are less and less able to fulfil the demands from work and family at the same time. The multiple demands for flexibility and availability can hardly be met any more. We have seen already developments of self-exploitation at the cost of other family members. Employed carers neglect their own reproduction and prioritise the needs of the workplace against the care needs of their children and/or dependent relatives. Children have to be brought to the workplace, older children are obliged to look after their younger siblings, children and dependent family members are left alone or are taken care of by professional services against their will.[55] Somatic illnesses and burn-out syndromes are increasing steadily, there is high fluctuation of employees in sectors and professions with tight working conditions, such as in professional care services, and the number of young men and women with unfulfilled wishes of becoming parents is increasing.[56] Family-friendly working environments are still the exception rather than the standard in German enterprises.

The emancipatory potential of the 'adult worker model' consists of the equal participation of men and women in the labour market and the chance for women to earn their own money for an independent living. However, these possibilities are not sufficiently realised due to the deficits in service provision and working conditions. The basic question is how care can be organised in a modern society. The traditional care responsibility of the family is strongly tied to the traditional sex division of labour and the male breadwinner family model. Thus, not only economic reasoning, but also feminist arguments promote the de-familisation of care in terms of an expansion of care services for children and the frail elderly. De-familisation is the precondition for an increase of female employment rates and improved financial means of women. However, a one-sided perspective on the 'right not to care' neglects the questions of how care can be organised satisfactorily outside the family by public and market-driven services, and to what extent a de-familisation of care would be possible and desirable.

Future developments

During the election campaign in the run-up to the national elections in September 2017, all of the parties (with exception of the right-wing populist AfD – Alternative für Deutschland) emphasised the importance of early education and care for reconciliation policy and promoted increases in the quantity and quality of childcare. While the Social Democrats promised childcare free of charge, the Christian Union, the Green Party and the Liberals opposed free childcare because they do not want to subsidise high earning parents, but would rather invest the money in improved quality of childcare. Social Democrats, Christian Democrats and the Green Party suggested expanding the right to a childcare place for children in primary school who still lack after-school care. Social Democrats and the Green Party even promoted the right to a full-time place in childcare from the first birthday of the child.[57]

In regard to childcare leave, the Social Democrats developed a new model of shared *Familienzeit* (family time) for work and family. If both parents reduce their weekly working time to twenty-six to thirty-six hours, each parent receives a cash transfer of 150€ per month (the so-called *Familiengeld*). The working time reduction can be subsidised for twenty-four months after the *Elterngeld* has ended.[58] The Christian Union and the Liberals criticised this proposal to patronise parents. The Green Party recommended the transformation of the *Elterngeld* into *KinderZeit Plus*. A paid leave of twenty-four months should be divided into eight months for each parent and eight months that can be freely divided between the parents.[59]

In addition to the existing ten days of paid care leave, the Social Democrats proposed three months of paid care leave with a replacement rate similar to the *Elterngeld*. Furthermore, caring relatives who reduce their working time to twenty-six to thirty-six hours per week should be entitled to a flat-rate benefit of 150€ per month for a maximum time span of two years. This *Familiengeld* for caring relatives could be received by two relatives of a dependent family member.[60] The Green Party suggested three months of paid care leave in addition to the already existing ten days.⁶¹ Neither the Christian Union nor the Liberals came up with any new proposals for care leave.

Since the elections were lost by the Social Democrats and the Christian Union, and the attempts to build a 'Jamaica-coalition' between the Christian Union, the Green Party and the Liberals failed, Germany has had another grand coalition between Social Democrats and the Christian Union since March 2018.⁶² The coalition agreement announced the introduction of a legal right to a childcare place for children in primary school until 2025.⁶³ Moreover, the coalition partners have agreed to increase financial support for children, especially in the context of low-income families by increasing existing cash transfers. All in all, it seems that German family policy does anticipate major reforms within the next four years.

Looking back at the beginning of the post-reunification period, we can see an expansion policy with regard to childcare and professional care services for the frail elderly during the last thirty years. In addition, care leave policies have been reformed in order to improve the possibilities for reconciling work and care. The major driving force was economic reasoning in order to enable female labour market participation within the framework of the 'adult worker model' and to keep costs for elderly care low by enabling female care work within the family. Long-standing feminist demands for gender equality in the labour market and within the family have been only secondary drivers of the policy changes. Nevertheless, the traditional male breadwinner model is substituted more and more by a one-and-a-half-earner model as well as by a two-full-time-earner model. However, the picture remains mixed and there is still a long way to go for gender equality in German families.

Notes

1   U. Klammer and C. Klenner, 'Geteilte Erwerbstätigkeit – gemeinsame Fürsorge. Strategien und Perspektiven der Kombination von Erwerbs- und Familienleben in Deutschland', in S. Leitner, I. Ostner and M. Schratzenstaller (eds), *Wohlfahrtsstaat und Geschlechterverhältnis im Umbruch. Was kommt nach dem Ernährermodell? Jahrbuch für Europa- und Nordamerika-Studien 7.* (Wiesbaden, 2004), pp. 177–207.

2. T. Meyer, 'Die Erosion des starken deutschen Brotverdienermodells. Sozioökonomische und institutionelle Faktoren', *Zeitschrift für Sozialreform* Vol. 44 (11/12) (1998), pp. 818–37.

3. The German *Länder* hold the legislative competency for childcare and the municipalities are responsible for investing in the expansion of kindergarten places. Therefore, the federal state was not allowed to directly invest in local childcare, but the financial means had to be provided by a complicated procedure included in the revenue allocation between the Federation and the *Länder*.

4. DJI – Deutsches Jugendinstitut (2002): Zahlenspiegel. Daten zu Tageseinrichtungen für Kinder. München: DJI.

5. In West Germany only 38 per cent of all places were full-time places, in East Germany the percentage was 74 per cent.

6. In the West, 55 per cent of mothers with a child aged three to six work less than thirty-two hours per week, 13 per cent work more than thirty-two hours per week. In the East, the percentage amounts to 36 per cent of mothers who work less than thirty-two hours per week and 37 per cent who work more than thirty-two hours per week (BMFSFJ 2014).

7. BMFSFJ – Bundesministerium für Familie, Senioren, Frauen und Jugend (2017): Kindertagesbetreuung Kompakt. Ausbaustand und Bedarf 2016. Berlin: BMFSFJ.

8. S. Gruescu and B. Rürup, 'Nachhaltige Familienpolitik', *Aus Politik und Zeitgeschichte* 23–4 (2005), pp. 3–6; M. Ristau, 'Der ökonomische Charme der Familie', *Aus Politik und Zeitgeschichte* 23–4 (2005), pp. 16–22.

9. DJI – Deutsches Jugendinstitut (2002): Zahlenspiegel. Daten zu Tageseinrichtungen für Kinder. München: DJI.

10. BMFSFJ – Bundesministerium für Familie, Senioren, Frauen und Jugend (2017): Kindertagesbetreuung Kompakt. Ausbaustand und Bedarf 2016. Berlin: BMFSFJ.

11. P. Bleses und E. Rose, *Deutungswandel der Sozialpolitik. Die Arbeitsmarkt- und Familienpolitik im parlamentarischen Diskurs* (Frankfurt am Main, 1998); W. Kolbe, *Elternschaft im Wohlfahrtsstaat: Schweden und die Bundesrepublik im Vergleich* (Frankfurt am Main, 2002).

12. H. Geissler, 'Die Anerkennung von Familienarbeit', in Bundesministerium für Familie und Senioren (ed.), *40 Jahre Familienpolitik in der Bundesrepublik Deutschland. Rückblick/Ausblick* (Neuwied, 1993), pp. 105–16.

13. Bleses and Rose, *Deutungswandel der Sozialpolitik*; R. Pettinger, 'Erziehungsgeld und Erziehungsurlaub: Anspruch und Wirklichkeit zweier

zentraler familienpolitischer Leistungen für junge Familien', in B. Jans, A. Habisch and E. Stutzer (eds), *Familienwissenschaftliche und familienpolitische Signale. Max Wingen zum 70. Geburtstag* (Grafschaft, 2000), pp. 243–54.

14 In the GDR a paid maternal leave existed since 1976. The leave was paid with 80 per cent of the former income and lasted six months, later twelve months.

15 S. Bothfeld, *Vom Erziehungsurlaub zur Elternzeit. Politisches Lernen im Reformprozess* (Frankfurt am Main, 2005).

16 E. Beck-Gernsheim, 'Leyen-Feminismus: Kinder, Krippen und Kulturkampf', *Blätter für deutsche und internationale Politik* Vol. 7 (2007), pp. 856–60.

17 S. Leitner, 'Ökonomische Funktionalität der Familienpolitik oder familienpolitische Funktionalisierung der Ökonomie?', in A. Evers and R. Heinze (eds), *Sozialpolitik. Ökonomisierung und Entgrenzung* (Wiesbaden, 2008), pp. 67–82.

18 A. von Wahl, 'From Family to Reconciliation Policy: How the Grand Coalition Reforms the German Welfare State', *German Politics and Society* Vol. 26, No. 3 (2008), pp. 25–49.

19 A. Rüling, 'Re-Framing of Childcare in Germany and England: From a Private Responsibility to an Economic Necessity'. CSGE Research Paper. (London and Berlin, 2008).

20 BMFSFJ – Bundesministerium für Familie, Senioren, Frauen und Jugend (2014): Dossier Müttererwerbstätigkeit. Erwerbstätigkeit, Erwerbsumfang und Erwerbsvolumen 2012. Berlin: BMFSFJ.

21 M. Keller and T. Haustein, 'Vereinbarkeit von Familie und Beruf. Ergebnisse des Mikrozensus 2013', *Wirtschaft und Statistik* Vol. 12 (2014), pp. 733–53.

22 Statistisches Bundesamt (2015): Öffentliche Sozialleistungen. Statistik zum Elterngeld. Beendete Leistungsbezüge für im Jahr 2013 geborene Kinder.

23 BMFSFJ – Bundesministerium für Familie, Senioren, Frauen und Jugend (2008): Evaluation des Gesetzes zum Elterngeld und zur Elternzeit. Endbericht 2008. Berlin: BMFSFJ.

24 BMFSFJ – Bundesministerium für Familie, Senioren, Frauen und Jugend (2009): Evaluationsbericht Bundeselterngeld- und Elternzeitgesetz 2009. Berlin: BMFSFJ.

25 S. Pfahl, S. Reuyß, D. Hobler and S. Weeber (2014): Nachhaltige Effekte der Elterngeldnutzung durch Väter. Gleichstellungspolitische Auswirkungen von Elterngeldmonaten durch erwerbstätige Väter auf betrieblicher und

partnerschaftlicher Ebene. Projektbericht. http://www.boeckler.de/pdf_fof/S-2012-572-3-5.pdf.
26 https://www.destatis.de/DE/ZahlenFakten/GesellschaftStaat/Soziales/Sozialleistungen/Elterngeld/Tabellen/BestandElterngeldbezuegeJahr2016.html, 14 November 2017.
27 Nevertheless, there are tax benefits in place for lone parents.
28 S. Leitner, *Varianten von Familialismus. Eine historisch vergleichende Analyse der Kinderbetreuungs- und Altenpflegepolitiken in kontinentaleuropäischen Wohlfahrtsstaaten* (Berlin, 2013).
29 'Ehe und Familie stehen unter dem besonderen Schutz des Staates.' (Art. 6 GG)
30 S. Leitner, 'Die Tour de force der Gleichstellung: Zwischensprints mit Hindernissen', in A. Gohr and M. Seeleib-Kaiser (eds), *Sozial- und Wirtschaftspolitik unter Rot-Grün* (Wiesbaden, 2003), pp. 249–64.
31 https://www.bundestag.de/parlament/plenum/abstimmung/abstimmung?id=486, 14 November 2017.
32 M. Bujard, 'Wie passt das zusammen? Familienbilder junger Menschen und Parteipositionen zur Familienpolitik', *Aus Politik und Zeitgeschichte* Vol. 67 (30–1) (2017), pp. 9–15.
33 OECD (2001): Starting Strong. Early Childhood Education and Care. Paris: OECD; OECD (2006): Starting Strong II. Early Childhood Education and Care. Paris: OECD.
34 OECD (2007): Babies and Bosses – Reconciling Work and Family Life: A Synthesis of Findings for OECD Countries. Paris: OECD.
35 W. Adema, N. Ali und O. Thévenon (2014): Changes in Family Policies and Outcomes: Is there Convergence? OECD Social, Employment and Migration Working Papers 157. Paris: OECD.
36 W. Adema, C. Clarke und V. Frey (2015): Paid Parental Leave: Lessons from OECD Countries and Selected U.S. States. OECD Social, Employment and Migration Working Papers 172. Paris: OECD.
37 OECD (2016a): Parental leave: Where are the fathers? Policy Brief March 2016. Paris: OECD.
38 OECD (2016b): Dare to Share – Deutschlands Weg zur Partnerschaftlichkeit in Familie und Beruf. Paris: OECD.
39 J. Lewis, 'The Decline of the Male Breadwinner Model: Implications for Work and Care', *Social Politics* Vol. 8, No. 2 (2001), pp. 152–69; J. Lewis and S. Giullari, 'The adult worker model family, gender equality and care: the search for new policy principles and the possibilities and problems of a capability approach', *Economy and Society* Vol. 34, No. 1 (2005), pp. 76–104.

40 EIGE – European Institute for Gender Equality (2015): Überprüfung der Vereinbarkeit von Arbeit, Familie und Privatleben in der Europäischen Union. Politikbericht. http://eige.europa.eu/rdc/eige-publications/reconciliation-work-family-and-private-life-european-union-policy-review, 04 October 2017.
41 OECD (1996): Caring for Frail Elderly People. Policies in Evolution. Paris: OECD; OECD (1998): The Caring World: An Analysis. Paris: OECD.
42 OECD (1996): Caring for Frail Elderly People. Policies in Evolution. Paris: OECD; OECD (2005): Long-term Care for Older People. Paris: OECD; F. Colombo, A. LLena-Nozal, J. Mercier and F. Tjadens (2011): Help Wanted? Providing and Paying for Long-term Care. Paris: OECD.
43 F. Colombo, A. LLena-Nozal, J. Mercier and F. Tjadens (2011): Help Wanted? Providing and Paying for Long-term Care. Paris: OECD.
44 http://www.gbe-bund.de, 19 October 2017.
45 D. Auth, *Pflegearbeit in Zeiten der Ökonomisierung. Wandel von Care-Regimen in Großbritannien, Schweden und Deutschland* (Münster, 2017).
46 Statistisches Bundesamt (2017): Pflegestatistik 2015. Pflege im Rahmen der Pflegeversicherung. Deutschlandergebnisse. Wiesbaden: Statistisches Bundesamt.
47 TNS Infratest Sozialforschung (2011): Abschlussbericht zur Studie "Wirkungen des Pflege-Weiterentwicklungsgesetzes". München: TNS.
48 C. Ungerson, 'Gender, Cash and Informal Care: European Perspectives and Dilemmas', *Journal of Social Policy* Vol. 24, No. 1 (1995), pp. 31–52; S. Leitner, *Varianten von Familialismus. Eine historisch vergleichende Analyse der Kinderbetreuungs- und Altenpflegepolitiken in kontinentaleuropäischen Wohlfahrtsstaaten* (Berlin, 2013).
49 D. Auth, 'Betreuungsgeld und Familienpflegezeit: Mehr Wahlfreiheit und bessere Vereinbarkeit?', *Femina Politica* Vol. 21, No. 1 (2012), pp. 135–40; S. Ehm and J. Rinderspacher, 'Ein Jahr Familienpflegezeitgesetz – Welche Erfahrungen gibt es und wie kann es weitergehen?', *Feministische Studien* Vol. 31, No. 2 (2013), pp. 315–23; S. Leitner and M. Vukoman, 'Zeit, Geld, Infrastruktur? Vereinbarkeitspolitik für pflegende Angehörige', *GENDER – Zeitschrift für Geschlecht, Kultur und Gesellschaft* Vol. 7, No. 1 (2015), pp. 97–112; B. Stiegler and D. Engelmann, *Zeit und Geld für pflegende Angehörige. Eckpunkte für eine geschlechtergerechte Gestaltung der Vereinbarkeit von Beruf und Pflege.* Wiso direkt. (Bonn, 2011).
50 F. Colombo, A. LLena-Nozal, J. Mercier and F. Tjadens (2011): Help Wanted? Providing and Paying for Long-term Care. Paris: OECD.

51 R. Müller, Rolf, R. Unger und H. Rothgang, 'Reicht eine zweijährige Familien-Pflegezeit für Arbeitnehmer?', *Soziale Sicherheit* 6–7 (2010), pp. 230–7.
52 Formerly parents with children under six years old were exempted from the work obligation.
53 K. Jürgens, 'Deutschland in der Reproduktionskrise', *Leviathan* 38 (2010), pp. 559–87.
54 K. Jurczyk, *Entgrenzte Arbeit – entgrenzte Familie. Grenzmanagement im Alltag als neue Herausforderung* (Berlin, 2009); I. Nowak, J. Hausotter and G. Winker, 'Entgrenzung in Industrie und Altenpflege: Perspektiven erweiterter Handlungsfähigkeit von Beschäftigten', *WSI Mitteilungen* Vol. 65, No. 4 (2012), pp. 272–80.
55 D. Auth, C. Klenner and S. Leitner, 'Neue Sorgekonflikte: Die Zumutungen des Adult worker model', in S. Völker and M. Amacker (eds), *Prekarisierungen. Arbeit, Sorge und Politik* (Weinheim/Basel, 2015), pp. 42–58.
56 Bundestherapeutenkammer 2013: BPtK-Studie zur Arbeits- und Erwerbsunfähigkeit, psychische Erkrankungen und gesundheitsbedingte Frühverrentung. http://www.bptk.de, 31 March 2017; M. Simon, P. Tackenberg, H. Hasselhorn, A. Kümmerling, A. Büscher, B. Müller, *Auswertung der ersten Befragung der NEXT-Studie in Deutschland* (2005). http://www.next.uni-wuppertal.de/index.php?artikel-und-berichte-1, 31 March 2017; C. Boll, H. Bonin, I. Gerlach, K. Hank et al. *Geburten und Kinderwünsche in Deutschland: Bestandsaufnahme, Einflussfaktoren und Datenquellen* (2013). http://www.zew.de/de/publikationen/publikation.php3?action=detail&nr=6950, 31 March 2017.
57 M. Bujard, 'Wie passt das zusammen? Familienbilder junger Menschen und Parteipositionen zur Familienpolitik', *Aus Politik und Zeitgeschichte* Vol. 67 (30–1) (2017), pp. 9–15.
58 https://www.spd.de/standpunkte/wir-machen-familien-stark/familienarbeitszeit, 15 November 2017.
59 https://www.gruene-bundestag.de/files/beschluesse/Beschluss_Zeitpolitik.pdf, 15 November 2017.
60 https://www.spd.de/standpunkte/wir-machen-familien-stark/familienarbeitszeit, 15 November 2017.
61 https://www.gruene-bundestag.de/files/beschluesse/Beschluss_Zeitpolitik.pdf, 15 November 2017.
62 https://www.bundeswahlleiter.de/bundestagswahlen/2017/ergebnisse/bund-99.html, 15 November 2017.

63 Bundesregierung (2017): Ein neuer Aufbruch für Europa. Eine neue Dynamik für Deutschland. Ein neuer Zusammenhalt für unser Land. Koalitionsvertrag zwischen CDU, CSU und SPD. 19. Legislaturperiode. https://www.bundesregierung.de/Content/DE/_Anlagen/2018/03/2018-03-14-koalitionsvertrag.pdf?__blob=publicationFile&v=5, 30 April 2018.

Conclusion

Lisa Pine

Each discrete period across the 150 years covered by this book was characterised – as every chapter demonstrates – by the interaction between continuity and change in the structure of the German family. This interplay also reflected the position of the family between private life and the state. The book has explained how discourses and policies across a variety of political ideologies – including liberal, National Socialist, Communist, social democratic and conservative – shaped and influenced the family in modern Germany. Across the entire modern era, the German family evidenced complex developments. Taken together, the chapters reveal the strong strands of continuity, especially in the domestic division of labour and assumptions about the role of mothers, while also tracing an arc of profound – if contested – transformation in the public roles of mothers and wives.

In terms of changes before 1900, we have seen how the new middle class led the way in family forms in Germany, distinctive from both the aristocracy and the working class. The middle-class family stood at the heart of bourgeois culture and values. Separated from the world of work and professional life, it was conceived of as a two-generation nuclear family, made up of father, mother and children. In bourgeois discourse, the family was viewed as a refuge from the outside world. It was a patriarchal family in which all members were subject to the father's authority. His wife was the custodian of the family, setting the rhythm and tone of family life, rearing children and managing the household and social arrangements. Middle-class marriage and married life were burdened with very high expectations, and so disappointments and shortcomings were inevitable in reality. In addition, girls and boys were reared with very specific gender ideals. There were substantial variations from these arrangements in both rural and urban working-class families in Imperial Germany. Perhaps most significantly, they differed in size: working-class families commonly had between five and ten children, as compared with two children in middle-class families. Yet we have seen that they all shared a more or less implicit comparison with the bourgeois family ideal. Gendered norms about fathers as breadwinners and women in the home, fulfilling maternal duties, came to represent a key aspect of social commentary and discourse in Imperial Germany.

The impact of the First World War on both German society and the family was profound and contributed to the considerations of Weimar policymakers. The trauma of defeat and revolution engendered a sense that the very survival of the nation was in danger. The death toll from the war and the plummeting birth rate brought about considerable debate, across the political spectrum from left to right, about how best to regenerate and rejuvenate the German family. Hyperinflation in 1923 and the impact of the Wall Street Crash in 1929 had serious economic implications for family life. Support for the family and policy towards marriage, divorce and motherhood changed during the Weimar era, as economic exigencies and ideological worldviews shifted and society modernised. The progressive and modern side of the Weimar Republic was characterised by changing attitudes towards sexuality, at least in the big cities. While eugenic concepts had started to creep into public and political discourse towards the end of the Weimar Republic, it was only under National Socialism that they became part of state policy and enshrined into law. Mother education and mother recuperation programmes were features of Nazi policy that continued earlier developments from the Weimar Republic, although with a much stronger ideological slant.

In the Third Reich, the family was heralded as 'the germ cell of the nation', the building block upon which the fortunes of the organic state would prosper or founder. The National Socialist regime implemented a wide array of policies aimed at the restoration of the family. To be sure, however, this applied only to approved families that the regime considered to be fit. For 'valuable' families, welfare measures and policies designed to encourage early marriages were put into place. At the same time, the Nazi government profoundly intervened in the lives of ordinary German families, with its regimentation of social life and its penetration of the private sphere. For 'unworthy' sectors of the population, whether on grounds of 'asociality', physical disability or mental illness, or 'racial inferiority', Nazi family policy was one of destruction. Its distinctive and radical policies marked out the Nazi dictatorship that followed the liberal democracy of the Weimar era, plunging the nation into another costly and devastating world war, with its impact and repercussions to be felt long after its demise.

As was the case after the First World War, the importance of the family formed part of the post-war discourse about reconstructing society after the Second World War. There was the problem – of even greater magnitude after 1945 than after 1918 – of a 'surplus' of women, brought about by the death toll of war. There was a determination to reject Nazi visions of the family and to reconstruct the German family. Furthermore, politicians in both West and East Germany cited family and gender policies in the other Germany as a reason to follow a different path.

In West Germany, throughout the 1950s, there were changes in attitudes towards both marriage and divorce. There was also a desire to restore the traditional German nuclear family on the male-breadwinner/female-homemaker model. This was proclaimed by Adenauer as a way to re-establish order to a society in disarray. The Federal Ministry of Family Affairs, established in 1953 and led by Franz-Josef Wuermeling created policies, such as the creation of child allowances, that were designed to support the male-breadwinner/female-homemaker family model. Yet simultaneously, shifting societal norms and openness to liberalisation also had some impact on West German politics and legislation. By the early 1960s, female labour was regarded as a way to help West German families engage in a growing consumer culture, but not as a way to women's economic independence or freedom.

Increased labour force participation and educational opportunities for women in West Germany during the 1960s–1980s challenged the male-breadwinner/female-homemaker model that formed the foundation of gender roles and family structures of the FRG. Progressive legislation in the FRG was epitomised by the 1976 law to reform marriage and divorce, which also addressed changes to the gendered division of labour in the family. In addition, the introduction of paid maternity leave policy in May 1979 recognised women's employment outside the home and helped to reconcile family and employment for women in West Germany. In 1986, *Erziehungsgeld*, a subsidy payable to either parent, replaced this. A partnership marriage, in which the father shared responsibilities in the home (or even took the main role in childcare), formed part of a new political and cultural discourse in the FRG in the 1970s and 1980s, although in reality, the male-breadwinner model remained strong. Partial reform of Paragraph 218, the abortion law, was also a significant policy change in 1976.

In the meantime, East German history took a different course, and in terms of the family, the most significant development was the rapidly rising percentage of working mothers. The SED's approach to modernising the family was pragmatic and reformist, not revolutionary. Yet throughout the course of four decades, changes were introduced in a variety of laws, for example in relation to abortion, and provisions were made that affected the East German family profoundly. In particular, Honnecker's programme of *Muttipolitik* brought about considerable change to the East German family in the 1970s and 1980s. Attitudes towards women at work had changed completely from the immediate post-war period. The GDR had forged a family model in which an employed and trained mother was the norm.

Since reunification, there has been a fundamental shift in family policy, which has left behind the male-breadwinner model and incorporated a new concept of shared parenthood, as well as the continuous labour market participation of both parents. This has been made possible by an expansion of public childcare and the introduction of earnings-related parental leave benefits. Greater gender equality in parenting has enhanced the participation of fathers in childcare. The traditional male-breadwinner/female-homemaker model has increasingly been replaced by a one-and-a-half-earner model or a two full-time-earner model. The trend towards the adult worker model for both sexes accords with gender equality arguments that contain shared responsibilities for childcare. New benefits of *Elterngeld* and *Elterngeld Plus* further help families to optimise their lifestyle choices in regard to employment and parental leave. Yet other policies, such as the progressive tax system (*Ehegattensplitting* – tax benefit for married couples), still support the old male-breadwinner model. As people live longer, new issues face the family in the twenty-first century, in particular, in regard to care for the aged and infirm.

We have traced significant changes in the history of the German family over the period from 1870 to the present day. There have been important transformations in attitudes, policies and legislation, at times reflecting the ideological tenets of particular governments. We have seen shifts in attitudes and legislation towards same-sex relationships, as well as in family models. We have examined changes in women's position in the family and at work over time. Relationships and structures of the family have evolved, as women earn a second wage (either as full-time or part-time earners). Not only has this brought about the possibility of a higher standard of living and the ability to buy time-saving devices, but also men's role has changed to incorporate more involvement in the household and the care of the children. This trend has become increasingly accepted and more commonplace and is indicative of shifting social attitudes. However, despite certain strides forward, there is still scope for further change in terms of many of the areas we have considered in this book. The family as an institution at the intersection between the state and private life has been subject to shifts based upon political ideologies and economic exigencies throughout the time period we have examined. Our endeavour in this book has been to fill the gap in the scholarly literature by tracing some of the broad trends and developments in the history of the family in modern and contemporary Germany, offering a thread through the different eras on themes that we consider significant to cover. Our aim was to provide a useful critical analysis of the subject, but we are aware that this could only cover a certain amount of ground within the scope of this volume. We hope that this book inspires and paves the way for further scholarship in this important field.

Select bibliography

Abrams, L. and Harvey, E. (eds), *Gender Relations in German History: Power, Agency and Experience from the Sixteenth to the Twentieth Century* (London, 1996).
Ariès, P., *Geschichte der Kindheit* (Munich, 1998).
Auth, D., *Pflegearbeit in Zeiten der Ökonomisierung. Wandel von Care-Regimen in Großbritannien, Schweden und Deutschland* (Münster, 2017).
Bessel, R., *Germany after the First World War* (Oxford, 1993).
Bessel, R. and Jessen, R. (eds), *Die Grenzen der Diktatur. Staat und Gesellschaft in der DDR* (Göttingen, 1996).
Betts, P., *Within Walls: Private Life in the German Democratic Republic* (Oxford, 2010).
Blasius, D., *Ehescheidungen in Deutschland 1794–1945. Scheidung und Scheidungsrecht in historischer Perspektive* (Göttingen, 1997).
Bleses, P. and Rose, E., *Deutungswandel der Sozialpolitik. Die Arbeitsmarkt- und Familienpolitik im parlamentarischen Diskurs* (Frankfurt am Main, 1998).
Boak, H., *Women in the Weimar Republic* (Oxford, 2015).
Bock, G. and Thane, P. (eds), *Maternity and Gender Policies: Women and the Rise of the European Welfare States 1880s–1950s* (London, 1994).
Bridenthal, R., Grossmann, A. and Kaplan, M. (eds), *When Biology Became Destiny: Women in Weimar and Nazi Germany* (New York, 1984).
Budde, G., *Auf dem Weg ins Bürgerleben. Kindheit und Erziehung in deutschen und englischen Bürgerfamilien, 1840–1914* (Göttingen, 1994).
Budde, G. (ed.), *Frauen arbeiten: weibliche Erwerbstätigkeit in Ost- und Westdeutschland nach 1945* (Göttingen, 1997).
Buske, S., *Fräulein Mutter und ihr Bastard: eine Geschichte der Unehelichkeit in Deutschland, 1900–1970* (Göttingen, 2004).
Chapoutot, J., *The Law of Blood: Thinking and Acting as a Nazi* (Cambridge, MA, 2018).
Daly, M., *The Gender Division of Welfare: The Impact of the British and German Welfare States* (Cambridge, 2000).
Daniel, U., *The War from Within: German Working-Class Women in the First World War* (Oxford, 1997).
Davidoff, L., Doolittle, M., Fink, J. and Holden, K., *The Family Story: Blood, Contract and Intimacy 1830–1960* (London, 1999).
Dollard, C., *The Surplus Woman: Unmarried in Imperial Germany, 1871–1918* (New York, 2009).
Eley, G. and Palmowski, J. (eds), *Citizenship and National Identity in Twentieth Century Germany* (Stanford, 2008).

Ericsson, K. and Simonsen, E. (eds), *Children of World War II: The Hidden Enemy Legacy* (Oxford and New York, 2005).

Evans, R. and Lee, W. (eds), *The German Family: Essays on the Social History of the Family in nineteenth- and twentieth-century Germany* (London, 1981).

Fenemore, M., *Sex, Thugs, and Rock 'N' Roll: Teenage Rebels in Cold-War East Germany* (New York, 2007).

Franzius, C., *Bonner Grundgesetz und Familienrecht: die Diskussion um die Gleichberechtigung von Mann und Frau in der westdeutschen Zivilrechtslehre der Nachkriegszeit (1945-1957)* (Frankfurt am Main, 2005).

Frevert, U., *Women in German History: From Bourgeois Emancipation to Sexual Liberation* (Oxford, 1997).

Ginsborg, P., *Family Politics: Domestic Life, Devastation and Survival 1900 to 1950* (New Haven and London, 2014).

Grau, G. (ed.), *Hidden Holocaust? Gay and Lesbian Persecution in Germany, 1933-1945* (London, 1995).

Grossmann, A., *Reforming Sex: The German Movement for Birth Control and Abortion Reform 1920-1950* (Oxford, 1995).

Hagemann, K., *Frauenalltag und Männerpolitik: Alltagsleben und gesellschaftliches Handeln von Arbeiterfrauen in der Weimarer Republik* (Bonn, 1990).

Hagemann, K., Jarausch, K. and Allemann-Ghionda, C. (eds), *Children, Families, and States: Time Policies of Childcare, Preschool, and Primary Education in Europe* (New York, 2011).

Hagemann, K. and Michel, S. (eds), *Gender and the Long Postwar: The United States and the Two Germanys, 1945-1989* (Baltimore, 2014).

Harsch, D., *Revenge of the Domestic: Women, the Family, and Communism in the German Democratic Republic* (Princeton, 2007).

Harvey, E., *Youth and the Welfare State in Weimar Germany* (Oxford, 1993).

Heineman, E., *What Difference Does a Husband Make? Women and Marital Status in Nazi and Postwar Germany* (Berkeley, 1999).

Helwig, G. and Nickel, H. (eds), *Frauen in Deutschland, 1945-1992* (Bonn, 1993).

Herzog, D., *Sex after Fascism: Memory and Morality in Twentieth-Century Germany* (Princeton, 2007).

Jurczyk, K., *Entgrenzte Arbeit – entgrenzte Familie. Grenzmanagement im Alltag als neue Herausforderung* (Berlin, 2009).

Kertzer, D. and Barbagli, M. (eds), *Family Life in the Twentieth Century* (New Haven and London, 2003).

Kiessling, F. and Rieger, B. (eds), *Mit dem Wandel leben: Neuorientierung und Tradition in der Bundesrepublik der 1950er und 60er Jahre* (Cologne, 2011).

Kocka, J. (ed.), *Bürgertum im 19. Jahrhundert. Deutschland im europäischen Vergleich*. 3 vols. (Munich, 1988).

Kuller, C., *Familienpolitik im föderativen Sozialstaat: die Formierung eines Politikfeldes in der Bundesrepublik 1949-1975* (Munich, 2004).

Kundrus, B., *Kriegerfrauen: Familienpolitik und Geschlechterverhältnisse im Ersten und Zweiten Weltkrieg* (Hamburg, 1995).

Leitner, S., *Varianten von Familialismus. Eine historisch vergleichende Analyse der Kinderbetreuungs- und Altenpflegepolitiken in kontinentaleuropäischen Wohlfahrtsstaaten* (Berlin, 2013).

Leitner, S., Ostner, I. and M. Schratzenstaller, M. (eds), *Wohlfahrtsstaat und Geschlechterverhältnis im Umbruch. Was kommt nach dem Ernährermodell? Jahrbuch für Europa- und Nordamerika-Studien 7* (Wiesbaden, 2004).

Leo, A. and König, C., *Die 'Wunschkindpille'. Weibliche Erfahrung und Staatliche Geburtenpolitik in der DDR* (Göttingen, 2015).

Lybeck, M., *Desiring Emancipation: New Women and Homosexuality in Germany, 1890–1933* (Albany, 2014).

Marhoefer, L., *Sex and the Weimar Republic: German Homosexual Emancipation and the Rise of the Nazis* (Toronto, 2015).

Massino, J. and Penn, S. (eds), *Gender and Everyday Life under State Socialism in East and Central Europe* (London, 2010).

Maynes, M. J. and Waltner, A., *The Family: A World History* (Oxford, 2012).

McLellan, J., *Love in the Time of Communism: Intimacy and Sexuality in the GDR* (Cambridge, 2011).

Michlic, J. (ed.), *Jewish Families in Europe, 1939-Present: History, Representation, and Memory* (Waltham, MA, 2017).

Mitterauer, M. and Sieder, R., *The European Family: Patriarchy to Partnership from the Middle Ages to the Present* (Oxford, 1982).

Moeller, R., *Protecting Motherhood: Women and the Family in the Politics of Postwar West Germany* (Berkeley, 1993).

Mouton, M., *From Nurturing the Nation to Purifying the Volk: Weimar and Nazi Family Policy, 1918–1945* (Cambridge, 2007).

Nave-Herz, R. (ed.), *Kontinuität und Wandel der Familie in Deutschland. Eine zeitgeschichtliche Analyse* (Stuttgart, 2002).

Niehuss, M., *Familie, Frau und Gesellschaft: Studien zur Strukturgeschichte der Familie in Westdeutschland 1945–1960* (Göttingen, 2001).

Obertreis, G., *Familienpolitik in der DDR 1945–1980* (Opladen, 1985).

Oertzen, C. von, *The Pleasure of a Surplus Income: Part-Time Work, Gender Politics, and Social Change in West Germany, 1955–1969* (New York, 2007).

Paulus, J., Silies, E. and Wolff, K. (eds), *Zeitgeschichte als Geschlechtergeschichte: Neue Perspektiven auf die Bundesrepublik* (Frankfurt am Main, 2012).

Pine, L., *Nazi Family Policy, 1933–1945* (Oxford, 1997).

Prost, A. and Vincent, G. (eds), *A History of Private Life. V: Riddles of Identity in Modern Times* (Harvard, 1991).

Riehl, W. H., *Die Familie* (Stuttgart, 1854).

Rölli-Alkemper, L., *Familie im Wiederaufbau: Katholizismus und bürgerliches Familienideal in der Bundesrepublik Deutschland 1945–1965* (Paderborn, 2000).

Roos, J., *Through the Lens of Gender: Prostitution Reform, Women's Emancipation, and German Democracy, 1919–1933* (Ann Arbor, 2010).

Rosenbaum, H., *Formen der Familie: Untersuchungen zum Zusammenhang von Familienverhältnissen, Sozialstruktur und sozialem Wandel in der deutschen Gesellschaft des 19. Jahrhunderts* (Frankfurt am Main, 1996).

Rouette, S., *Sozialpolitik als Geschlechterpolitik: die Regulierung der Frauenarbeit nach dem Ersten Weltkrieg* (Frankfurt am Main, 1993).

Shorter, E., *The Making of the Modern Family* (New York, 1975).

Sieder, R., *Sozialgeschichte der Familie* (Frankfurt am Main, 1987).

Silies, E., *Liebe, Lust, und Last. Die Pille als weibliche Generationserfahrung in der Bundesrepublik 1960–1980* (Göttingen, 2010).

Skinner, Q. (ed.), *Families and States in Western Europe* (Cambridge, 2011).

Steinhausen, G., *Häusliches und gesellschaftliches Leben im 19. Jahrhundert* (Berlin, 1898).

Therborn, G., *Between Sex and Power: Family in the World, 1900–2000* (London and New York, 2004).

Timm, A., *The Politics of Fertility in Twentieth-Century Berlin* (Cambridge, 2010).

Trappe, H., *Emanzipation oder Zwang? Frauen in der DDR zwischen Beruf, Familie und Sozialpolitik* (Berlin, 1995).

Usborne, C., *Politics of the Body: Women's Reproductive Rights and Duties* (Ann Arbor, 1992).

Usborne, C., *Cultures of Abortion in Weimar Germany* (Oxford and New York, 2007).

Vaizey, H., *Surviving Hitler's War: Family Life in Germany, 1939–48* (Basingstoke, 2010).

Völker, S. and M. Amacker, M. (eds), *Prekarisierungen. Arbeit, Sorge und Politik* (Weinheim and Basel, 2015).

Weber-Kellermann, I., *Die deutsche Familie. Versuch einer Sozialgeschichte* (Frankfurt am Main, 1974).

Weindling, P., *Health, Race and German Politics between Unification and Nazism, 1870–1945* (Cambridge, 1997).

Whisnant, C., *Male Homosexuality in West Germany: Between Persecution and Freedom, 1945–69* (London, 2012).

Wiliarty, S., *The CDU and the Politics of Gender in Germany: Bringing Women to the Party* (New York, 2010).

Index

abortion 52, 62, 69, 70–71, 74, 192
   access to 81
   after reunification of Germany 203
   Democratic Women's League data on 180–181
   Lebensborn agency struggle against 101
   legalisation of 185–186
   partial reform of 232
   punishments for 94
   at Ravensbrück concentration camp 106
   during the Weimar era 77
Adenauer, Konrad 120, 125, 128, 129, 132, 151, 231
adult worker model 22, 214, 218–220, 222, 232
adultery 73, 75, 191, 192
age of consent 82, 149, 193
agricultural families, division of labour in 6
Aktionsrat der Befreiung der Frau (Action Council for the Liberation of Women) 158, 159
alimony 73, 74, 75–76, 177, 183
Allied Control Council 17, 123
Ariès, Philippe 10, 37
Article 3 124, 132
Article 6 124, 211
'Aryans' 13, 92, 93, 94, 104, 106, 109
'asociality' 104–105
autonomy 158

Bäumer, Gertrud 37
Bebel, August, *Woman and Socialism* 52
Bell, Johannes 74
Benjamin, Hilde 177
Berlin, Battle of 172
Bertram, Cardinal Adolf 73
bestiality 148, 149
Betreuungsgeld (cash transfer for childcare) 213
Bevolkerungspolitik (population policy) 59, 77, 85

Biess, Frank 142
birth control *see* contraception
birth rate 180, 204
   by end of the 1970s 19
   incentives to increase 13, 91, 92
   out-of-wedlock 119–120, 122
   during the Weimar era 60, 77
   in West Germany, 1950–90 145–146
Bismarck, Otto von 127
Bock, Gisela 112, 160
Bolsheviks 174
Borner, Holger 153
bourgeois families *see* middle-class families
boys, middle class 38–39
breadwinners 3
Brigitte 154, 160, 161–162
Budde, Gunilla 9, 10
Busch, Wilhelm 36

capitalism 158
care insurance 210, 211, 216, 217
Carney, Amy 92
Catholic Church 135, 142, 150
   marriage clinics 69
   view on Christian Marriage 71
Centre Party 69, 73, 74
Chapoutot, Johann 92
child development 184
child support 75–76
childcare 100, 159, 221, 222
   in East Germany after World War Two 181–182
   in Germany since reunification 201
   Guidelines for Day Nurseries 100
   impact of international organisations on childcare policies 213–215
   public 21, 203–205, 232
   in West Germany 152
childcare leave 205–208, 214, 221
childhood, discovery of 10, 37
childrearing 37

240

Index

children
    adjusting to family life after the Second World War 111
    illegitimate 12, 81, 101
    number in families 38
    socialisation of young 142
Christian Democratic Employees Association (CDA) 156
Christian Democratic Union (CDU) 17, 18, 123, 129, 131, 142, 151, 207, 221
    Women's Union 151–152, 156
    Youth Union 156
Christian Social Union (CSU) 123, 142
Civil Code *see* German Civil Code of 1900
civil servants, married female 127
Cold War 17, 134, 151
collective intervention 184
Communist Party 74, 123
concentration camps
    Bergen-Belsen 107
    Buchenwald 194
    deliberate starving of babies in 106–107
    Ravensbrück 106, 107, 194
    Sachsenhausen 194
conscription 10, 14
contraception 66, 67, 68–69, 70, 81, 94, 147, 180
counselling centres 184
    marriage and sexual 173, 191, 192
    pregnancy 180
    state-supported marriage 69–70, 71
Criminal Code 94
Cross of Honour of the German Mother 13, 94, 95, 105

das ganze Haus ('the whole household') 4, 9
Dehler, Thomas 128
Delcke, Maren 162
Deutscher Bund für Volksaufklarung und Erbkunde (German League for Regeneration and Heredity) 64
Dewor, Peter 162
Die Frau von heute 182
Die neue Ordnung 156
division of labour in the household 3, 163, 188
divorce 67, 72–77, 149–150, 183, 184
    1938 law 13, 94
    1977 law 18, 19

court proceedings 190
grounds for 187–188
guilt clause 73, 74, 148, 154
impact on fatherhood 162
marriage after 76–77, 149
openness towards 122
rates of 120
DNVP *see* German National People's Party (DNVP)
Dollard, Catherine 120
Duncombe, Jean 22

Early Childhood Education and Care (ECEC) 213
East German families
    between 1949 and 1990 19, 171–200
    after the Second World War (1945–1949) 172–173
East Germany
    early Five Year Plans 175
    employment 177–179
    family law in 183–184
    gender relations in 188
    heterosexuality in 190–193
    homosexuality legislation 193–194
    institutional childcare 181–182
    marriages 186–188
    mechanisation of the household 182
    Muttipolitik, 1971–89 185–186
    parents and children 188–190
    reproductive and natalism policies 179–181
education 9–10, 175
    academic secondary schools 39
    early education and care 221
    on marital health issues 67–68
Ehegattensplitting (tax benefit for married couples) 202, 210, 233
elderly people 215–218, 222
elections, September 2017 221
Elterngeld 207, 219, 232
Elterngeld Plus 209–210, 232
employment
    maternal 19–20
    part-time 179
equality 125–126, 133, 215
equality clause 124
Erziehungsgeld (parental benefit) 157, 206, 232

Erziehungsurlaub (parental leave period) 206
eugenics 64, 66, 80, 230
Eulenburg Affair 37
Europe 2020 214
European Council 214
European Institute for Gender Equality 215
European Union (EU) 213
  employment strategy 21, 202, 214, 215
Eyck, Helene 33–34

families
  approved and non-approved 112
  communication during periods of separation 110
  contemporary policy since reunification 20–21
  early modern period 4
  in Imperial Germany 9, 27–58
  Industrial Revolution and 4–5
  inferior 103–107
  post-war debates 133
  state's right to intervene in 63–64
family law
  East Germany 183–184
  married women's rights in 128
family models 130
family policies 133–134
  since German reunification 201–228
fathers, employment rates of 208
Federal Constitutional Court 213
Federal Ministry of Family Affairs 129, 231
Federal Republic of Germany (FRG) *see* West Germany
Federation for the Protection of Mothers 69
Federation of German Women's Organisations (BDF) 67
Fichte, Johann Gottlieb 30
films
  The Legend of Paul and Paula 188
  Solo Sunny 188
First Law for the Reform of Marriage and Family Law 154, 161
First World War 10, 117, 230
  Germany after the 60
  letters written during the 54–55
Focke, Katharina 141, 153, 154
Fontane, Theodor 35

Frauenpolitik ('women's policy') 176, 194
Free Democratic Party of Germany (FDP) 123, 152
Freeland, Jane 118
FRG *see* West Germany
Frick, Wilhelm 92
Friedan, Betty, *The Feminine Mystique* 161
Froebel, Friedrich 38

GDR *see* East Germany
gender equality 21
  in the labour market 202
gender roles in the family 3, 62, 111
gender-related legislation and policies 135
Gerhard, Ute 158
German Civil Code of 1900 8, 18, 75, 126
  Paragraph 1356 154, 161
German Communist Party (KPD) 71, 93
German Democratic Republic *see* East Germany
German families *see* families
German League for Regeneration and Heredity 64
German National People's Party (DNVP) 66, 69, 73
German Organisation of Law 73
German plays 27
German Society for Racial Hygiene 68
Ginsborg, Paul 92, 110
girls, expectations of 41–42
Gleichberechtigungsgesetz (Equal Rights Act) 130
Godesberger Programme platform of 1959 153
Goebbels, Joseph 13, 93, 112
Göhre, Paul 51
Great Depression (1929) 12, 65, 71, 85–86
Green Party 211, 221
Grimm, Jacob and Wilhelm 27
Grossmann, Atina 70
Grotjahn, Alfred 67
Guest Worker programme 152
Guggemoos, Georg 76
Guidelines for the Practical Housewife 97
'gypsy' clans 105

Hagemann, Karen 142, 152
Hagemeyer, Maria 126, 128
Harsch, Donna 19–20, 118

Hausmutter ('mistress of the household') 4, 5, 6
Hausvater ('patriarch') 4, 5, 6
health education 99
health insurance 210
healthcare, of children 99
Heide, Christine 162
Heineman, Elizabeth D. 121
Herder, Johann Gottfried, *Adrastea* 29
Herzog, Dagmar 190
   Sex after Fascism 118
heterosexuality 190–193
Hilfswerk 'Mutter und Kind' (Mother and Child Relief Agency) 95–101, 103
Himmler, Heinrich 92, 94, 101, 102, 106
Hirtsiefer, Heinrich 69, 79
Hitler, Adolf 12, 92, 112
Holocaust, the 106
home care (*Pflegegeld*), cash benefit 216, 217, 219
homophobia 193–194
homosexuality 81, 82, 132–133
   in East Germany 193–194
   partnerships 37, 211
   in the Third Reich 107–109
Honecker, Erich 185, 194–195, 232
honeymoons 32
Honour Books, awarded to large families 95
households, female-headed 131, 173
housemaids 42–46
housewives 161
housework 84, 161
   electrification of 182
Houskova, Hanka 106

Imperial Germany 10, 27–58, 120, 230
infant mortality 77, 78, 81, 99, 102
inflation, after the First World War 11, 65, 78, 230

Jensen, Anni 153
Jews
   Nazi discriminatory policies towards 105
   prevention of marriage to 'Aryans' 104
journeyman artisans 49
Junge Sozialdemokraten (Young Social Democrats/Jusos) 153

Kaiser, Robert 95
kindergartens 84–85, 181, 203–204
   Harvest kindergartens 100–101
Kinderladen 159
Kinderladenbewegung (Store Front Daycare Movement) 159
Knauer, Rudolf 82
Kohl, Helmut 157
Kolbe, Wiebke 142

labour market policy 21, 202, 214, 219
labour shortages 134, 177
Lange, Helene 37
laundries 182
Law for Combatting Venereal Diseases 81
Law for Maternity Benefits and Maternity Welfare 78
Law for the Prevention of Hereditarily Diseased Offspring 13, 104
Law for the Protection of Mother and Child and the Rights of Women 179–181
Law for the Protection of Working Mothers and the Rights of Women 126–127
League for Child Rich Families 71
Lebensborn ('Well of Life') organisation 13, 101–103
Leitner, Sigrid 20–22
Lepsius, Renate 155
lesbianism 107–109, 132
letters
   bridal 30
   wartime 110
Lex Heinze 148
Lisboa-Strategy 214
Luders, Marie Elisabeth 73
Ludwig, Emil 38
Lybeck, Marti 81

Mabry, Hannelore 158
maidservants 42–45
male-breadwinner/ female-homemaker family model 130, 135, 141, 142, 143, 149–150, 164, 231–232
   Christian Democrats and the 129, 133
   in families with young children 208–210

Guest Worker programme and the 152
persistence of 210–213
Women's movement and the 157–158
Mannheimer Declaration 156
marriage 8, 30–31, 147
   after divorce 76–77
   age difference between husband and wife 32–33
   certificate of fitness to marry 104
   egalitarian socialist 187
   failure of 117
   rate after the First World War 60
   in rural areas 186–187
   same-sex 143
   surveys on the importance of 121–122
   systematic intermarriage 31
   urban-dwelling 186
   during the Weimar era 65–72
Marriage Health Law 13, 104
Marriage Loan Scheme 13, 93
Marsden, Dennis 22
Marshall Plan 123
maternity leave 232
maternity welfare law 78
Mayer, August 69
Meisinger, Josef 108
middle-class families 5–6, 7–8, 9, 28–46, 229
   female subordination 29
   feudalisation of 46–48
   number of children in 230
migrant guest worker programme 144
Ministry of Family Affairs 207
Moeller, Robert G. 132, 142
mother advice centres 79–80
Mother and Child, Department of (in the Ministry of Health) 179, 181
motherhood
   in 1970s West Germany 141
   in Imperial Germany 34
   during the Weimar era 77–85
mothers
   employment of 19–20, 208
   help and advice centres 98–99
   recuperation for 97–98
   schools for 83
   size of families and employment of 147
Mother's Day 82
Mouton, Michelle 11–12

Muttererholung ('mother recuperation') programmes 84
Mutterschutz (mother's protection) law 17, 127, 155
Muttipolitik (mother's policy) 185–186, 232

National Socialists *see* Nazis
Nationalsozialistische Volkswohlfahrt (NSV or National Socialist People's Welfare) 95–96
Nave-Herz, Rosemarie 147, 149
Nazis 12–14, 86
   family policies 91–116
   health policy 99
   interventions into family life 112
Neubert, Rudolf 191–192
   The New Marriage Book 191
   The Question of Sex. A Book for Young People 191
'new family man' 161
'New Woman' 65, 80, 157
Nolan, Mary 112
non-marriage partnerships 149
nuclear family 19, 52
Nuremberg Laws 13, 104

old age care 22
   work and 215–218
'one-year volunteer' 48
Organisation for Economic Cooperation and Development (OECD) 213, 214, 215, 218
Orientierungsrahmen '85 (Orientation Framework) 153

Paragraph 175 81, 132, 147, 193
Paragraph 175a 107–108
Paragraph 175b 108
Paragraph 218 19, 70, 71, 232
Paragraph 297 82
parental leave 22, 157, 206, 208–210
parental leave benefit 21, 201, 206, 232
Parsons, Talcott 3
Partnerehe (partnership marriage) 161, 162
Pflegegeld (cash benefit for homecare) 216, 217, 219
Pill, the 147, 192

Pine, Lisa 66
Pius XI, Pope 71
pregnant workers 127
Pross, Helga, *The Realities of Women* 161
prostitution 81
Protestant church 135
Protestant Union for Health 71
Protestant Women's Aid Society 84
Protestant Women's League 187
Prussian Legal Code 1794 36

Radbruch, Gustav 73
Raphael, Lutz 141
Ravensbrück concentration camp 106
Red Army 172–173
Reich Central Office for the Combating of Homosexuality and Abortion 108
Reich Health Education Council 71
Reich Youth Welfare Law of 1922 81
Reichsbund der Kinderreichen (RdK, National League of Large Families) 94–95
reunification of Germany 20
    German family policy since 201–228, 232
Riehl, Wilhelm Heinrich 33, 41, 53
Romantic writers 30
Roos, Julia 81
Rotteck, Carl and Carl Welcker, *Staats-Lexikon* 27
Rousseau, Jean-Jacques 37
Ruble, Alexandria 16
rural labourers 49

Sachse, Carola 118
same-sex couples 211
Sander, Helke 158
Schelsky, Helmut, *Changes in the German Family in the Present Day* 117
Schmitt-Maass, Hety 151
Schoppmann, Claudia 109
Schröder, Hannelore 160
Schubnell, Hermann 145, 146
Second World War 16
    and family life 14–16
    gender imbalance after 120–121
    impact on family life 109–111
    policy for 'unworthy' sectors of the population 231

sex education 191
sexual enlightenment 192
sexuality 80–81
Silies, Eva-Maria 147
Simmel, Georg 40
single parent homes 19
single women 36, 81, 85, 120, 131
Social Democratic Party (SPD) 52, 62–63, 67, 123, 129, 132, 206, 211, 222
    childcare leave 221
    'Guidelines for Social Democratic Family Policy' 151
    legislation for working mothers 127
    promotion of the father as sole family breadwinner 51
    rift between Christian Democrats and 17
    women's movement 53
Socialist Unity Party (SED) 124, 125, 171–172
    policies and social consequences, 1950-1970 176–177
    vision of the family 173–176
sodomy 193
Sombart, Werner 52
Soviet zone of occupation (SBZ) 172
SPD 151, 152–153
    Arbeitsgemeinschaft sozialdemokratischer Frauen (AsF or Working Group of Social Democratic Women) 153
Stasi, the 194
state benefits 63
state youth departments 76
sterilisation 13, 66, 104
Stern 160, 161, 162
Stillich, Oskar 44
Stüwe, Wilhelm 95
Summers, Sarah 18

Tagesmutter Modellprojekt (Nanny Model Project) 153–154
tax benefits
    married couples 210
    for married couples with one earner or low-earning second earner 202
tax system 233
Third Reich 230
    divorce law 94

families during the 91–116
family in the 12–13
traditional male breadwinner model 202, 218
'traditional' male breadwinner/female homemaker family model 125
Treber, Leonie 118
Truman, Harry S. 123
Truman Doctrine 123

Ulbricht, Walter 178, 185
unemployment benefits 219
Unity of Economic and Social Policy' 185
Unterspann, Ingeborg 141
upper class families 6–7
Usborne, Cornelie 70–71

Vaizey, Hester 110, 111
Valentova, Eliska 106
venereal disease 81
von Hollander, Walther 117
von Rosen, Kathinka 45

Wages for Housework campaign 159–160
Wander, Maxie, *Guten Morgen Du Schone* 188
Wandervogel movement 54
Washington Convention of 1919 79
Weber, Max 40
Weber-Kellermann, Ingeborg 112
Weimar Republic 59–90, 230
  attitude towards families 60–65
  families during the 85–86
  marriage 65–72
  tradition and modernity in 11–12
Weitz, Eric 64
Welber, Wilhelm 32
welfare, for mothers who had recently given birth 96–97
West German families
  1948–61 post-war crisis 123–130
  in 1950s 117–140
  1960s to 1980s 141–170
  from the 1960s to the 1980s 18
  changing demographics between 1945 and 1961 119–122
  legislating 150–157
  outliers in the 1950s 130–133

West German Trade Union Federation (DGB) 154
West Germany
  in the 1950s 231
  demographic changes 1960–89 143–150
  effects of the Second World War on 16
  gender roles and family structures of 231
  Grundgesetz (Basic Law) 124
  women's movement and the family 157–163
Western Allies 16, 17
Westphalia 82, 83
wet nurses 35
Wex, Helga 156
Whisnant, Clayton J. 132
widow pensions 210–211
widower pensions 210–211
Wilhelmine *Gymnasium* 39
Willmott, Peter 3
women
  average age of marriage for 149
  employed in West Germany (1950–1989) 143–144
  fertility and ability to reproduce 106
  part-time employment of 151
  rights in marriage and the family 123
  unmarried. *see* single women
  working outside the home 83
'Women's Communique' 178
women's movement 156, 164
working mothers 127
  East Germany 171
  in East Germany after World War Two 232
working times, attitudes towards the ideal weekly working times of parents with a child aged 2 years 211–212
working-class families
  in Imperial Germany 49–53
  during the late nineteenth century 10
  number of children in 230
  urban 50
Wuermeling, Franz-Josef 129, 131, 231

Young, Michael 3
youth movement 54

www.ingramcontent.com/pod-product-compliance
Lightning Source LLC
Chambersburg PA
CBHW070030010526
44117CB00011B/1770